# Death's Dream Kingdom

# Death's Dream Kingdom

## The American Psyche Since 9-11

Walter A. Davis

Pluto Press
LONDON • ANN ARBOR, MI

First published 2006 by Pluto Press
345 Archway Road, London N6 5AA
and 839 Greene Street, Ann Arbor, MI 48106

www.plutobooks.com

Copyright © Walter A. Davis 2006

The right of Walter A. Davis to be identified as the author of this work
has been asserted by him in accordance with the Copyright, Designs
and Patents Act 1988.

British Library Cataloguing in Publication Data
A catalogue record for this book is available from the British Library

ISBN    0 7453 2469 X hardback
ISBN    0 7453 2468 1 paperback

Library of Congress Cataloging in Publication Data applied for

10   9   8   7   6   5   4   3   2   1

Designed and produced for Pluto Press by
Chase Publishing Services Ltd, Fortescue, Sidmouth, EX10 9QG, England
Typeset from disk by Stanford DTP Services, Northampton
Printed and bound in the United States of America by
Maple-Vail Book Manufacturing Group

*To*
*Rowan Williams*
*Archbishop of Canterbury*
*and*
*in America*
*to those who have kept faith with the spirit of the Sixties*

*If the book we are reading does not wake us, as with a fist hammering on our skull, why then do we read it? Good God, we would also be happy if we had no books, and such books as make us happy we could, if need be, write ourselves. But what we must have are those books which come upon us like ill-fortune, and distress us deeply, like the death of one we love better than ourselves, like suicide. A book must be an ice-axe to break the sea frozen inside us.*

Franz Kafka, *Diaries*

# Contents

# Acknowledgements

There is one consolation to the melancholy of things completed: the opportunity to thank those who helped along the way. This work owes a large debt to the work and the example of Ruth Stein whose own book on the psychoanalysis of religious terrorism will appear shortly. It was my good fortune to be invited by Ruth to participate in an on-line seminar on fundamentalism and terrorism conducted by *PsyBC*. I want to thank the founder of *PsyBC*, Dan Hill, for including me in the forum and the other participants: Richard Koenigsberg, Charles Strozier, James W. Jones, Ana-Maria Rizzuto, Dan Merkur, and Dan Shaw. The interchanges of the forum galvanized my thoughts on a number of topics. A large debt of another kind is owed to Hannah Berkowitz. As a good Luddite I frequently make major mistakes working by computer. Hannah is always there to bail me out and set things right. Hers too is the credit for my website which she recently designed to aid readers of this book: http://www. walteradavis.com. (Readers who wish can contact me through the website or at davis.65@osu.edu.)

I have also had the benefit of a number of friends who have read portions of the work and responded with incisive comments that made my work harder but hopefully the book better. As but a partial token of my gratitude thanks to: Todd McGowan, Howard Beckwith, Nick Kaldis, Virginia Hill, Kara J. Kostiuk, Alex Blazer, Christopher Shinn, Paul Eisenstein, Lois Tyson, Stephen Davis, Greg Forter, Gretchen Cline, Guy Rowland, Jon Mills, Adam Engel, Daniel DeQuincy, Janet Pfunder, Jon Mills, Donna Bentolila, Paul Whalen, the late Gary Heim, Liz Burbank, Shahram Vahdany, Chris McMahon, Salwa Ghaly, Jonathan Lewis, Gerry Gargiulo, Susan Block, Rachel Newcombe, George Snedeker, Tadit Anderson, Mark Bracher, James Kozicki, and Ghislaine Boulanger. A special word of thanks to Michael Eigen for encouragement and support on numerous occasions. And deep appreciation to Jeffrey St. Clair, the editor of *Counterpunch* who enabled me to try out earlier versions of some of these chapters online and to those readers of *Counterpunch* who were good enough to write me. An earlier version of Chapter 3 appeared in *Socialism and Democracy*.

# Preface: The Way We Were

"We must finally relearn what we forgot ... that humanitarian and moral arguments are not merely deceitful ideology. Rather, they can and must become central social forces."

Herbert Marcuse, *The Problem of Violence*

"If *liberty* means anything at all, it means the right to tell people what they do not want to hear."

George Orwell, *Notes on Nationalism*

The word American in the subtitle of this work was originally spelled Amerikan, the spelling used on the left in the 1960s to indicate a fascist direction in our politics that seems mild compared with our current situation. That spelling was a gesture of hope. America is not Amerika. Not yet. But it could become so, which is why we must understand Bush and Company better than they understand themselves. In them many disorders rise to the surface: an economic pillage rivaling the robber barons; a political agency savaging the Constitution and the Bill of Rights; a social agenda catering to everything reactionary in the religious right. All these are also signs of a deeper disorder of the American character or psyche requiring an in-depth psychoanalytic examination. But the method for undertaking such an examination does not exist and any desire for it was lost long ago in the flight of American culture from the psyche. My goal is to reverse that situation by developing a method that will enable us to recover and radicalize a psychoanalytic way of examining political and cultural events. To put the proposition in concrete terms, the reactions of the Bush administration to the trauma of September 11, 2001 brought an underlying psychosis to the surface. An event that should have led to restrained and far-reaching reflections on America's place in the world led instead to a hysterical acting out that continues to project globally the demands of a bullying vision that is also uncannily suited to the designs of global capitalism. Dubya is a fundamentalist crusader in the service of several masters. His deepest service perhaps is to cover the void at the center of American society. A culture of narcissism, religious infantilization and infatuation with violent computer games as the only ways to shock a benumbed sensibility into the illusion that it feels, finds in Dubya the perfect model of the collective hysteria that achieved its latest, but by no means its last, expression in the Schiavo case. Whenever traumatic historical events such as 9-11 happen the only response of such a sensibility is the *projection* of a grandiose and omnipotent attitude toward history that enables the American people to bathe themselves collectively in the belief that we are that blessed City on a Hill called upon by the Lord to rid the world of evil. For in the high stakes poker game called history the next move must always be more extreme.

Profound changes have been in process in America since 9-11 and those changes put new problems on the agenda of the left. Among them, I'll show, is the need to recover the *kind* of psychoanalytic Marxism that was one of the achievements of Adorno, Marcuse and other early members of the Frankfurt School and which has become but a dim and fading memory in the work of Habermas. My effort will not be to revive their methods *per se* but to reconstitute what a psychoanalytic way of thinking can contribute to an understanding of contemporary history. (I should add here that the psychoanalytic method I develop involves a rejection of most of American psychoanalysis—which is little more than the mental health wing of adaptation to capitalist society—as well as a detailed critique of Lacan whose thought constitutes a moment or component of the theory I'll develop here.) Having so bluntly identified my thought as psychoanalytic, I want immediately to extend my hand, palm open, to the reader with a simple request. Forget popular commonplaces about Freud and all the prejudices against psychoanalysis that have by now become a settled part of both the academic and the popular landscape and consider the possibility that the collective resistance to psychoanalysis may be one of the essential and most successful operations of capitalist ideology. I promise in return that you won't find here the kind of dogmatic and reductive pontificating that so often characterizes official Freudian thought, especially when it comes to "psychohistory."[1] After Shakespeare, Freud is the greatest thinker I've encountered, but one won't find here any of his concepts that hasn't been filtered through a reflection that has included Hegel, Heidegger, Sartre, and Marx (among others) as equal participants. The dogmatic application of fixed Freudian concepts as if they held the key to History is one of the reasons why psychoanalysis has fallen out of favor, except among what are finally coterie writers who recycle little more than a precious jargon as if iteration were proof of immutable truth. In my view, every concept in the Freudian canon requires a reinterpretation which will only be possible when we regain contact with what is most radical in Freud's thought and that of the few followers who remained faithful to what is most unsettling in psychoanalysis: its insight into the ineradicably tragic dimension of the psyche and of history. This dimension, I hope to show, must become the center of leftist thought if we're to overcome the system of rationalistic and metaphysical guarantees that continue to blind us to history.[2] A quick take on the left: the assumption that final victory is in the cards, made necessary *a priori* by the laws of history, the humanistic urgings of our essential nature, or the consciousness of the proletariat. A quick take on the history of psychoanalysis: a repeated repression of its radical discoveries. Their recovery, I'll show, is what will enable us to overcome the dilemmas in which the left is mired.

But I fear this discussion is becoming too academic when my initial procedure in the book proper will offer the reader something quite different. Every psychological idea developed there will come drenched in particulars. In a sense the first half of the book is a primer of sorts, a movement from the more obvious ways a psychoanalytic sensibility can help us understand key events since 9-11 to the more complex psychoanalytic understanding that evolves from those examinations. No special knowledge of psychoanalysis is needed to understand the first four chapters, which are also the most topical ones in the book. They offer, in effect, concrete training in how to think along psychological lines while illustrating the kind of insights into contemporary events that such a perspective can provide. The book then moves gradually yet progressively toward more complex issues and more complex ways of thinking psychoanalytically. Here too, however, the reader will never be asked to conceptualize what I haven't first enabled them to experience in more primary ways.

In the same concretizing spirit, the first part of the book will conclude with a critique of the two paradigms that currently control the way that psychoanalytic thought is employed on the left for purposes of political and cultural critique. Moreover, I use as examples two recent books—Lifton's *Superpower Syndrome* and Žižek's *Welcome to the Desert of the Real*—which apply those two paradigms to 9-11. It'll come as a shock to Bill O'Reilly, Sean Hannity and William Bennett but thinking on the left, unlike its counterfeit on the right, is not monolithic. One of my purposes, in fact, is to establish the necessity of continuing self-critique if we on the left are to overcome the contradictions that dog us. Critique, however, is only as good as the new analyses to which it leads. They form the larger and more theoretical second part of the book. Here too, however, all concepts will remain tied to the analysis of specific events and phenomena. *Terror, evil, fundamentalism.* At Dubya's insistence these three topics have become the primary agenda of intellectual reflection today. In Dubya's mouth, of course, the three terms are crass ideological manipulation deployed to create a mass hysteria that can be ratcheted up whenever it serves the designs of domestic or international terror. Rather that simply crying mystification, however, our response must be to think these three terms through in a rigorous way, thereby rescuing them not only from Dubya but from the number of academic conferences now being organized to assure that these hot, new academic commodities get parsed and parceled out in all the properly decorous and disciplinary ways. In opposition to both practices, Chapter 7 takes up the psychology of (Christian) fundamentalism. Chapter 8 looks at (domestic) terrorism. Chapter 9 then attempts to develop a concept of evil that will take us beyond the pivotal contributions that Immanuel Kant and Hannah Arendt made to its understanding. This examination enables me in Chapter 10 to take up the issue of ethics and replace abstract moralism with an existential ethic that is fully situated in the world.

The book thereby turns on a frank appeal to experience. My effort is not just to change the way readers will think about certain events, but to effect a deeper change in the reader's emotional and psychological being. The goal is to offer readers with each chapter an experience of progressively deeper insights into themselves and, specifically, insights into the ways in which we are part of the problem rather than the solution precisely because we've lost sight of the psychological truth expressed in one of Marx's deepest insights: "To be radical is to go to the roots; but the root is man himself." Though we're loath to acknowledge it, a common tendency whenever thought gets close to the psyche is to apply defenses to banish the unwelcome intruder. Some of these take the form of theoretical objections: Is psychoanalysis a science? Can any sense be made of pseudo-concepts such as Thanatos and the Unconscious? Others practical: How can any of this psychological stuff be relevant to political action? And some are purely emotional. I hope this book will reverse all of these practices by producing an inner transformation that will free us from the system of guarantees on which all of them are based. A critique of the guarantees that inform the Western Logos or *ratio* is a large issue, which I've pursued in philosophic and methodological terms in *Deracination*. Here I extend that analysis by applying it to a specific historical and political situation.

I should add that for me psychoanalysis offers no exclusive purchase on the truth about history. Our situation calls for many analyses. Economic explanations, geopolitical perspectives, sociological and statistical analyses, studies in terms of international law and the history of American foreign policy are needed. Dubya is the general term we give to a complex of historical problems and tendencies that currently intersect in a way that makes ours a moment fraught with danger—and opportunity. Danger of the sort Walter Benjamin spoke of, when possibilities flare up that must be seized or lost forever. Opportunity of the sort that comes when dialectical connections that usually evade us can be made because the need for them has become through the news a daily Artaudian pressure on the nerves. Thanks to Dubya Inc. ours is perhaps a privileged ideological moment in which many branches of knowledge come together in what may emerge as a new understanding of ideology and its operation.

My contribution to that hypothetical construct will focus on what is neglected when ideology is seen primarily as a matter of the beliefs and ideas that blind people to their historical situation. Such analyses don't go deep enough because they neglect the emotional and psychological glue that holds the ideological edifice together. Ideology is not primarily the operation of quasi-rational processes through which subjects "think" about their world. As we'll see in chapters 1–4, it's primarily a matter of the fantasies or fantasmatic structures that subjects project onto history in order to assure the fulfillment of deep emotional needs. We believe x, y, and z because these beliefs satisfy certain emotional needs that have become psychologically necessary; i.e., needs that the collective subject of ideology must defend because without them the sense of identity and purpose collapses. A great case in point, as we'll see, is the neocon belief about how the Iraqis would welcome us with open arms as prelude to democracy sweeping the Middle East. A focus on the emotional roots of ideology aligns my work in some ways with that of Lacan and Žižek, but as Chapter 6 will show, within that shared concern lies a fundamental difference between the general structural malaise Lacan and Žižek describe and the far more concrete historical analyses that my method makes possible; and with as its concrete yield an understanding of the underlying psychotic condition that Dubya brings to the surface. Contra Žižek, ideology is not an attempt to escape the Trauma of the Real. It's an attempt to prevent the implosion or dissolution of the subject into very precise forms of social fragmentation that can only be exorcized by projecting apocalyptic desires and delusions upon History. As we'll see, this understanding of ideology offers a concrete way to read key events since 9-11.

History is what hurts. The deepest reason why this oft cited maxim of the left is true is seldom acknowledged. History hurts because it can become the scene of profound and irreversible changes in the collective psyche. We live in such a moment. And we'll only begin to understand it and our responsibility toward it when we realize that no transcendental, theological, or humanistic guarantee protects us from history; protects us, to put it concretely, from the prospect that *1984* remains a profound book—about the future. There is no guarantee of humanistic renewal, nor is there anything in the Constitution and the Bill of Rights that can't be abrogated if the tendencies represented by Dubya and Co. come to fruition. We love to think that human nature provides certain ethical guarantees that cannot be lost—this being perhaps the best example of how many a good leftist is also a prisoner of ideology—but the hard truth of history is that everything is contingent. Contingency is the only reality and to know that is to realize that everything we value can become as extinct as the species that are now leaving us every day forever. Nothing protects us from history, which is why our engagement in and responsibility for it must be absolute.

"But what about the terrorists over there? What about Islamic fundamentalism? And what about the evil of people like Osama bin Laden and Saddam Hussein?" There are, I think, two useful responses to such questions when they come from legitimately concerned readers and not from fascists like O'Reilly and Limbaugh. First, in studying any problem it is always best to begin at home, for it's there that experience enables one to cut quickly to the bone. For example, we need not spend the next six months cribbing distortions of Islam in order to understand the fundamentalist psyche. The thing's on display daily, in our midst, avid for expression. Second, one only earns the ethical right to raise questions about another culture after one has had the decency to raise those very questions about one's own. Reversing that order is the prime gesture of ideology. And if there's any doubt about that point Dubya has laid it to rest. No one has shown better than he how to use evil, terror, and fundamentalism for purposes of othering and Orientalism and in order to prohibit the kind of criticism that's needed if we're to address the collective disorder that he represents.

But for the nonce and because we'll be studying ideology as fantasy, flash forward. Let's indulge the fantasy that so often comforts us in dark times. Perhaps we'll thereby gain something beyond fantasy. It didn't happen! All the dire predictions of another generation of leftist pessimists failed to materialize. Dubya overshot his mark with the social security legislation the way Hillary Clinton did with the health care program. As with LBJ and tricky Dick, *hubris* again saved us from disaster, though only by the skin of teeth growing very thin. Dubya overreached in the Middle East too. The neocons salivated for four years for regime change in Iran, Syria, and North Korea but the interminable ground war in Iraq betrayed their hopes. Etc. Early in his second term the air went out of Dubya's balloon. The duck quacked sooner than he himself predicted. And in 2008 Dubya retired to Crawford and Cheney went to his eternal reward without wreaking the havoc that had once danced like sugarplums in their brains. Books like the one you are about to read were rendered obsolete, consigned to the flames of a resurgent liberalism, that of a victorious Democratic Party composed of what we used to call Rockefeller Republicans—the vital center moving ever rightward of people eager to go Van Winkle-like to sleep again. Until the next time—which is something about history that the right understands. That is why in the winter's of their discontent they're always making plans for the next step. Reagan to Bush to "the future, Mr. Gittes," as Noah Cross put it in *Chinatown* when asked to state that motive that is even more precious than money. The future. That, in one sense, is what this book is about: an effort to offer what we need to know so that we can fight it each time it comes. Who knows, maybe we'll get so good at this that we'll fight it the other times too.

But all this is but prologue to the swelling act that Dubya exploited for the designs of the imperial theme. Two planes plunged into a building and something exploded in the American psyche. One result was the psychotic response that continues to advance its agenda domestically and globally. The only meaningful reply is to constitute its absolute antithesis. That is the overarching purpose of this book. As you'll see, the movement from Chapter 1 to Chapter 10 is the movement from a collective psychosis to the deep psychological changes we must make in ourselves in order to attain in the tragic the only adequate stance toward our historical situation. But as with all voyages of discovery and change, the map is not the territory. The only way to know what must be done is by immersing ourselves in the process. That effort begins in Chapter 1 with an inquiry into the image and what images reveal about the emotional and psychological roots of ideology.

The Ides of March, 2005

# Part One
# The Belly of the Beast

# 1
# 911– America

"A screaming comes across the sky."

Thomas Pynchon, *Gravity's Rainbow*

"...every image of the past that is not recognized by the present as one of its own concerns threatens to disappear irretrievably."

Walter Benjamin, *Theses on the Philosophy of History*

Gandhi on a hunger strike to protest fighting between Hindu and Muslim after the Partition is confronted by a man in agony. "I am going to hell. I killed an innocent child. My son was slain and in my rage I killed a Muslim child. Gandhi's reply: "I know a way out of hell. Go, find a homeless Muslim child, adopt him and raise him as your own. But raise him in the Muslim religion."[1] Gandhi knew a way out of hell. I think I know a way in—and why it is the route we must follow in addressing 9-11.

Trauma occurs when something happens that shatters the ego and its defenses. An event persists as an image that awakens other images buried in the psyche, images bound to repressed memories that bring with their return an anxiety that threatens psychic dissolution. The hidden, buried history of one's life presents itself as an awareness one can no longer escape, a self-knowledge one must now construct since that act is the only route to "recovery."

Can what is true for individuals also be true for nations? And thus with respect to 9-11, perhaps our task is not to resolve the trauma but to do all in our power to assure that it is fully constituted? But for that to happen it is not enough to cite the traumatic images that were blazed into the nation's consciousness that day: a plane embedded surrealistically in a building; bodies falling from the sky; that great granite elevator going down; the terrible black cloud rushing forth to engulf a fleeing multitude; and then the countless dead, buried alive, passing in endless queue across the shattered landscape of the nation's consciousness. Nor is it enough to note the precise correspondence of these images to the anxieties that define the psychotic register of the psyche: falling endlessly, going to pieces, collapsing in on oneself, losing all orientation, delivered over to a claustrophobic world of inescapable, ceaseless suffering.[2] Something more is needed for an event to traumatize the collective psyche. Images from the present must speak to other images tied to memories buried deep in the nation's history; to things forgotten, ungrieved, vigorously denied; things in the past that have never been confronted and worked through. On 9-11 did many Americans perhaps realize, if only for a moment, that we were now experiencing, in diminished form, what it was like to be in Hiroshima city on August 6, 1945 when in an instant an entire city disappeared in a flash of light that vaporized over 200,000 souls, condemning the survivors to a condition of nameless dread, to wandering directionless in a landscape become nightmare?

## GROUND ZERO AS IMAGE

What's in a name? Ground zero, the term now used to designate the rubble of what was once the World Trade Center, was the term coined in Alamogordo, New Mexico to identify the epicenter where the first atomic bomb was detonated. It was then used to locate the same place in Hiroshima and Nagasaki so that we could measure with precision the force of the bomb and gauge its effects.

Image is the native language of anxiety, the language the psyche uses in an effort to mediate the emotional and psychological impact of events. As such, a language of images has much in common with the logic of the dream, a logic of hidden and unexpected connections, of abrupt shifts and apparent discontinuities in which image succeeds image in the drama of a psyche seeking a concrete way to embody its condition. In *image* we find a mode of cognition that is prior to the conceptual order, with a revelatory power beyond the concept's range of disclosure.[3] To apprehend what image reveals requires a hermeneutic of engagement.[4] Rather than address 9-11 from some objective stance above the rubble, secure in ideologies that enable one to dispense healing insights to an anguished nation, we must find a way to get inside the event by following the path Walter Benjamin outlined for the dialectical historian: to arrest those images that flare up at a moment of crisis and attempt to internalize and articulate their significance before they disappear, perhaps irretrievably, in the predictable rush toward ideological reaffirmations—and national healing.

## MOURNING vs EVACUATION

And so, we return to ground zero and two possibilities—one idealistic, the other ratified by events. The idealistic possibility: Hiroshima, unfinished business deep in the American psyche, returned on 9-11 to trouble the nation with afterthought and forethought? A mourning process long deferred would then have commenced with the recognition that guilt is not a psychological condition to be avoided at all costs but the primary source of knowledge and inner transformation. Internalizing that recognition would have led us to the true origin of ethics: the realization of what we've done to others when our deeds are done to us. Ground zero would thus signify our transformation from subjects bent on rectitude and revenge to ones capable of reflection and restraint; capable of pursuing justice through international law, through the presentation of carefully gathered evidence to the United Nations and the World Court. 9-11 would have led us to a recognition of the duties of world citizenship and thereby a way of honoring the innocent victims of terror with a fitting memorial.

But of course none of this happened. Nor could it. Indeed, the suggestion raises strong objections, even outrage, because we've learned to recite, by rote, what has now become a national article of faith: that the bombings of Hiroshima and Nagasaki were justified, almost idealistic acts, undertaken with reluctance, as "the least abhorrent choice" but finally the only way to end the war thereby saving perhaps a million lives. This explanation was first articulated in an article ghostwritten for Secretary of State Henry Stimson by his aide McGeorge Bundy (1947). It is a pretty story, the only problem being Bundy's admission in a book published shortly before his death that the entire thing was a fabrication, a deliberate myth, carefully constructed after the fact[5] to disguise the actual reasons why we dropped the bomb: (1) to avenge Pearl Harbor, (2) to justify the amount of money spent developing the bomb, (3) to create laboratories so that our scientific, medical, and military personnel could study the effects of the bomb, and (4) to impress the Russians and the rest of the world with this opening salvo in the Cold War.[6] The act, moreover, abrogated all distinctions between combatant and non-combatant, the object of military action now being an entire city, of no military significance, its inhabitants indifferently identified as a single mass delivered to death in an effort, as General Leslie Groves put it, "to inflict the maximum moral and psychological damage on the enemy".[7] Hiroshima, in short, was the first act of global terrorism, the harbinger of acts that would derive their rebarbative logic from the way in which America on August 6, 1945 consigned humanistic considerations to the dustbin of history.

And that is but the beginning. For the motives for bombing Hiroshima drew their power from deeper psychological forces that rose to the surface again in the way the term ground zero was actually deployed in the days following 9-11. Calling upon a primary mechanism of projection and denial—the reversal of meaning—appropriating ground zero offered us a way to identify ourselves as the innocent victims of a terror that we claimed as unprecedented—and that we demanded the whole world acknowledge as such. From which follows, of necessity, the parade of heroic images whereby we rise phoenix-like from the ashes, united as a Nation that, having recovered its essence, goes forth to reaffirm the ideals it represents by undertaking the deeds needed to cleanse the world of yet another evil. John Wayne lives. The projector has started running and on the screen of the national psyche we see projected another movie full of patriotic sentiment and patriotic gore. Flags a-burstin the heroic dead of 9-11 are resurrected in the acts of war we undertake in their name, their image blending and fading into the images of our triumphant military action in Afghanistan, Iraq or any other place we designate as a haven of "terrorism." America has once again found a way to think of history as the inevitable progress of an ahistorical Essence, a way to exploit a traumatic event in order to reassert the ideological guarantees that make it impossible for us to learn from history. On a psychological level an even greater boon is thereby guaranteed: the evacuation of all inner conflict through a projective identification that is unlimited in its scope and that can find new objects any time it needs them.

## THE PSYCHE THAT DROPPED THE BOMB

The bomb provided the template for that transformation because the psyche first found in it the possibility of an unprecedented self-mediation: the chance to take the anxieties that define the psyche and resolve them at what I term the sublime register.[8] This is the register that operates whenever the psyche seeks a way to turn a situation of abject weakness into a confirmation of omnipotent power. In 1945 in Alamogordo the human mind ascended to a condition it had long dreamed of: nature's secrets and her might were now harnessed to our will. The human mind had finally triumphed over the otherness of nature. Nature's power, unleashed as never before, served to confirm our power to overcome all inner limitations. The sequel thus beckoned. For if we found ourselves abject objects of the other's wrath at Pearl Harbor, we now had a way to effect a complete and lasting transformation of that situation. Projective identification finds in the bomb a way to take everything weak and vulnerable in oneself and invest it in an other who is reduced to an object of contempt and obliteration. The resulting mania banishes any return of depressive anxieties. In the bomb the manic triad—triumph, contempt, and dismissal[9]—celebrates its Sabbath.[10] Metapsychologically, the transformation is complete and can be schematized thus: abjection reversed; blockage overcome; aggression unbound. Narcissistic grandiosity thereby finds the fullest possible expansion, its perfect phallic mirror, in the mushroom cloud rising above the eviscerated landscape as proof of the bomb's power to compel submission. Evacuation of inner conflict thereby attains an exorcism of an unprecedented order: a psychotic attack on linking[11] that is totalizing in its scope and that scoffs at all humanistic considerations. Thanatos in the bomb achieves the condition Freud feared: a condition in which death has been fully eroticized, with pleasure or *jouissance* the releasing of a destructiveness that voids all inner tensions in an aggression that has the blessing of the superego, an aggression that feels righteous. As confirmation consider this, but one example among many: Navy Day, October 1945, a crowd of 120,000 gather in the Los Angeles Coliseum to celebrate a simulated re-enactment of the bombing of Hiroshima, complete with a mushroom cloud that rises from the 50-yard line to the joyful cheers of that rapt throng.[12] The first Super Bowl. The society of the spectacle[13] here announces its truth as a mass audience *cums* to the ritual that confers on it a lasting, ghostly identity: the howl of joy that rises as a hymn of praise to the burgeoning cloud is the new American collectivity in Hosanna before the image of its inhumanity as it blossoms before them, big with the future.

From which follows a quick tour of the underside of American history from 1945 to the present. The debacle of Vietnam. The error: the image came home to roost. Each night with the evening news America supped full with horror. The lesson: no more images. The solution: Iraq I, the Nintendo war, a war represented on TV as a video game. No images of the 100,000 Iraqi dead entered the American conscience to trouble our sleep. Instead, with victory the proclamation of George H.W. Bush: "We've finally put an end to Vietnam syndrome." The lesson of history learned, the son now deploys it globally in a war against "terror," where, he informs us, much will happen that we will never hear about or see. Extremes meet: the image is banished but the promise of global action is affirmed. Dubya is an apt pupil. He knows that in order to resolve the trauma of 9-11 he must satisfy an outraged public by finding a way to repeat the psychological operations perfected in Hiroshima. He knows that nothing less than a global war against "terrorism" will suffice. But he also knows that the pleasure of the image must be replaced by another kind of satisfaction, one appropriate to the information age, an age in which pleasure has itself become virtual. Subjects formed by what is today perhaps the primary relationship—worship of the computer—find it natural to imagine scorched earths as so many blips on a computer screen with disavowal already in place and a pleasure united to Thanatos assured through the reduction of the human to the statistical and the boundless power one feels in manipulating, at the speed of light, a world so rendered into one's hands. The society of the spectacle—a society that needed Hiroshima and Navy Day in the L.A. Coliseum—is replaced by the society of the virtual. The postmodern subject has entered a condition of bliss, the hegemony of Thanatos assured by the sacrifice of the image. We no longer need it because we've abstracted ourselves into another realm in which in line with our own inner deadening we now experience reality as no more than flows of information denuded of human meaning. Mass carnage grows apace: over a million Iraqi civilians have now died as a result of our sanctions; more civilians ("collateral damage") have now died in Afghanistan as a result of our bombings than perished at the WTC. But the knowledge of these things has become virtual, disembodied, imageless and thus is always already fading, leaving no ethical residue in the national consciousness.

## AFTER SUCH KNOWLEDGE, WHAT FORGIVENESS?

What, then, are the possibilities of healing and renewal that we can derive from an understanding of America's response to 9-11? A responsible reply must begin with the recognition that it was through America that terror on a global scale first came into the world and that we remain its primary global practitioner. For internalizing that fact delivers a death blow to the belief that "catharsis" and "renewal" require the reassertion of adolescent myths about ourselves and our place in history. Historical memory must become instead the movement toward a tragic culture: one for whom memory is conscience and not hagiography; for whom the past weighs like a nightmare precisely because it has not been constituted. That is the true meaning of Hiroshima. Ground zero haunts us not because we feel guilt about it but because we don't. Or, more concretely, because guilt for us is that which we must evacuate. That is why, whenever we are traumatized, we repeat the psychological operations we perfected in Hiroshima in a progressive self-reification that we will remain powerless to reverse as long as we refuse to internalize what actually happened on August 6, 1945. But to do that we must begin the long, hard task of rooting out everything in our culture that weds us to the psyche that dropped the bomb. Such an effort requires, as we'll see, freeing ourselves from our own liberal myth that admitting error assures renewal and a reclamation of the ideals that make American history the story of inevitable progress.[14] What Hiroshima teaches us, on the contrary, is that history remains irreversible in its tragic consequences until we find for our history an equivalent of Gandhi's ethic: a way out of hell that sustains trauma and depressive mourning as the destiny of historical subjects who know that reversal begins only when we are willing to plumb the depths of our collective disorder. A tragic understanding of history assures us no catharsis, no renewal, no guarantees. What it offers instead is the realization that to sustain and deepen the trauma is our only hope.[15]

For the alternative is truly horrifying: the Bush doctrine, a blank check for whatever carnage will be needed to satisfy our bloodlust and preserve our "right" to ravage the planet's resources. Because one fact above all others is, as Marx would say, "determinative in the last instance" of what is going on in the world today. 5 percent of the world's population consume 25 percent of its resources—and they do so by exerting control over the destiny of other countries. Bin Laden is a symptom, a nostalgic religious fanatic, but his fanaticism derives from a condition that is actual. In Rio de Janeiro, at the one ecological conference he attended, the first President Bush delivered a proclamation even more chilling than his crowing about Vietnam syndrome: "The American way of life is not negotiable." As long as that dogma remains in place there will be many more ground zeroes.

# 2
# Living in Death's Dream Kingdom:
# The Psychotic Core of Capitalist Ideology

"The National Government will regard it as its first and foremost duty to revive in the nation the spirit of unity and cooperation. It will preserve and defend those basic principles on which our nation has been built. It regards Christianity as the foundation of our national morality, and the family as the basis of national life."

Adolf Hitler, My New World Order,
Proclamation to the German Nation, February 1, 1933

Here are ten quick lessons toward developing a concept of ideology adequate to our historical situation. In contrast to those who would separate ideology from psychology, each lesson shows a way in which ideology depends on psychological principles for its realization. We can't understand—and resist—the working of capitalist ideology until we understand its psychological foundations. I hasten to add, however, that while the categories I use here are psychoanalytic, one of the main purposes of this chapter is to expose the bankruptcy of American psychoanalysis, the history of which has been shaped by the desire to provide engineering for adaptation of the ego to the system.

## IDEOLOGY AS DELUSIONAL FANTASY

*Lesson One.* "The occupation of Iraq will be an enormous success because once free of their shackles the Iraqi people will embrace us as their liberators." "Democracy in Iraq will be a model for the spread of democratic governments throughout the Middle East." "Our actions in Iraq will bring a solution to the Palestinian problem." Etc. The true significance of such beliefs is that those who put them forth actually believe them. Such beliefs are not the cynical, deceptive cover for something else, but true articles of faith. Capitalist ideology isn't a false consciousness that can be corrected by reality testing. It's a deliberate self-deception of a delusional order, a fantasy or *fantasmatic* consciousness[1] that is imposed on history so that all contingencies will submit to the force of beliefs that cannot be challenged, modified, or reflected upon. Those who create ideology are not master deceivers, they are true believers. Fantasies are essential to ideology because they provide the frame that is imposed upon historical events to deliver us from traumatic realities. As Marx taught, ideology renders history unknowable. What he didn't see is what Freud enables us to add: it does so for psychological reasons.

This understanding of ideology, like the nine that follow, transform our task. There is not some correct, reasonable consciousness behind ideology to which we can appeal in order to get rid of ideological distortions, come to our senses, and change our policies. No such consciousness is possible. The fantasmatic distortions are essential to the maintenance of the capitalist system. Without them it implodes. *Ideology isn't false consciousness. It's fantasmatic consciousness, the creation of illusions and self-delusions.*

*Lesson Two. Ground zero.* As Chapter 1 showed, the appropriation of this term to refer to the site of what was the World Trade Center illustrates the basic psychological operation that sustains ideology: the *inversion* or *reversal of meaning.* That operation sets the stage for employment of the most primitive psychotic defense mechanisms— *evacuation* and *projective identification*—in order to cleanse the collective consciousness of any possibility of learning from history. Surplus aggression is thereby liberated as a justified attack on an "evil" that has been placed totally outside us. The result of these psychological operations is the solidification of the only relation ideology can form to history. Ideology takes the past and inverts its meaning in order to repeat again what was done before. In this repetition compulsion History doesn't repeat itself as farce however; it repeats itself as expanded aggression. *Ideology isn't based on false ideas. It's based on the necessity of employing primitive, psychotic defense mechanisms in order to exorcise traumatic events.*

*Lesson Three.* Instead of declaring war on Al Qaeda, Dubya declared war on Terrorism. Moreover, that glorious battle had to come cloaked in theological terms so that a desire for omnipotence could find in global actions a way to confirm an infantile identity. Through a battle of good against evil, all inner disorders are placed outside us. Historical action thereby becomes the reaffirmation of an ahistorical essence. Action must serve omnipotent desire by constituting the next step in a progress toward the end of history. Being unable to learn from history and seeking to bring about the end of history—recall here this post-Cold-War boast by Francis Fukuyama and others—are functions of the same underlying psychotic desire, which today shapes both policy studies and military action. The psychotic hatred of reality requires the extinction of all otherness. Putting an end to history is its defining project. The ghostly peace it seeks is only attained when nothing any longer exists that could oppose its logic. This understanding of ideology mandates a further transformation of our task. Marx spoke of liberating the historical, rational kernel from the mystical shell of the Hegelian dialectic. For us, at a later stage of history, a new task beckons: *to liberate the psychotic kernel from the fantasmatic shell.*

Ideology is grounded in necessities far deeper than popular beliefs and prejudices. Such beliefs maintain their hold only because they serve a deeper necessity. Understanding the psychological defense-mechanism of *inversion* enables us to get at that lower layer. Inversion occurs when we turn something upside down or inside out in order to deny an impossible condition. That condition, I suggest, is the psychotic anxiety that is at the center of American society, the void we incessantly flee and deny. Fantasms provide the frame that makes reality endurable because fantasies are acts of magical reasoning that give evacuation and projective identification a way to fashion an omnipotent identity, which whenever challenged moves toward psychosis. Psychotic necessity is thus the true reason why Empire is the destiny we now brazenly announce to an incredulous world. *Ideology derives from the psychotic register of the psyche and performs the three operations required to satisfy the inversion that defines psychosis: i.e., projective identification, evacuation, and surplus aggression. These are the means whereby one locates an inner disorder in an external object so that by attacking and annihilating that object one exorcises what one cannot face about oneself.*

*Lesson Four.* In the age of hyperreality and simulation, predicting and producing the future necessarily become inseparable. John Poindexter (of earlier Reagan Iran–Contra fame) was, until recently, the head of TIAP, the Terrorist Information Awareness Program of DARPA (The Defense Advanced Research Projects Agency) where he set in motion the since cancelled PAM, the Policy Analysis Market, where anyone who wanted could bet money on the date for events such as the following: the death of Saddam Hussein or Yasser Arafat, the next major terrorist attack in the U.S., the discovery of a weapon of mass destruction (WMD) in Iraq, the assassination of Ariel Sharon. The official rationale: the Defense Department would thereby get statistical "information" providing a reliable index of future events.

Sybil the Soothsayer dressed out in computer garb. The Senatorial outcry that nixed the project (temporarily) was nothing to the hue and cry that then went up within the intelligence community at this affront to the technological imperative. Once again short-sighted politicians deprived us of "a way of capturing people's collective wisdom" and binding it to "a tool with a strong history of accurately predicting future events."[2] Also, fantasmatically, a chance opportunity to tap into terrorist's plans, since a primary rationale behind the proposal—backed, supposedly, by scientific data about insider trading on the stock of American Airlines and United in the days before 9-11—is that terrorists are finally good capitalists too and won't be able to resist the temptation to cash in on their actions. As apologists for PAM indignantly note, similar computer wagering systems correctly picked 35 of the 40 Oscar nominees in the eight biggest categories in 2002 and have shown scientifically that the price of orange juice is an accurate predictor of the weather in Florida![3] The speciousness of this argument isn't irrelevant; it's the point. For what PAM offers is a fantasmatic satisfaction of the cardinal imperative of capitalist ideology: a fetishization and worship of the market as the privileged space for the projection of fantasies, fears, and desires.

Freud saw religion as collective neurosis. In PAM technology creates for capitalist ideology a sacred space. For the deepest fantasy fueling this thing—the shared dream of the stock broker and the Department of Homeland Security—is the dream of omniscience, the belief that we can know and control the future before it happens. All we have to do is provide a space to which all psyches will be drawn as to a gigantic magnet, addicted to what market capitalism promises, the simultaneity of wealth, knowledge, and power. There is, indeed, something autoerotic about the whole scheme. The informing belief of necessity is that capitalism has already conquered. Terrorists are, finally, just like us. They too can't resist the market. From which follows, however, the paranoid suspicion that the fantasy necessarily generates. Suppose terrorists make bets to deliberately put us off their tracks? Well, the market has long taught us how to stay one step ahead. After all, we rule the world because we play this game better than anyone else. And thus we find in the further reaches of PAM the realization for our time of MAD and its dream of perfecting the logic of deterrence (i.e., "if the Russians think we'll send our nukes if they send theirs then they won't and so we can, etc."). PAM is not a crackpot scheme, it's a necessary madness, a madness that reveals the nature of the system, the kind of thing it must produce to satisfy both libidinal and paranoid imperatives.

Those who know the work of Thomas Pynchon can see why such examples prove that he (not Marx) is our Vergil who provides in *Gravity's Rainbow* a model for ideological inquiry. Pynchon's basic insight is that the most extreme, bizarre acts and fantasies reveal in the guise of a desperate pseudo-rationality the madness and irrationality that inform the system as a whole. Texts such as PAM are privileged objects of ideological critique because they show that the underlying psychosis moves with obsessional insistence to what will finally be a condition of pure noise, information cancelling itself as it grows skyward in pure worship of itself. As PAM shows, the great benefit of "Pynchonian" ideological analysis is that it enables us to put an end to the base–superstructure concept of ideology which has so often had the deleterious effect of isolating then deifying hard-headed economic analysis while confining everything else to superstructural insignificance. But as PAM illustrates, the economic and the fantasmatic are inseparable components of a system that is, of necessity, fantastically fantasmatic. That is why Cheney and the others can whisper to one another, in one and the same breath that "it's about the *oil*, stupid," and that "capitalism will bring the blessing of progress and freedom to the entire world in a final triumph of good over evil." *The inherent logic of ideology demands the formulation of policies and projects in which the underlying rationality takes the form of pseudo-rational ideas. Such policies are surreal texts that must be read as pure wish fulfillments that derive from the ideological Unconscious, that register at the core of ideology that knows no No and must therefore project a dream-state in which all contradictions are annulled and all desires fulfilled.*

*Lesson Five.* Omnipotent desire begets paranoia. Or, to put it in political terms, *global terrorism requires domestic terrorism.* That is why the First Patriot Act begets the second and will no doubt beget the third. Why if you smoke pot you support terrorism and if you criticize Bush's policies you give aid and comfort to the "enemy." Why *Roe* v. *Wade* must be dismantled and gay marriage made a primary campaign issue, all the better to motivate the knee-jerks of docile subjects compelled to defeat those who support the cancer eating away at our moral fabric. The essential drive of ideology is to extinguish everything that poses the threat of otherness, everything that brings anxiety to a mind like Ashcroft's by raising the specter of citizens who are anything but obedient, respectful—and afraid.

Ideology is inherently fascistic and surveillance is its priest because the inherent goal of ideology is to totalize the operations needed to give it omnipotent control over all possible contingencies. History only makes sense to Dubya and Company when projected on the inner screen of psychotic anxieties. Ideology doesn't blind us to history. It rejects history before the fact by projecting a future in which all otherness has been eliminated. *Ideology is driven by an obsessional need to totalize a desire for omnipotence. That effort is ruled by the contradiction that defines obsessionalism: the production of new uncertainties, renewed paranoia, and the consequent projection of a demand that can be satisfied only when history is over and all otherness extinguished.*

### CAPITALISM AS FULFILLMENT OF THE IDEOLOGICAL ENTERPRISE

*Lesson Six.* We thus attain the only ideologically adequate definition of capitalism—a definition which dances simultaneously to economic and psychological imperatives. Capitalism is the reduction of all human relations to the profit motive in an expansionism that is necessarily global and must eliminate everything opposed to its logic. Subjects who internalize capitalism thus necessarily desire to possess "all good things" in a logic of accumulation that is infantile since it can tolerate no contradictions or limitations. Choosing among a conflict of goods is unintelligible and repugnant. Annexation is the only operation that makes sense to a consciousness that has internalized capitalism. But annexation to what? To a psychic economy that takes as its primary task the elimination of everything within the "self" that does not conform to the logic of capitalism. Through the perfection of that operation one attains the only goal that has value: that blissful state of affirmation of a subject obsessed of necessity with sign-exchange value—with obtaining what Rilke termed "money's genitals," the objects one surrounds oneself with in order to satisfy the narcissistic fixation and conceal the narcissistic void that capitalism necessarily produces. A "self" that has reduced itself to the condition of a thing must perforce obsessively proclaim, through the possession of things, a phantom identity. That is why capitalism produces as the primary form of social interaction the age of Happy Talk—the compulsive and compulsory reassurance that one is, indeed, the realization of all human values and has the proof: one "feels good about oneself" and is unable to feel any other way. *Capitalist ideology fuses economic and psychological imperatives. The result is a mass subject in thrall to collective fantasms, a subject whose inwardness mirrors the void at the center of the system. The pursuit of narcissistic "identity" and the fetishization of commodities are inseparable and finally indistinguishable processes.*

*Lesson Seven.* Compulsory happiness brings us to the role in ideology of what should have been its primary critic. In using psychoanalytic categories to analyze ideology, my effort is to reclaim all that is dangerous and radical in Freud's legacy in order to combat what has happened to psychoanalysis in America. For in America psychoanalysis is by and large the "identity wing" of the ideological project. This wing performs perhaps the most important function: social engineering in order to create subjects bound to the social system as the very condition of mental health and ego identity. Playing that role has been the through-line of psychoanalytic ego psychology from Heinz Hartmann's fetishization of *adaptation* to the current fruition of that project: the creation, as a therapeutic ideal, of "selves" that are so well adapted to the system that anything troubling or traumatic has but one meaning and serves but one purpose: an occasion to prove that a strong, stable ego-identity always moves *from* and *to* the reaffirmation of all the ideological beliefs and guarantees and one's *identification* with them. *Ego psychology* is social engineering as ideological justification. And it works because thanks to the trickle-down effect of such thinking in popular discourse and in the media, we are now bound psychologically as a nation to the cruelest necessity: the internalization *en masse* of affirmative ways of feeling that wed subjects to the system because such feelings constitute the only way they can relate to experience. Feeling good must perforce be enacted with the rigidity and regularity of a behavioral law of stimulus–response in service to the underling rule: one should never have bad feelings; indeed, all feelings labeled "negative" must be shunned. This is why 9-11 was a *trauma that could not be responded to traumatically.* Instead, the trauma had to be resolved with good feelings restored and as quickly as possible. Any response to events that sustains pain is by definition bad. Faced with trauma, psychology performs what is for capitalism its function—putting Humpty Dumpty back together again by helping the populace reaffirm the founding emotional belief: that every trauma must be resolved through recovery of those positive feelings without which, we are told, life would be meaningless.

Our task thus entails a new psychological imperative. To free ourselves from capitalist ideology we must free ourselves from all the psychological needs and feelings that have for most of us attained the status of unquestioned emotional necessities. If we are to free ourselves from capitalism's monopoly over emotional experience, tragic self-overcoming and not adaptation must become the relationship we live to ourselves. *Psychology is the capstone of the ideological process. Its function under capitalism is social engineering: the transformation of quiet desperation into the noisy affirmation of docile subjects wedded to the collective hosannah that deprives them of inwardness.*

*Lesson Eight.* The opposite drive, however, has today assumed control over what should be the primary site of resistance. I refer to what has happened in the arts since 9-11: not just the cancellation in New York, in Princeton, and elsewhere of "shows deemed inappropriate at this time" because they ask us to question when what everyone wants from the arts now is the warm bath of positive feelings; but also the proliferation of works that perform one of the two functions that capitalism assigns to art: (1) mindless entertainment that relieves us of our burdens while programming us to desire more mindless entertainment; and worse, (2) false resolution of trauma through the offering of those *structures of feeling* that are the aesthetic wing of ideology.[4] I refer to the general belief that the role of serious art is to produce a "catharsis" that discharges the burden of painful feelings thereby restoring us to a "humanity" that is essentialistic and ahistorical. Such an aesthetic cannot learn from history because it has "always already" *transcended* it. What it regards as its superior "humanism" really amounts, however, to little more than *a priori* emotional needs imposed on events in order to protect and reaffirm a system of beliefs that has as its informing purpose a "metaphysical" containment of the tragic.[5] Art as oppositional discourse thereby receives from this ideology what it must henceforth take as its task: the *deracination* of every "structure of feeling" that weds art to the effort to please audiences and reaffirm their identities. Culture remains oppositional only if it refuses to compromise its *negativity*. By that standard, I would suggest, the arts have never been in a worse condition than they are now. *Ideology is the means through which the sources of resistance are contained a priori by structures of feeling that dictate the response to traumatic events so that any possibility of knowledge and genuine change is rendered impossible. Far from incidental, this is the ideological formation that holds the entire ideological edifice in place, determining what we must feel and predetermining what we cannot know. In its working upon feeling, ideology is inherently behaviorist. Its effort is to create a populace bound to ideology by emotional stimulus–response mechanisms that cause its subjects to salivate to certain beliefs the way Pavlov's dogs salivated to the bell.*

*Lesson Nine.* On August 6, 2003, as an official "commemoration" of the 58th anniversary of Hiroshima, a top secret meeting was held at the U.S. Strategic Command Center in Omaha, Nebraska. Over 150 top U.S. officials and military contractors attended. Vice President Cheney was reportedly there as was Keith Payne, the man most often seen as the prototype for Dr. Strangelove. (It was Payne who in 1980 opined that the U.S. could absorb losses of 20 million in a nuclear war with Russia and win.) Congressional staff members and committee staff members were barred from the meeting. Its primary purpose was to discuss various proposals for production of tactical high-yield, earth-penetrating nuclear weapons. Such weapons are thought to have many uses, including (fantastically) the ability to incinerate biological and chemical weapons.[6]

The search is over. We finally know where the WMD are—and why they haunt us as something we must project as "out there somewhere" ... in Iraq ... or, as one pundit suggested, already smuggled out and hiding somewhere else. (The WMD functions as Bush and Company's Lacanian *objet a*.) For the imagination of nuclear winter there will always be such conferences where, as in PAM, contradictions come together as in the logic of the dream, a logic where desire cannot be negated and where expression of the deepest unconscious wish-structure is assured. *A specter is haunting Amerika, the specter of Hiroshima.* What we did then must be repeated, if only in fantasy (and supposedly in a diminished form) in order to again exorcise the *disavowed* memory of Hiroshima from our collective psyche. Nuclear fear swept America after 1945 as our bad conscience: the recognition that what we'd done could be done to us. But as in *Macbeth* fear for us can only be the *return of projections* which must be evacuated again by an even greater projection of the founding act. Thus the hydrogen bomb. Star wars. And for the twenty-first century and a new historical situation—the Age of Empire or State Terrorism and counterterrorism—the production of new tactical nuclear weapons as both practical and justifiable. In that extreme, historical irony and dark intentionality meet. Our actions in Iraq proliferated the nuclear threat by teaching all nations (North Korea, Iran) that the only way to *deter* American aggression is by getting the bomb. What the conference in Omaha enables us to intimate about the future thus squares with what after fifty years we now know about why Hiroshima and Nagasaki were incinerated. Those motives remain at the core of our policy toward the world. Once again history does not repeat itself as farce; it repeats itself as psychotic necessity. *Ideology guarantees the continued projection of the founding psychosis as the blank check on which the entire edifice draws for its sustenance; for in its work ideology forms a circle that cannot be broken into, one which resolves experience and history into the ceaseless repetition of the same.*

*Lesson Ten.* There is a deeper, psychological reason why our leaders must find ways to "commemorate" Hiroshima. Psychosis is the attempt to attain certainty through the *manic triad*—triumph, contempt, and dismissal. Thereby the other is made the object of an aggression that obliterates all humanistic and ethical restraints. The narcissistic grandiosity thereby unleashed is wedded to the ultimate inversion: *Thanatos eroticized* provides the one and only, supreme and irresistible, libidinal pleasure—the pleasure of unleashing a destructiveness that voids all inner tensions, thereby completing the project of ideology by putting an end to all doubts and fears. Fortuitously, the same day as the Omaha conference Studs Terkel interviewed Paul Tibbetts, the man who dropped the first bomb and who has proudly proclaimed on countless occasions that he's never felt a moment's regret. To him is thus reserved what was in Omaha also the last word. Studs Terkel: "One last thing, when you hear people say, 'Let's nuke 'em,' 'Let's nuke these people,' what do you think?" Tibbets: "Oh, I wouldn't hesitate if I had the choice. I'd wipe 'em out. You're gonna kill innocent people at the same time ... That's their tough luck for being there."[7] *Ideology is the wedding of everything to the eroticization of Thanatos.*

That eroticization *is* the through-line of recent American history, the key to understanding the true goal of capitalist ideology: to create a historical situation in which all human relations have become relations among things. To know the future mandated by that imperative the best text remains a great poem Robert Lowell wrote in 1967 entitled "Waking Early Sunday Moring." Lowell there identified global war as our monotonous sublime.[8]

*Monotonous* because it's the repetition compulsion of those unable to react to history in any other way. *Sublime* because it evacuates all inner anxiety by creating the only object that can fill such beings with wonder: the scorched earths in which they realize the objective correlative of their own inner condition.

In view of such a situation the task of resistance is clear. We must continue to constitute the trauma of 9-11 and refuse any and all attempts to dissolve it. This is the only response that seizes trauma not as an occasion to prove once again that ideology blinds us to history but in order to show that sustaining trauma is the act that enables us to know history for the first time through the act of apprehending—at the very moment they go into operation—the psychological mechanisms whereby it is denied. This epistemological opportunity speaks, moreover, to a deeper imperative. It is the only basis for an *ethic* that maintains solidarity with the victims. As Walter Benjamin taught, the dead remain in danger. Not just of being appropriated by the monsters who claim to act in their name, but of us whenever we sacrifice our solidarity with the dead in order to satisfy our psychological and emotional needs.

# 3

# Passion of the Christ in Abu Ghraib

### THE MISFIT'S DILEMMA

"It's no real pleasure in life."

The Misfit in Flannery O'Connor's
*A Good Man is Hard to Find*

"When thinking comes to a stand still in a constellation saturated with tension—there the dialectical image appears."
Walter Benjamin

The previous chapters reveal emotion as the glue that holds together the entire ideological edifice. My focus here is on how it takes root through images, symbols, and symbolic actions. It is here that we'll find the psychological forces that hold other ideological formations in place, giving them the power to compel allegiance, often long after their contradictions have become apparent. Unfortunately, ideology is still thought of as primarily a study of the ideas, beliefs, commonplaces, and attitudes that blind people to a correct understanding of their historical situation. Ideological analysis so conceived concentrates on how a world in the head is maintained through a sort of reasoning, however flawed. The psyche, which is where the real action is, thereby escapes detection and critique. We lose sight of the primacy fact: that human beings are creatures ruled by emotions that we refuse to examine or alter even after those emotions have proven themselves thoroughly incompatible with our situation. How else can we explain tearful, cheering throngs transfixed by the words "Habemus Papam" (We Have a Pope) heralding the ascension of a reactionary beyond belief? Ideology is so hard to subvert not because the beliefs and ideas are solid but because they draw on and satisfy underlying emotions. Get people to invest enough emotion in a flag or an image (Christ on the Cross, the Twin Towers aflame) or a symbolic act (the fantasy of ridding the world of evil) and it is a thing of comparative ease to enlist their continuing support in discredited ideas and policies, lies readily embraced because they feed underlying emotional needs. To dislodge ideological blinders we have to get at the emotional and psychological register where the actual processes of ideological formation take place. This requires a new kind of ideological analysis. As Walter Benjamin and Theodor Adorno saw, it is in image that the historian finds the secret dream life of a culture. Image must, accordingly, become the primary object of ideological analysis because it reveals what other ideological formations conceal. That is so because from the beginning image is foremost in the formation and self-regulation of the psyche. We don't know the world of our most intimate concerns through concepts that are arrived at through rational, quasi-deliberative processes; we know it through images that engage us emotionally because they embody our dreams, our fantasies, and our discontents in forms that draw on the primary processes through which the psyche relates to itself in depth.[1] The world of image to which we would return is, however, far different from the one that Benjamin and Adorno inhabited. Always historicize! This, the first and last commandment of leftist inquiry, implies the search for images that will reveal how our historical situation differs from the past. Historical inquiry is the search for those events that are singular because they reveal something new, because in and through them the collective psyche takes a leap toward something new and potentially irreversible.[2] The task of ideological critique is to identify and comprehend such events. This is also its inherent challenge, since nothing is harder to understand than the new—an event such as Hiroshima, Auschwitz, 9-11. Such events shatter extant ways of thinking. That shattering persists in the images that define those events. They point thought toward places it cannot go unless one allows the image to continue to work emotionally and psychologically within one's consciousness.

In terms of rigorous criteria few things that happen qualify as events. And seldom is the response to an image developed with the frightening clarity of the American response to 9-11 as analyzed in Chapter 1. I want to argue here that the same revelatory status should be given to a recent film by Mel Gibson and to what happened in Abu Ghraib. I hope to show, moreover, that the three events are necessarily connected developments in the historical unfolding of a single disorder. To combat that disorder, however, our first order of business must be to comprehend how image and emotion operate in the psyche. Thanks to Mel Gibson we have at our disposal a particularly revealing example, a privileged sign of the times and of what Christianity has become in Amerika.

## MOVIE-GOERS IN THE HANDS OF AN ANGRY FILM-MAKER

We should take seriously the testimony of vast audiences that watching this film was one of their deepest religious experiences. Demonstrating how the film operates in the psyche will thus enable us to gauge the extreme emotional register at which religion today works. For Gibson is a master of the image and its ability to work on the deepest registers of the psyche.

The following scene occurs early in Gibson's film. As the bound Jesus is being led to prison he is dropped over a wall. The rope catches just before he will hit the ground. We hear the crunch of bone, see the broken Jesus dangling, suffering what must be a shock to the entire system. (We would see the same image again, soon, in the news, April 4, 2004. Only this time it would come to us from Fallujah: the photo of the charred body of an American hung from a bridge over the Euphrates.) The scene in Gibson's film has no biblical source and thus is particularly revealing in a film that claims absolute fidelity to the Gospels, which Gibson refuses to submit to one iota of historical scholarship. "It is as it was," such was the *imprimatur* that Gibson's publicists claimed John Paul II pronounced after viewing the film. The scene under discussion is in the film, however, because it serves a far greater exigency than the "truth." Gibson knows what films do, what his audience craves. He is impatient to get the blood sport underway in what will become two hours of unrelieved sadomasochism, making *Passion* the longest piece of snuff porn on record.

The day I saw the film—the day it opened, in what I took as my atheistic responsibility—the theater was packed as would be theaters throughout the country for the next few weeks. There they sat with buckets full of buttered popcorn, large containers of coke, working men in shirt sleeves with pot bellies beside their even larger Fraus (the McDonald's generation), tears streaming down their faces, moved as they had not been by any film in memory. Some actually cried out. Others gasped. Repeatedly.

How do we account for the unprecedented success of this film, its status as a true event in the development of Amerikan fundamentalist religiosity?

Gibson as film-maker pays strict allegiance to the lesson that for him forms the totality of cinematic art. Cinema makes possible the systematic administration of repeated shocks to the nervous system, creating visceral affects that operate by a mechanism that delivers the psyche of the audience to the ministry of the special effects department. For Gibson we live indeed in unprecedented times. Film is the art form that enables us, for the first time in Western history, to experience the Passion as it was for eyewitnesses. Gibson knows—and the unprecedented popular success of his film testifies to the fact—that today's mass audience is only capable of a single operation, which must perforce be repeated endlessly through the production of new and greater shocks to the system. The ooohs and aaahs, the gasps of shocked amazement at each new special effect are the audience's tribute to the film-maker's success in devising new and bloodier ways to assault their sensibilities.

Film is, as Bertolucci said, an animal act, the immediacy of a convulsive experience that eludes reflective consciousness. As such, film is the greatest tool of propaganda yet invented. Its inherent power is to work directly on the response mechanism of the human being in order to effect permanent alterations in one's ability to feel. (Think of Gibson as the anti-Kubrick, *Passion* as an unrepentant *Clockwork Orange*.) Gibson has mastered the single principle that informs this art. He knows what the audience wants. How much of it they want. And he's smart enough not to let anything get in the way. All complexities, any attempt to represent the inwardness of Jesus, are and must be sacrificed to the bloodbath. Christ's suffering must remain a purely physical spectacle. About all one can say about this Christ is that he is the greatest athlete of his time, in perfect shape for the marathon he must run.

Of necessity Gibson reduces the Passion to a mechanical sequence of sadomasochistic shocks, which must be repeated, each more brutal than the last and with less time intervening. The inability to feel in any other way—even over the Christ—is the true testimony Gibson's film offers to the ruling principle of mainline Hollywood cinema. Gibson knew his film would be a megahit because it makes the Amerikan audience the offer they can't refuse: the pleasure of sadomasochistic cruelty. Protestations of piety disguise the true object of this film: to brutalize the audience by offering them the most extreme experience yet captured on film of the primary thing they go to the movies for—a feast of violence. By masking an orgy of violence as an act of piety Gibson offers the audience a way through their tears both to deny and to feel good about the sadomasochistic process needed to generate those tears. Having paid that price they get a final benefit: identification with God's rage. For Gibson's audience is crying only on the outside. Inside they've been ripened for *projective identification*; i.e., an evacuation on some target of the cumulative rage that has built up in them. At the film's end, having glutted their appetite for sadomasochistic stimuli, they leave the theater full of rage and with a new need: a target on which to vent that rage. It is a mistake to fixate on the film's patent anti-Semitism. Gibson's true achievement is the creation of a war readiness readily transferrable to Islam.

Rene Girard, ever hopeful that Christianity holds the solution to escalating violence, said this: "religion puts a veil over the subject of vengeance."[3] Gibson rends it, letting us see beneath that veil the insatiable lust of a mindless cruelty. This is not only the pleasure that the murderers of Christ indulge. It's what the film-maker takes repeated, orgasmic delight in. It's Gibson's own arm, we are told, that drives the nail through Christ's hand, Gibson's own blood-curdling scream the soundtrack offers in response to that blow. Such is true autoaffection for a compulsive sadomasochist. No doubt the pleasure of repeated reviewing is why he recently re-cut the entire film, just in time for an Easter re-release. But Gibson's delight is one he fully shares with the audience. The death of affect requires extreme affects repeated and with an accelerating extremity. Otherwise the audience sinks into lethargy, returning to the void. Sadomasochistic pleasure has become the only affect that assures them that they are alive. In this sense Gibson is their Saviour, the savage god.

The goal of his film is not purification or faith or love or piety. It's the sadomasochistic bludgeoning of the audience so that they will become abject subjects on their knees, but full of rage, eager to "do unto others" the violence that has been done to their psyches. There is no contradiction here; rather a confirmation of the way in which Eros and Thanatos become one in Gibson's film. The libidinous and the violently aggressive here fuse in a new constellation that transforms the basic condition of cinematic pleasure. Contra Laura Mulvey, the gaze of the camera is now fixated not on eroticized (though passive) women but on suffering male bodies in extremes of excruciating pain.[4] The Nazi pleasure dome is achieved. In the Christ Gibson finds the homoerotic urtext behind the Nazi love of the beautiful blonde boy, his taut body blossoming with his own blood at each bite of the whip.

Gibson's film thus stands as a sign of the desperation that underlies the pieties of mainstream American religiosity. This is both Gibson's "genius" and his hidden despair. He may loudly proclaim his Christianity, but the world he lives in is one of utter brutalization, his project as film-maker the same as the one that informs porn:

to reduce the psyche of the audience to a mechanism that cums by command whenever triggered by the one thing that excites it: cruelty. As such, *Passion* offers us a privileged insight into the fundamentalist Amerikan psyche, a way to understand what's really going on in the prayer breakfasts that have become a daily necessity at the White House.

For there they were, afterward, those same men and women I'd heard moaning and shrieking for the past two hours, standing in the lobby, dazed and confused, unable to leave the theater, tears streaming down their faces but with a new look in their eyes—that of a rage already on the lookout for anyone who did not share or dared to question the verities of their feelings. Such are the glad tidings according to Mel: when most devout and most perverse the Amerikan is the same, a psyche excited only by extremes of sadomasochism. Marx was wrong. Capitalism won't dispense with religion. It will require one kind of religion. Bush and Ashcroft represent its benign—if mindless—face. Gibson gives us its true visage.

His significance for an ideological and historical understanding of emotion is considerable, since what his film dramatizes with unexampled clarity is how an ideology operates directly on the psyche to bring about fundamental changes both in the principles of its self-regulation and the actions that will be required to provide that psyche the satisfaction it seeks. As such, Passion is not just an expression of what I term 9-11 syndrome; it's a blueprint for Abu Ghraib. I hasten to add what should be obvious. This is not a sociological question of whether the seven perpetrators of Abu Ghraib saw Gibson's film or are born-again Christians. My concern is to comprehend a collective psyche that operates in many places and in many ways. Gibson offers one way for it to act out, as ritual, its sadomasochistic needs. The perverse artists of Abu Ghraib found another.

Gibson gives us an in-depth look at what is actually going on in the fundamentalist psyche and how its extremities mirror the psychotic and narcissistic needs of the culture at large. Prior to Gibson, over 50 million Amerikans declared themselves fundamentalist or born-again Christians. Such sociological data is helpful though far from sufficient to account for Gibson. For Gibson is a traditional Catholic anti-Vatican II reactionary who represents beliefs that were covertly supported by Karol Wyotka (John Paul II).[5] Gibson's significance, however, extends well beyond the designs of Opus Dei. Thanks to Gibson the ranks of the born-again have grown, if not officially, in a far more important way: psychologically. Such is the power of art and why cultural practices should become a primary object of ideological study. Once films like Gibson's become the primary means by which audiences react to the cinematic representation of experience, the thing they crave in going to the movies—and Gibson's film is but one example of the prevailing sadomasochism of mainline Hollywood cinema—it's just a matter of time before the political manifestation of this way of feeling will find its Leader. Which, of course, it has. Subjects formed by images to feel a certain way will of necessity act on what they've felt. The way they've been formed to feel will perforce become the content of their being, the essence of their religion. Psyches formed by the Christianity Gibson represents seek of necessity actions that crave a particular form of jouissance: one in which orgiastic pleasure comes from abolishing all inner restraints and committing the kind of dehumanizing deeds required to make one feel better than one has ever felt before. Abu Ghraib beckons.

Two theoretical points by way of transition to the theater of cruelty fashioned in Abu Ghraib. Thanks to Gibson we now have a better understanding of image as emotion. Image is the assault that emotion makes upon the psyche and what is opened up to transformation as a result. We will only begin to understand this ideological process when we develop a theory of emotion that breaks with the understanding of emotion that has characterized the intellectualist tradition in its abiding attempt to make emotion something secondary: as when emotion is seen as a byproduct of ideas; a loss of rational control; a release of tension; a sign of irrationality; a purely biological or neurological event. In contrast to all these views and their common effort to isolate rationality from taint, we must begin to see emotion as the primary way in which the psyche regulates and empowers itself in a world where knowledge is not primarily a matter of logic or rationality but rather the projection of psychological needs and complexes upon events. I hasten to add, the corrective to the ideological manipulation of emotion is not the impossible pursuit of a standpoint free of emotion, but as will be shown below a full and historical engagement of the radical possibility implicit in emotion: the discovery, through tragic self-overcoming, of emotions that have the power to deracinate the kinds of emotions Gibson indulges.

There is reason to be thankful for Gibson. For the main thing his film reveals is that today everything is played out at the psychotic register of the psyche. That register is what was rent open by 9-11, what Dubya and Co. have been acting out ever since and what

Gibson brings to a grotesquely sublime and finalizing condition. Psychoanalytic theories that remain within the orbit of neurosis and normalcy are unable to deal with the present historical situation, which is defined by what happens when traumatic events create catastrophic anxiety in a collectivity threatened with psychological fragmentation and dissolution under the sway of a nameless terror. Such was the impact of 9-11 on a collectivity already working overtime to deny the void at the center of a desperate narcissism. It now faced a new task. But getting the necessary emotional satisfaction of its condition through a film is one thing. What's needed is action, rituals to consecrate worship to the savage god of sadomasochistic excess. We are ready to enter Abu Ghraib.

## THE NON-ACCIDENTAL TOURIST

If *The Passion of the Christ* is the high point in the emotional expression of fundamentalist Christianity, Abu Ghraib is equally extreme in its attempt to attack and belittle another religion. The two acts derive, moreover, from the same psychodynamic principle: the sadomasochistic need for extreme images of brutalization and suffering that must be repeated and maximized in order to create in a mass audience the only feeling of which they are capable: the glee that comes from participation in spectacles of cruelty.

Abu Ghraib, as Seymour Hersh has shown, had its genesis in a reading by Bush's neocon luminaries of Raphael Patai's *The Arab Mind* (1973) and specifically a single chapter in that unremarkable book, Chapter VIII "The Realm of Sex."[6] Reading no doubt with their hands in their pants, a light went on in the neocon darkness. The way to control the other, the Arab, is to use their sexual beliefs and practices to humiliate them and thereby destroy their attachment to the principle that gives their life meaning. Abu Ghraib is the acting out of that project. The language of transmission—how the idea got from Perle and Wolfowitz to Rumsfeld to Sanchez to Karpinski to Garner, England et al.—isn't all that important. What matters is the message, which is assured at each step along the way because it addresses the same shared psychological disorder.

Neocon ideology is a fantasmatic dream state. We've now learned much about the naïve beliefs that inform neocon thinking, such as the assurance that following the blitzkreig in Iraq, Democracy would sweep the Middle East. The tortures devised by ordinary American soldiers at Abu Ghraib prison give us the other side of the neocon fantasm, the perverse corollary to the airy nothing on which it bases its political articles of faith. Such is the genius of the actors who arrange the tableaux and pose themselves for the camera eye in Abu Ghraib. A terrible envy underlies what happened in Abu Ghraib, an envy that has been working on the psychotic register of the American psyche since 9-11. Islamic fundamentalists have something we lack. They're willing to die for their religion. Only one response to such an affront is possible. They must be forced to violate their religious beliefs and to do so as part of a perverse ritual. In this regard two images from Abu Ghraib are especially revealing. The man masturbating before his torturers forced while doing so to curse Islam. The father and son, hoods ripped off, confronting one another's nakedness.

Just as any piece of writing has an implicit audience, any posed photograph is self-representation before an ideal viewer. The key to the project of Abu Ghraib is the desire to be the one in the picture frame who bears the gaze that is simultaneously directed at the prisoner's abjection and the camera's eye. One is thereby assured of a triumph over the abject otherness that the former represents and the identity that the latter alone confers. As such Abu Ghraib is the staging of self for what Lacanians call the Big Other—that ultimate paternal principle of authority and meaning whose approval one seeks. Abu Ghraib tears away all other masks, revealing that the true father of the American Imaginary is not Billy Graham or Dubya or Scalia or even Reagan. The true father is "the obscene father of enjoyment."[7] But in confirming this Lacanian idea Abu Ghraib gives it a new twist. For in epiphanizing the commandment to enjoy it overturns that imperative. Contra Lacan, enjoyment fails because it is meant to relieve a psychotic condition. That is why it must take horrifying forms, in a repetition compulsion dictated by a quantitative logic of increased cruelty since for the commodified self no inner source of creative invention remains. The torturers of Abu Ghraib are condemned to the incessant aping of the idiot grin, the phallic pose that mimes the identity they seek. That, in fact, is why one must be photographed and those photographs endlessly circulated to the only audience they can have: those who will gape back, *interpellated* by them, hailed as subjects who say the yes of recognition to this mirroring of their own mindless stare. Abu Ghraib reveals the Amerikan as a serial killer trapped in the necessity that defines that condition: repetition but always with a new excess because every action returns one to a psychic void. That void is the condition of affectlessness. Its result: the inability to feel except through the sadomasochistic acts through which one tries to convince oneself that one is alive.

Abu Ghraib also signals a transformation in the nature of Tourism. As we all know, our boys and girls now go off to war armed with digital cameras. Writing is a dying art, but those left behind on the homefront can expect a frequent supply of photographs. Many of these photos bear a family resemblance to those taken at Abu Ghraib. We, not the Japanese, are now the tourists who must photograph everything. But with a fundamental difference. The Japanese tourist is a subject respectfully posed before the object—be it the Grand Canyon, the Mississippi, Disneyworld, the Golden Arches. The American tourist, in contrast, focuses the camera on the self: Kilroy in Baghdad, the grin, the leer, the phallic posturing, the gesture of appropriation applied to every aspect of the domestic space of the other. Abu Ghraib is a stark revelation of the perverse desire that fuels that need. One goal of these pictures is to give the folks back home a taste of what they're missing. Abu Ghraib as an Amerikan kasbah, true Orientalism. If there is a measure of cruelty toward that audience in these pictures, it's a function of their smug assertiveness. "This is what I got by enlisting, what you're missing out on." A deeper function, of course, is to send back home the message that the media can't broadcast. "This, rest assured, is what we're doing to those vermin who caused 9-11."

The most striking thing in the faces and postures of the Americans at Abu Ghraib is their commodified nature. Nothing can be spontaneous about their pleasure. One has seen all of this before. Countless times. In porn. Such is the mindless leer on Private England's face, the staple of the woman in porn, offering herself to the camera in that look that epitomizes the Playboy bunny; the idiot look of one trying to persuade herself and the male viewer that this is what female pleasure looks like: the "come take me any way you want me I live just to please you" come on. Such is the phallic assertiveness of Spc. Garner's posture, Duke Wayne proud above a tangle of naked Arab men, secure in the smug assurance that brutality is the true mark of macho identity.

In Abu Ghraib sexual debasement is staged as an act of violence on a passive victim who is forced to perform perverse actions for the sexual satisfaction of agents who make no attempt to hide the glee they derive from their perversity. As such Abu Ghraib is not the staging of sexuality but a perverse parody of it. The attempt of these soldiers is to convince themselves that they have what the photographs reveal they lack: an autonomous sexual identity. The empty mindless looks on the faces are the most revealing thing about these photographs. Like Gibson's *Passion*, Abu Ghraib is a desperate attempt to flee the void which only serves to reveal it. The death of affect is here the truth of subjectivity. That is why sadomasochism again strides forth to fill the breach as the one sexual expression adequate to the *fascism of the heart*: the reduction of the other to the conditions of a thing in order to celebrate a feeling of power that is openly contemptuous of all moral and human restraints.

Friends and relatives are quick to tell us that the Americans pictured at Abu Ghraib were typical kids, kind, helpful, friendly, all-round regular guys and gals. There is no reason to doubt this account or the uncanny way it witnesses to the condition that characterizes the American subject today: the split between a benign, average public self and the underlying void that self-hypnotic conformity is meant to conceal. The result: a festering disorder wedded to the perverse fantasies that alone give one a sense of being. Abu Ghraib is a message from the heart of the American psyche back to the heartland. It broadcasts the good news: the pleasure and the self-certainty that come from cruelty.

It is easy to say that Abu Ghraib represents the acting out of a fantasy. But rather than mitigate what happens there, this idea should be developed in the most rigorous way. For fantasy is serious business. It is an attempt by the psyche to imagine or perform an action that will free it from its deepest conflicts while realizing its deepest desires. By this definition Abu Ghraib is an act of genius, a psychoanalytic masterpiece. For everything here is sexual—both the humiliation forced upon the victim and the identity claimed through that action. The latter, however, is a sham, which is what the commodified looks reveal. The mindless grin, the obscene leer is the copy of a copy of a copy, an imitation that has no source because it was already in its pornographic genesis a fantasy meant to counterfeit sexual pleasure for the camera.

Abu Ghraib is both homage to and imitation of the Chief. For the parent text is Bush on the aircraft carrier *Lincoln*, unable to delay his orgasm any longer, needing to crow "We're #1" to the world with that smug smile of superiority that is the only thing he learned at Yale. But this too is imitation, the military garb and the phallic posturing a reincarnation of President Bill Pullman in Osama bin Laden's favorite film, *Independence Day*. Abu Ghraib mirrors as privilege and pleasure the contempt of Bushian unilateralism for the rest of the world, for all conventions, Geneva or otherwise, that would restrain the thrust of Empire. What the Bush doctrine proclaimed abstractly, Abu Ghraib acts out at the psychotic register. Mindless bullying is the American sublime. The grinning, idiotic face is the objective correlative of the only response that the Amerikan can have to the trauma of 9-11, since surplus revenge has historically provided us with the only way post-trauma to once again feel good about ourselves. Hiroshima *vivant*. As Private England said: "This wasn't punishment. This was sport." Because the actors of Abu Ghraib—and they were nothing if not performers—acted from the psychotic register of the American unconscious their actions are uniquely revelatory of what official policies conceal—and solicit. For about one thing there should be no doubt: Abu Ghraib was an act of worship, the creation of a ritual like the Mass, celebrating the fundamental article of the new faith: the sanctity of psychological cruelty.

In all these ways Abu Ghraib is far more than an Atrocity Exhibition. Like Gibson's film it offers us a privileged window into the collective psyche. Two things proceed from the void: the desire to exploit suffering for sadomasochistic pleasure and the desire, whenever the opportunity presents itself, to take perverse pleasure in doing unto helpless victims what the torturers of Christ did to Him in Gibson's film.

Ideological scrutiny here applies, however, to more than the obvious targets. We've been offered a series of explanations for Abu Ghraib. All are wrong and all are necessary because they supplement one another in the support of a shared collective ideology. This ideology cuts across differences between liberals and conservatives and points to something shared that ideological critique must expose. This is moreover where the most strenuous objections will arise, since our inquiry will now impinge on *guarantees* that claim wide allegiance because they satisfy the one superordinate thing that all ideologies offer: the belief that there are certain values and ideals that can be placed outside history and that no traumatic events can eradicate. In support of this underlying need we've been offered a series of explanations of Abu Ghraib that supplement one another in their effort to limit the disruptive significance of that event and thereby exorcize the thing we refuse to think: that history cuts to the quick with nothing in the order of "human nature" protected from what it may bring to pass. (1) Abu Ghraib was an exception, not a sign of a systemic disorder. (2) It was the act of a few bad apples (in contrast to the 99.9 percent of our boys and girls in uniform). (3) It was a result of instructions from above reflecting a pathology confined to the upper reaches of the Bush administration and not America in general. (4) It was a function of the situation—of what Robert J. Lifton calls "an atrocity-producing situation"; i.e., such things always happen in wars of oppression.[8] The combined weight of these explanations assures us once again that there is nothing new under the sun, no evidence in Abu Ghraib of a new pathology nor of a historical change in the psyche. (5) And so we can rest assured, as reported in one of the first psychological essays on Abu Ghraib, that "experts in the history and psychology of torture say" that "the U.S. troops who abused Iraqis at the Abu Ghraib prison near Baghdad were most likely not pathological sadists but ordinary people who felt they were doing the dirty work needed to win the war."[9] Explanations of Abu Ghraib thus present something like what happens when members of Congress put aside "partisan disagreements" to report on matters we can all agree on. It's then that we should get nervous—and keen in our interest. Because one thing then is certain: some ideological commonplace is forthcoming, dressed in the demand that the public at large concur. So, with respect to the above series of explanations, which one you pick doesn't matter, since the function of the series is to assure that history is denied. What could have been known is thereby lost; namely, that Abu Ghraib is a *singular event* revealing a collective pathology enacting what makes this event unique: *the use of their religion to destroy subjects and thereby justify the contempt one feels for their religion.* Abu Ghraib, I suggest, is in fact the coming of something new under the sun. Moreover, this is the understanding we must try to produce because it's the one that sets our teeth on edge, the one capable of maximizing rather than short-circuiting the trauma of that event. Ideology works best when it tricks us into accepting false alternatives. Our debates thereby assure that we'll miss the necessary connections. Abu Ghraib, however, is not a matter of either/or, as in the above series, but of both/and, revealing the unity of a purpose that stretches from top to bottom because it derives from the underlying pathology that informs the whole. Making the necessary connections that ideology strives to render impossible is the goal of dialectical or Marxist understanding.

The explanations offered of Abu Ghraib prevent our knowing it as an unprecedented event, a historical singularity, and as such a break with the past and a tiger's leap into the future. It is easy to say that sadistic sexual torture is endemic to wartime. In that, of course,

Abu Ghraib is hardly unique. What's unique here is the religious connection. In Abu Ghraib sexual humiliation is used to force individuals representative of a people to violate their deepest religious beliefs in order to reduce them psychologically to a condition of permanent abjection. Let us not understate the goal of torture at Abu Ghraib: to destroy the soul—the ability to go on being—of those one tortures. And lest one miss the point, walk for five minutes in the shoes of the men who had to say this to themselves: *I betrayed my religion in order to save my life.*

Abu Ghraib, like Gibson's *Passion*, is the antithesis of a purification ritual. Nothing is discharged. The Amerikan desire dances to a different necessity. To inflict one's condition on the other. If you eat dung that means I don't have to. The pleasure Gibson offers is the same one that one finds on the faces of the Americans at Abu Ghraib. That is so because both draw on the same disorder. The void as the lethargy that gnaws at one from within until one is delivered from it by a new shock to the system through a brutalization one suffers or one that one inflicts. Only so can one feel or, what amounts to the same thing, convince oneself that one feels. Inadvertently Gibson reveals the truth. When at its most devout and its most perverse the Amerikan is the same.

A Spinozistic conclusion, a lesson in how to use mechanistic explanations when they are historically appropriate. To summarize with the bluntness the subject deserves, Abu Ghraib enacts what the life of feeling now is for the average American. Sadomasochism is the one constant because historically it now constitutes the only way to convince oneself that one is alive. When we indulge it on behalf of those we "love," we get choked up with emotion. When we indulge it on behalf of those we hate, we take joy in expressing the manic triad: triumph, contempt, and dismissal projected onto an object of rage in order to give us the sense of victory over all inner conflicts. The Amerikan psyche oscillates between these two behaviors because it is, qua psyche, no more than their underlying necessity: for new and ever greater shocks to the system as the only way to deliver oneself from despair. From which follow a few of what Spinoza would term adequate ideas regarding three words that Dubya glibly employs for transparent ideological ends. To know what terror, fundamentalism, and evil are one need go no further than Abu Ghraib. If, unlike Bush and the media, we want to think about these topics in non jingoistic ways there is no better place to begin than Abu Ghraib. Terror is the attempt through humiliation and cruelty to destroy another's psyche in order to confer on oneself the absolute status that comes with the liberation of a power free of restraint that can be indulged as an end in itself. What is fundamentalism? Here's a definition offered by many historians of religion: voluntary enslavement in the joy of mindlessness and obedience. The Germans have a word for it: *Kadavergehorsamkeit*—to obey like a corpse. In this too Abu Ghraib provides a chilling model of how true believers behave; nay, how they worship. There is, of course, no word quicker to Dubya's lips than evil. Here's a definition that might give even him pause. Evil is the desire to destroy people in their soul and to feel righteous in doing so.

Two theoretical points by way of transition to our concluding sections. Image is where the psyche gives itself away, revealing what other ideological formations conceal. Accordingly, the primary object of ideological study is what, following Adorno and Benjamin, I term the dialectical image. Such images lay bare the fundamental contradictions of a society, arresting both heart and mind because they reveal the disorder that defines a historical situation. As Gibson and Abu Ghraib reveal, in our time the disorder is *the eroticization of Thanatos*[10] and the underlying psychosis that makes that eroticization the only way Amerika can respond to traumatic events. The images Gibson and Abu Ghraib offer are *sublime* in the full Kantian meaning of that term: they represent the innermost needs of the psyche realized in phenomena. The sublime power of such images is a function of their effort to finalize a way of being in a way that will hypnotize the psyche and compel submission to a power that overcomes all resistance. It is Thanatos that finds in Gibson and Abu Ghraib images that transform the rage defining the Amerikan psyche into an object of worship. In these images destructiveness is celebrated both as an end in itself and as a force that persists long after it has destroyed everything opposed to its will.[11] If we want to get inside Thanatos, see how it works, and thereby find a way to reverse its telos, we must comprehend the function that such images have in the sick psyche. A dialectical image has the power to compel allegiance because it speaks directly *from* and *to* the psyche's deepest desires. It cuts through all defenses, displacements, and delays, offering the bliss of a massive unbinding. As we'll see, the only way to combat such images is to create images of an equal power and an opposed telos: i.e., images in which Eros is reclaimed, Orpheus-like, from situations dominated by death.

But to undertake that task we must purge ourselves of the thing in ourselves that stands in the way. I have termed it the guarantees. By that term I refer to all those assurances we set up *a priori* to protect ourselves from the reality of historical trauma. The significance of events—the Shoah, Hiroshima, 9-11—is their power to call such guarantees into question by exposing cherished beliefs to the claims of darker views and by forcing us to think in radically new ways, considering things about the human being that we've persistently denied or marginalized. One dimension of any traumatic event is the shock it brings to traditional ways of thinking. That's why the dominant response to any historical trauma is the attempt to restore the guarantees by finding a way to impose them on the event in order to contain and interpret it. The ideological function of the guarantee is thereby demonstrated. A way has been found to limit the impact of the event by picturing it as an aberration, a temporary departure from values and beliefs that can always be recovered because they constitute something essentialistic or universal about "human nature." Something trans-historical. History may disrupt our essence but it cannot destroy it. The concept of human nature—in all the variants constituting the philosophic and psychological history of that idea from Plato and Aristotle through American self psychology—is the primary way in which we endeavor to deny history.

An event is traumatic precisely because it suggests that history occurs beyond the limits we want to impose on it and therefore may move in directions that have nothing to do with "human nature" or the cherished beliefs and values we derive from that concept. Events put us as subjects—and as thinkers—into a traumatic relationship to both ourselves and our world. The anxiety at the center of thought is revealed. Ideologists rush in to fill that void and restore the guarantees. Our effort must be to do the opposite and thereby sustain the vital possibility implicit in an event. That possibility is to sustain a break with the guarantees and thereby find for history a radically different way of thinking. To put it concretely, a trauma cannot be resolved until it's been constituted. The Western Logos is a monument to the effort to avoid that task; indeed, to render it impossible *a priori*. To reverse that tradition the things above all we must rid ourselves of are the desire and demand for resolution. The recycling of the guarantees must give way to an existentializing imperative: to constitute and work within trauma in a way that addresses the psyche at the same register as Gibson and Abu Ghraib do by creating images, symbolic actions, and emotions that are of equal depth but that move us in an antithetical direction—toward the inner transformation needed to purge ourselves of Thanatos. Such an effort, however, cannot itself be yet another variant of the guarantees as happens when Love and Eros are posited as ahistorical values. If anything, the possibility of Love is far more difficult and exacting than death because it can only arise by reversing the prior force that death has within us. The following two sections offer a brief picture of the kind of agonistic process such an effort entails in order to whet our appetitie for something that should by now be evident. The critique of ideology cannot be a merely intellectual exercise. It must be the activation within our psyche of a countervailing drama.

## THE PRINCIPLE OF HOPE: OR, *THE LATE LATE LATE SHOW*

"The last image was too immediate for any eye to register."
Thomas Pynchon, *Gravity's Rainbow*

"Paranoia is the ability to make connections."
From the sayings of Thomas the Elder

In ideological analysis we so often fail to attain anything truly hopeful because the need for hope clicks in too early, preventing us from perceiving the depth of the problem. People keep asking for a leftist principle of Hope and keep looking for it in some set of intellectualist guarantees, as if there were some essentialist humanism that remains untrammelled by history, some Habermasian communicative competence that can provide fixed *a priori* norms for what counts as thought, some system of values that will somehow enable us to rise phoenix-like from our darkest analyses restored to an a-historical essence.

My analysis suggests that we've got to start looking for hope and constructing that principle in a new way. All is action, image, emotion. Reason is but the cutting edge of passions. Drama is our destiny. We are shaped as subjects through process of symbolic action and interaction. What we need accordingly is analyses that will begin with the Waste Land and find within it forces, tendencies, and directions that generate the possibility of genuine reversals, reversals that come perhaps only when we push the disorder to the end of the line. Taking up this task entails admitting that a film such as Gibson's taps into feelings that are far more central than we want to admit. Our task, like that articulated in the motto of the great community activist Saul

Alinsky, is to "rub raw the sores of discontent." Ideological critiques that stay in the ballpark of reason are fine but the only ones that can produce change must attempt to act on the psyche at the same register Gibson gets to but in a way that reverses what a work like his does there. As we'll see shortly, we need to construct fantasies that take the horror manifested in Gibson and Abu Ghraib and reverse it by activating within the same conflicted space emotions of an antithetical order.

Perhaps one reason we can't fathom contemporary history and plumb the psychotic bases of American ideology is that we've not yet learned how to read Pynchon's *Gravity's Rainbow*. Pynchon's achievement derives from his effort to write from within the psychotic space that the bomb tore open in the psyche. I hope on another occasion to offer an extended discussion of what this seminal work thereby offers the student of ideology. For now I must condense that contribution into three concepts: (1) Pynchon reveals the constitutional stupidity of official rationality and its underlying madness. Thus, for example, the fetishizing of any and all information, as if there was a precious secret that each inmate of Abu Ghraib or Guantanamo could render up to Cheney, Rumsfeld, Rice, et al. (2) The excessive actions that official rationality requires are a result of the underlying paranoia in its insatiable search for omnipotent control. (3) The System as a whole is fatally wedded to the effort to transform Eros into Thanatos so that there will finally only be one thing—the imposition of technoscientific rationality globally. Such is the categorical imperative of late capitalism in its Empire phase. Interrogation of images remains the way to combat it because image reveals what rationality conceals. Its full power to work in us can today only be reawakened by desperate measures. For since 9-11 we've been given three commands with respect to the image. First, not to picture the World Trade Center (now cropped from many movies) because, as one psychologist put it, that image now only reawakens traumatic pain. Second, not to picture the faces of our own dead lest that image deliver us from statistical abstraction into an awareness of the human costs of an unnecessary war. Third, not to view, or, now that the cat's out of the bag, to severely restrict the viewing of, the (by all means cropped) images from Abu Ghraib.

This last command proved impossible, however, because it violated a deeper imperative. *And so early in 2006 a new show took to the airwaves becoming a megahit of unforseen proportions, the most watched show in television history, a surprising occurrence given the fact that the show played every night from midnght to 7:00 a.m., ending only when a sleepless nation readied itself for work with its daily prayer, the morning news. Only one restriction was placed on this new show. By order of Attorney General Gonzalez no one was allowed to tape it under penalty of being incarcerated in Guantanamo under suspicion of terrorist activity. (Those who don't know that everything we do electronically is now monitored must go immediately to the back of the class.) There was one other condition, but it operated at first spectrally. Each night our show was preceded by Ted Koppel's* Nightline, *which was always the same now—a processional of the faces of our dead from the Iraq conflict filling the screen one by one while their names entered our ears: Paul Smith ... Therrel Childers ... Matthew Milczark ... Jocelyn Carrasquillo ... Thomas Thigpen Sr ... Henry Ybarra III ... Fernando Mendezaceves ... Nathan Brown ... Algernon Adams ... Ninety minutes of this or however long it takes for all the faces of the dead to have their moment on the screen. Followed by what everyone eagerly awaited—*The Late Late Late Show. *It too took the same form nightly, the endless repetition for six hours of a film composed of all the images that had been collected from Abu Ghraib. Uncropped genitally, but with the eyes covered. Images looped into one another in a film that never ended—a perpetual orgy. Mel the Baptist was long forgotten, his movie but a dim prefiguring of a pleasure that had now found its proper form—but be reminded with the prohibition against taping. And so there they sat, every night, a hungry public waiting for the show to begin, avid to spend another sleepless night transfixed before those images that must be seen again and again because they alone had the power to produce a paroxysm of pleasure. Soon most viewers in fact found it most satisfying to watch the show with their neighbors and co-workers. Super Bowl-type parties with wife swapping and group sex became a national craze. Every night—starting at midnight sharp. But then almost immediately, despite the clamor one could now hear from every household, the show did not begin on time. 1:01, 1:05, 2:10, the hour of the wolf, 4:07, 6:15 as images from Koppel's show spilled over, taking up more and more air time, invading the temple of pleasure with the detritus of history. Until there came a desperateness in the audience as the pressure built to wring some last tortured pleasure from the night. Until eventually nothing remained of the images the public craved except the last few that flickered in the last few moments just before dawn. But in those moments fevered viewers groped one another in a violent effort to get off one last time before the images that triggered their orgasm vanished forever, and they could only sit gaping at the faces of those dead sacrificed to what might finally be perceived as another Amerikan folly. Only there* *was no one left who could see it that way. Only the undead gazing at the dead in blank incomprehension.*

To clarify the concepts of image and event as a contrast both to the paragraph above and to Gibson's film, let me offer a few comments here on Michael Moore's fine film *Fahrenheit 9-11*. Moore's film is a significant political act and a dazzling piece of propaganda, but it is not an event. It isn't and couldn't be—even if it has attracted as many viewers as Gibson and even if it had propelled Kerry into the White House—because Moore does not speak *to*, *from*, and *within* the psychic register that Gibson works on. Except for a few brief moments, Moore's film does not descend to the place in the psyche where the action is. As a result it cannot alter that condition. Moore is a superb gonzo-satirist who has done wonders in alerting a mass audience to the corruption and venality of corporate Amerika. What he can't do—because he doesn't try—is get into the deeper psychic terrain.

But to engage it directly is to engage it tragically and to activate the massive resistances that rise up whenever art tries to get an audience to experience how sick they are. The chances of success of such projects are today slim, especially when one suggests to liberal, rationalistic, academic audiences that they'll remain part of the problem as long as we continue to approach ideology as if we could in studying it occupy a purely intellectual space and not a tragic one. A concluding effort on behalf of the latter possibility follows.

### ENDGAME: THE CHRIST OF ABU GHRAIB

"And if there is still one hellish, truly accursed thing in our time, it is our artistic dallying with forms, instead of being like victims burnt at the stake, signalling through the flames."

Antonin Artaud, The Theater and its Double

There is in Abu Ghraib one photo that escapes the camera. The photo of a hooded prisoner standing on a box with his arms outstretched, electrical wires attached to his hands, his feet, his genitals, the arms extended downward, palms open—in a gesture of supplication, acceptance, forgiveness? This image is uncanny and arresting because of its allusive, iconic power. For those aware of it, an unmistakable allusion to the beginning of Beckett's *Endgame*. "Me to play." For the general culture, an echo of another kind, the resonance of the image that enters the Amerikan psyche in a momentary arresting of desire.

For the allusion is unmistakable. How could the prisoner know it? How dare he? ... This is the Christ being given over by Pilate to his crucifiers, extending his arms downward, palms open toward the crowd in the expression of his inconceivable willingness to take on their sins. There is a delicacy to this figure and a tense athleticism. Forced on the stage of another's disorder, this prisoner performs as Artaud said the actor must. "The actor is an athlete of the heart." Which is why this man triumphs over the camera. They will not be able to look at this image for long and yet they will not be able to forget it. Like the image of the dying Joe Christmas, it will haunt them. It will not, however, be able to work creatively within them because the psychic register it addresses has already been rendered irretrievably dead. This image can only call them to a shame they are no longer able to feel, a change of heart they will find impossible. Thanks to Mel Gibson and his ilk. And yet in spite of them the miraculous occurs. *An image calls the psyche to itself.*

The theater of cruelty that Antonin Artaud called for is incarnated by the Christ of Abu Ghraib. As Artaud taught, "an image is true insofar as it is violent." This violence, however, is the antithesis of that practiced by Mel Gibson and the torturers of Abu Ghraib. Emotion here shatters all stimulus–response mechanisms. We are forced to feel and live out an *agon* of primary emotions that have the power to strip away all the hiding places of the psyche, revealing the rule of Thanatos. As this image works within we feel the burden of all we'd have to change in order to reverse the force of Thanatos that ideology and mass culture has planted and nurtured in us. The theater Artaud dreamed of is the search for images that are *cruel* because they wrench us free from the cycle of mechanical, repetitive sadomasochism that porn, Gibson, and Abu Ghraib feed on. We are jolted back into *life* as the struggle to purge our psyche of the forces of *death*. Gibson or Artaud—that is the choice we face. This is not the place to offer a full explanation of Artaud's concept of a theater dedicated to the agonistic experiencing of what I call primary emotions.[12] Suffice to say that Artaud is concerned with eradicating all defenses and displacements so that the psyche brought before the anxiety of its condition experiences the need to take up a task that was perhaps best formulated by what deSade, the Artaudian protagonist of Peter Weiss' play *Marat/Sade*, says to one of the first great revolutionary students of ideology: "Marat these cells of the inner self are worse than the deepest stone dungeon. And as long as they remain locked, all your revolution is but a prison mutiny to be put down by corrupted fellow prisoners."[13]

Mel Gibson's project, in effect, is to destroy the possibility of Artaud's theater of cruelty by reducing our ability to feel to the mechanical reproduction of shocks that jolt the conditioned subject back into the only thing that exists for it. Cruelty. Artaud's project is to destroy that mechanism so that we can begin to feel again the *agon* of what it is to feel. That project finds one of its transcendent embodiments in the actions of a prisoner in Abu Ghraib who found a way to signal through the flames.

# 4

# Weapons of Mass Destruction Found in Iraq

## LAUGH-IN BRINGS YOU THE NEWS

The US Code, Title 50, Chapter 40, Sec. 2302 defines a weapon of mass destruction as follows: "The term 'weapon of mass destruction' means any weapon or device that is intended, or has the capability, to cause death or serious bodily injury to a significant number of people through the release, dissemination, or impact of (A) toxic or poisonous chemicals or their precursors, (B) a disease organism, or (C) radiation or radioactivity."

The reader over my shoulder can no longer withhold a fundamental objection. Renewing the dialectic of Eros and Thanatos as a way of understanding contemporary history may be speculatively satisfying, but what possible relevance can it have to actual U.S. policies and actions? As Robert McNamara taught us, everything now is essentially a matter of technoscientific rationality[1] and thus the function of a way of thinking that has nothing to do with deep psychological conflicts. Political culture has in fact purged itself of such things. Objective calculation within the world of *Realpolitik* is all that is the case today. Dark forces in the psyche have nothing to do with it. Confronted with such an objection the psychoanalytic historian can only reply by endorsing the wisdom of Wittgenstein: "look and see." In fact, let's drench ourselves in the empirical. Maybe it's there that Thanatos will reveal itself in its true visage.

Depleted uranium (DU) is a waste product of the uranium enrichment process that fuels both our nuclear weapons and civilian nuclear power programs. In fact, over 99 percent of the uranium enrichment process results in this waste product, which has a half-life of 4.5 billion years. DU is both a toxic heavy metal and a radiological poison. The U.S. currently has over 10 million tons of DU. The disposal of nuclear waste is, of course, one of the unintended consequences of the development of nuclear power. Fortunately, a solution to the problem of DU has been found. DU is now used in virtually every weapon employed by the U.S. in Iraq (and earlier in Afghanistan and in Kosovo). To cite the most conspicuous example: every penetrator rod in a shell shot from an Abrams tank contains 10 pounds of DU. DU is selected for weapons for three reasons: it's cheap (made available to arms manufacturers free of charge) and easy to develop; it's heavy, 1.7 times the density of lead and thus most effective at killing because it penetrates anything it hits; and it's pyrophoric, igniting and burning on contact with air and breaking up on contact with its target into extremely small particles of radioactive dust which is dispersed into the atmosphere. The result: permanent contamination of air, water, and soil.[2]

DU was first used by the U.S. in Desert Storm. The amount used was between 315 and 350 tons. Five times as much was used during the 2003 invasion of Iraq. Over a third of the U.S. soldiers who served in the first Gulf War are now permanently disabled. The Department of Energy and the Department of Defense of course continue to deny that DU has any harmful effects. A U.N. sub-commission on human rights has ruled that DU, which fits the definition of a "dirty bomb," is an illegal weapon.[3]

Huge chunks of radioactive debris full of DU now litter the cities and countryside of Iraq. Fine radioactive dust permeates the entire country. The problem of clean-up is insoluble. The entire ecosystem of Iraq is permanently contaminated. The Iraqi people are the new *hibakusha*. Their fate, like that of the "survivors" of Hiroshima and Nagasaki, is a condition of death-in-life. The long-term health effects of DU on the Iraqi people (and on our own troops) are incalculable. There is no mask or protective clothing that can be devised to prevent radioactive dust from entering the lungs or penetrating the skin. Moreover, DU targets the DNA and the Master Code (histone), altering the genetic future of exposed populations. Because it is the perfect weapon for delivering nanoparticles of poison, radiation, and nano-pollution directly into living cells, DU is the perfect weapon for extinguishing entire populations. The Iraqi's are not alone. Vast regions of the Middle East, Central Asia, and the Balkans have been permanently contaminated with radioactive dust and debris.[4]

These facts are worth bearing in mind the next time we are told what has now become a bipartisan article of faith: the Iraqi people are better off with Saddam Hussein gone. Or as Bill Maher put it on his show of September 24, 2004: "Eventually they're better off."

We need a new term to describe our actions in Iraq. Genocide is inadequate. Thus: *ecocide* (from Gr *oikos*, house; and *-cide*, the destruction of). Ecology has two referents. It refers to that branch of biology that deals with the relations between living organisms and their environment and that branch of sociology that deals with relations among human groups with reference to material resources and consequent social and cultural patterns. The destruction of both is the goal of ecocide. *Ecocide is the deliberate production of a condition of permanent radiological, biological, and chemical contamination whereby death comes to inhabit an entire ecosystem.* A condition of ecocide exists when life itself and all possibilities of its renewal are being systematically destroyed in an identifiable geographical area, which is also defined in terms of specifiable racial and religious characteristics. As is now known, the cumulative result of such actions may bring about for the entire planet the condition of *homo sacer* described by Giorgio Agamben.[5] The European Council on Radiation Risk, for example, calculated the damage to human health of the low-level radiation thus far released into the atmosphere from nuclear weapons testing to be 61,600,000 deaths by cancer alone. Moreover, in our wars since 1991 the U.S. has now released in terms of global atmospheric pollution the equivalent of 400,000 Nagasaki bombs.[6]

## APPOINTMENT IN SAMARRA

"—the little lower layer. All visible objects, man, are but as pasteboard masks. But in each event—in the living act, the undoubted deed—there, some unknown but still reasoning thing puts forth the mouldings of its features from behind the unreasoning mask. If man will strike, strike through the mask."

Ahab in Herman Melville's *Moby Dick*

Does the situation described above offer us an intimation of what Sigmund Freud had in mind when he spoke of a pure culture of Thanatos?

But it's always a good idea when seeking an explanation of the human motives behind actions to stick with the empirical. With stated intentions and official rationales. Otherwise we give ourselves over to psychobabble. Despite official denial by the Department of Defense that DU is harmful, a series of explanations are now in place to account for the development and use of DU weapons. DU is cost-effective, militarily efficient, and turns to productive use a waste product we'd otherwise have to dispose of at great cost. With motives and intentions thus circumscribed, the decision to use DU in weaponry need not raise the specter of anything dark in the psyche. It's all a matter of pragmatic efficiency with a little capitalist profit motive thrown in for good measure. There's only one thing wrong with this explanation. It leaves out the basis for the calculus. There's every reason to use DU and no reason not to use it if, and only if, one rationale informs all decisions. *How to maximize death, regardless of consequences or alternatives.* Introduce any countervailing motives and the entire chain of decisions becomes questionable. Conscious, stated intentions then reveal themselves as functions of something else that has been conveniently rendered unconscious. What looks like a purely pragmatic matter devoid of psychological motives now reveals the opposite: the fact that Thanatos so inhabits the system that the absence of anything opposed to it "goes without saying." Thanatos has become what Wittgenstein called a "form of life,"[7] a way of being so deeply rooted that it operates automatically, habitually, and of necessity. It has become a collective unconscious. And as such it is no longer accessible to those whose intentions conceal and reveal it. The reason for sticking with the empirical is now clear. There is something insane in the empirical. That is what the historian must uncover.

Before we ask ourselves how this situation came to pass we need to ask another question. For it's easy to claim we don't know about such things because the media refuses to tell us about them. There's another reason for our ignorance, however, and it's the one we need to confront. I refer to the possibility that we choose our ignorance because otherwise we'd lose the system of guarantees we depend on for our identity and our understanding of history. As Barbara Bush put it in telling Diane Sawyer why she doesn't watch the news: "Why should we hear about body bags, and deaths, and how many, what day it's gonna happen, and how many this or what do you suppose? Or, I mean, it's, it's not relevant. So, why should I waste my beautiful mind on something like that?"[8] It would be easy to deride Mrs. Bush, to congratulate oneself on not sharing her attitude. What I hope to show, however, is that on an essential level, one determinative in the last instance, we are in full agreement with her and delude ourselves as long as we think otherwise.

## THE FATAL LURE OF GUARANTEES

"The purpose of thought is to eliminate the contingent." Georg Hegel

Recently, my mother died. At the end of her funeral the priest left us with these words as a final reminder of what had been said repeatedly in a variety of ways for the past two days: "We who leave here in sorrow know that we will one day be reunited with her in joy." My concern here is not with the ontological status of this preposterous belief, but with its psychological function as a guarantee that offers human beings a way to deprive death of its finality. And the terror that prospect entails. The function of guarantees is to enable human beings to bear events and contingencies that would otherwise be too traumatic. There is much that we can face apparently only by denying. Such perhaps is one accurate estimation of what it means to be a human being, to remain a child of one's needs and desires disguising that fact in the form of beliefs and ideas.

The primary purpose of religion, philosophy, and culture has been to provide conceptual, psychological, and emotional guarantees so that traumatic events become part of a larger framework that assures the realization of our hopes and dreams. Without such supports, most people supposedly would find life unlivable. Through the ministry of the guarantees we banish those thoughts and feelings that we are convinced would deprive life of meaning, plunging us into despair. Experience, accordingly, becomes the movement *from* and *to* the affirmation of the guarantees through their imposition on events. The main line of Western philosophy can most profitably be seen as a series of efforts to provide a ground for the guarantees. That effort achieves one of its culminations in Hegel who defined the purpose of philosophy as the elimination of the contingent. As father of the philosophy of history, he offered that new discipline a single goal: to demonstrate that the rational is real and the real rational; that history is the story of progress, liberty, the realization of a universal humanity. Or, to put it in vulgar terms, democracy and civilization are on the march and will soon sweep the entire Middle East.

In order to triumph over the contingencies of existence—doubt about oneself, one's place in the world, and one's final end—many guarantees are needed. Moreover, they must form a *system* of reinforcing beliefs such that if one guarantee is threatened other guarantees come in to fill the breach. Thereby the function of the system as a whole is assured. Within the system of guarantees one guarantee, however, is superordinate. The belief that human nature is basically good. As *animal rationale* we are endowed with an ahistorical essence that cannot be lost. Evil is an aberration. Consequently, there's always reason for hope and the belief that no matter how bad things get we'll always find a way to recover everything that the guarantees assure.

What follows is a brief and by no means exhaustive description of the system of guarantees. One need not believe all of it for the system to hold. Guarantees are superfluous. If they collapse at one point, their hold becomes even stronger at another. That is one reason why the death of God gave birth to so many secular religions. The best way to read what follows accordingly is for each reader to locate the guarantees that have the greatest hold over them, since in them one will find what controls one's response to traumatic events. Or, to put it in other terms, what one must overcome in oneself in order to experience the ontological force of existence, contingency, and history. Perhaps one only begins to know, to think, and to respond appropriately to events once the entire system of guarantees has been eradicated.

Here then a list of the central planks in that edifice.

*Religious*: A loving creator with a redemptive purpose assures us of the triumph of goodness and the rewards of eternal life.

*Philosophic*: Rationality gives meaning, direction, and pragmatic efficiency to the human mind and all the purposeful activities in which we engage.

*Scientific*: Science is the fulfillment of reason and through its development we will harness nature to our needs. This guarantee gives birth to another: the technological imperative, which teaches us that all technological developments are good. (Or, in any case, that the die is cast since all technological problems require for their solution the development of new technologies.)

*Historical*: History is the story of progress: the development of those universal values through which eventually the real becomes rational and the rational real. Through that long march all contingencies are eventually overcome. A political corollary: the democratic ideal as realized in the United States is an ultimate good; its benefits should thus be extended to all humanity.

*Economic*: Capitalism, the economic realization both of reason and of human nature, is the global principle that will bring the greatest good to all. Therefore, any actions required to advance it are both necessary and good.

The deepest guarantees, however, address us on a far more personal level.

*Psychological*: We have an identity, a self, that is strong and once attained can never be lost. Trauma is but the occasion for its recovery. There is nothing fundamentally dark or disordered in the psyche, nor do our actions derive from repressed or unconscious forces. The intentions we give offer a full account of our actions, and thus the limit of our responsibility.

*Emotional*: The innermost need of human beings is to feel good about themselves. Whatever threatens that feeling must be exorcised. Health, normalcy, and productivity depend on avoiding negative feelings. Hope and optimism aren't just healthy attitudes; they are requirements of our nature. Biologically wired. We cannot remain for long in trauma. Recovery, moreover, must restore our faith in the guarantees and our hopes for the future. The need for hope is, in fact, the capstone of the entire system of guarantees. Yet it too apparently has a history. Today over 10 million of our children are on prescription drugs to prevent depression and anxiety. Informed of this fact by Bill Maher, the French actress Julie Delphy spoke the spontaneous wisdom of an archaic culture: "Don't they know that depression is a good thing; that it's something you have to go through in order to grow?" Not anymore.

The key to understanding the power of the guarantees is to understand the fears that they exorcise. Thanks to religion, death, suffering, and evil are deprived of their power. Through the attainment of reason, all other forms of consciousness and what they might reveal are put in their place. Poetic knowing is deprived both of its legitimacy and its terror. Science, as fulfillment of reason, assures us of domination over nature. What Heidegger termed technoscientific rationality becomes the measure of what is real. Belief in historical progress banishes the recurrent suspicion that history may lack direction or, even worse, move to the darkest of ends. The condition is thereby set that makes it impossible for us to experience traumatic events such as 9-11 except as occasions to take whatever actions are needed to reaffirm our goodness and restore our guarantees. It is in the personal order, however, that the guarantees do their deepest work. Psychologically, belief in the self or self-identity exorcises the most frightening contingency: that there is a void at the center of the American psyche with panic anxiety and its corollary, compulsive consumption, the expression of a desperate non-identity. That specter brings us before the greatest fear: that our psyche, not our conscious, deliberative intentions, is the author of our actions, an author who will do anything in order to feel safe, secure, and righteous. All of our emotional needs then stand forth under the rule of a single necessity: the need to feel good about oneself at whatever cost and to sustain hope by banishing anything that would trouble us. Resolution, catharsis (i.e., the discharge of painful tensions or awareness), and renewal emerge as the needs that bind us with an iron necessity to the guarantees and all that they make it impossible for us to know. It is easy to deprecate Dubya and, apparently, to hold onto the idea that he's a temporary aberration. But the problem goes deeper. To revive a battle cry from the 1960s, insofar as one is wedded to any one of the guarantees one is part of the problem and not the solution. For the grandest function of the system of guarantees, as a whole and in each one of its parts, is to blind us to history.

And so to take up again the question stated previously, how did the situation now being created in Iraq come about? The next three sections constitute an attempt to answer that question by constructing for America a repressed history.

## THE NUCLEAR UNCONSCIOUS

" ... he begins to expand, an uncontainable light ... hero and horror, engineer and Ariadne consumed, molten inside the light of himself, the mad exploding of himself ...."

Thomas Pynchon, *Gravity's Rainbow*

To recapitulate historical facts that it took over 50 years to rescue from myth: the United States did not bomb Hiroshima and Nagasaki "to end the war and save countless lives." It did so for four reasons (and in the knowledge that a defeated Japan was pursuing terms of surrender through several diplomatic channels): (1) to avenge Pearl Harbor, (2) to justify the amount of money spent developing the bomb, (3) to create a laboratory whereby our scientific, medical, and military personnel could study its effects, and (4) to impress the Russians—and the world—with this opening salvo of the Cold War. In short, Hiroshima was the first act of global terrorism. That story couldn't be told, however, and still encounters strenuous resistance from most Americans, because it exposes too many of the guarantees we want to have about our nation and its actions in history.

Those actions also gave birth to another myth and another skewed history. The mythical story of the development of "the peaceful atom." No sooner were the tidings of the Nuclear Age broadcast to a terrified world than we heard promises of a nuclear Utopia. Through those promises a collective fantasy was created about the guarantees that the peaceful atom gave us about the *future*. Entire cities would have all their energy needs met for the cost of a nickel. Etc. Now 50 years later we find that we can't get rid of the nuclear waste we've created. Nuclear technology, it turns out, is the least cost-effective and most environmentally destructive source of energy ever developed. What it provides—less that 20 percent of our electrical energy—comes at a cost of trillions of dollars and at the expense of the safe and clean technologies (wind, solar) that we must soon develop *if there is to be a future*. What we now know is that nuclear power was a mistake from the start and should have been aborted in its inception. (It also had among its unintended consequences a loss of life of those living near or downwind of our reactors that now well exceeds the combined loss of life in Hiroshima and Nagasaki.)[9] But to learn of such things points to something even more troubling: the recognition that the peaceful atom was always a fantasy, created after the fact for motives that had nothing to do with official ideological proclamations.

Robert Oppenheimer made two prescient observations. "The use of the bomb was implicit in its invention." "We [the scientists] did the devil's work." Opie's error was his belated belief that by recalling us to humanistic beliefs it would be possible to reverse the process begun in Los Alamos. The humanistic reflections that preoccupied his final years offer one of the clearest examples of the effort to reassert essentialistic ahistorical guarantees as a way of cleansing our collective hands of history. What Oppenheimer hoped to exorcise was the specter that there are certain actions that are irreversible, giving history a totally new direction that permits no return to the way things once were. Perhaps there are events that mark fundamental turning points in which the human psyche—with no essential, ahistorical nature to protect it—makes a quantum leap into a new way of being, embracing a logic that will propel it to move in new, unseen, and unwanted directions.

Oppenheimer offers us a picture of the Los Alamos scientists that exposes the official ideology of science. He and his colleagues know what their discoveries will lead to but dissemble that knowledge. As Freud could have taught them, hiding something from one's consciousness empowers it. The rush to the bomb that seized them fulfilled a desire that had little to do with value-free objective inquiry. "Devil's work" is of a different order and draws on something else in the psyche. Here, briefly, is one way to constitute its meaning. In inventing the bomb the scientists of Alamogordo realized the two sublime motives that have informed the history of science: the effort to know the secrets of nature and to harness them to our will so that its power becomes an extension of our power to overcome any and all limitations, moral as well as physical. The belated effort of Leo

Szilard and others to draw up a petition to the President banning the use of the bomb and Oppenheimer's intervention reminding them that doing so oversteps their role as scientists are the comedy of a reaction formation: the effort to restore the *a priori* cleanliness of hands that are already dirty, the nostalgic attempt to arrest a historical process that has already broken free of them as Edward Teller would soon reveal.

Once the bomb was used, the consequences of devil's work announced themselves. Nuclear fear became condition general in the United States, producing for the first time a collective national psyche. What we did to the other we could expect in return. Projection and denial thus assumed command over both consciousness and policy. Globally. The only way to make ourselves safe from ourselves was through the production of more nuclear weapons. Like Macbeth, we had to repeat our deed, increasing its scope each time, as if somehow this would undo the original error. Teller's hydrogen bomb provides succor to a quest for power fueled by the engines of guilt and fear. The whole world became a prisoner to the logic of Mutual Assured Destruction. Bush's recent actions in Iraq merely ratify once again the basic truth: the only way to prevent U.S. aggression is to develop one's own nuclear arsenal. MAD offers the only certitude, security, and "peace of mind" that is now possible. A psychotic peace. Devil's work thereby evolves the condition demanded by the Thanatos that the bomb released in the psyche. *Death has cut itself loose from anything that could restrain it.* What began as a fantasy of unlimited power ends in the assurance of total annihilation.

While we've resisted this knowledge, there is another knowledge fatally tied to it that we've resisted with even greater fervor. Namely, the true story of "the peaceful atom" as a continuation of the same thanatopic process under the guise of a protracted search for a *felix culpa*. For expiation and redemption. To expel any lingering (unconscious) guilt over having dropped the bomb. How else but by finding in the atom a new guarantee which would enable us to claim that everything we did from the start stemmed from good motives and served finally to bring about a greater good. Technoscientific rationality as secular theodicy. The peaceful atom as messianic historiography. Our faith in this new faith, like our rush to the bomb, could not be questioned. The two main dogmas of this faith in fact necessarily gave birth to a historical process that could not be halted since any negative results could only lead to a further investment in the process. Dogma one: Technoscientific rationality, the new Logos which will finally reveal the truth of everything, always produces good results in the end. All that's needed is to develop the appropriate technology. Dogma two: That development is mandated. Technology is the only thing that can save us, since all technical problems require new technological developments for their solution. Like the rush to the bomb, there is no way to halt or question *the technological imperative* no matter how troubling the results and the ensuing technological problems they pose such as how to clean up the vast amount of nuclear waste and radiation that now poison the atmosphere. Having committed ourselves to "the peaceful atom" in order to deny and repress guilt over the bomb, we found ourselves wed to the development of civilian nuclear power because it fulfilled both a psychological necessity and what had become a technological imperative. Like the logic of nuclear weaponry leading of necessity to MAD, the peaceful atom was fatally tied to a logic incapable of preventing the movement to the situation we now face. We've been promised the benefits of the peaceful atom for over 50 years. The results are now in. Since 1945 Dr. Strangelove has operated simultaneously on two fronts. The result: the production of massive piles of nuclear waste with destructive capacities we have no way to contain. (Try sometime devising a warning sign that can be easily deciphered 4.5 billion years from now.) Such is the nature of "devil's work." Every step you take trying to get out of it only leads you deeper into it.

Hegel found in "the cunning of reason" a way to redeem any and every historical situation. All evils are but apparent; even the darkest events serve the course of progress. 1945 inaugurates a different logic, calling for an antithetical understanding. The primary lesson is that history lets loose consequences that cannot be controlled, that every action taken to make us safe from the destructiveness we introduced into the world by turning that destructiveness to a good end only proliferates the very evil it would reverse. There was no way to foresee or prevent the situation pursuit of the peaceful atom would create because belief in it derived from the same grandiose fantasy that fueled the bomb. Its task was in fact even more grandiose. Utopian and messianic. Otherwise the unthinkable: history would have to be conceived in a radically different way. But that idea is more terrifying than the magnitude of the nuclear pollution that now confronts us because it forces us to see that nothing protects us from history and the irreversible changes that certain events bring about. There are no guarantees. Nothing in the conceptual, psychological, or emotional orders that we can call on to deliver us. We face, instead, a different task: we must deracinate the entire system of guarantees because it is the main thing that stands between a correct understanding of our situation and, of even greater importance, how we must *learn to feel* in the face of it. Einstein said the bomb changed everything except the way we think. That task still beckons.

The development traced above offers us a way to understand the movement of the Nuclear Unconscious from 1945 to the present. As a history defined by what I call the Macbeth principle: to live with the guilt of a deed one repeats that deed until one is no longer troubled by it; or what amounts to the same thing, until nothing else exists. In a world ruled by Thanatos the psychological transformation required takes place through increasingly more rebarbative actions through which one progressively eviscerates the voice of conscience. Eventually it becomes so thin that it's transformed into its opposite: the fanatical voice of a fundamentalism proclaiming its rectitude. We're ready for a tour of Bush's Amerika.

## THE FANTASMATIC BECOMES THE REAL

"The rational is real and the real rational."
Georg Hegel

Here is one way to describe American foreign policy since 9-11. Long before Dubya's ascension fantasies of democracy sweeping the Middle East danced like sugarplums in the neocon imaginary. 9-11, however, upped the ante. As return of the repressed, a terrifying case of the chickens coming home to roost, it raised the specter of Hiroshima. A new exorcism was needed. Projection and denial were once again called on to provide the only possible psychological response. By appropriating Ground Zero as a symbol of what had happened to us we became fantasmatically the innocent victims of an unmotivated and unprecedented terror. Thus Bush's "they hate us because they're jealous of our freedom." Our duty became clear: to rid the world of evil. The trauma of 9-11 was thus transformed into the only thing that it could be: the occasion for unleashing destructive rage toward any object deemed the target of our wrath. Pre-emptive unilateralism is psychologically necessary to the fantasmatic demand for grandiose action as the only means of restoration. Reality be damned. Thus, the unleashing of a weapon of mass destruction, depleted uranium, on a country, people, race, and religion that deserve that fate for being the *non-cause* of 9-11. The psychotic need to proclaim fantasy over against any correction by reality has become peremptory. We have attained a Cartesian certitude that the Iraqi people (and then the entire Middle East) will embrace us for setting them free; and surface evidence to the contrary we see new signs of progress toward that goal each day.

Only our hold on Iraq deteriorates more every day. None of the things the fantasy assured happens. Two things do happen, however, providing a new confirmation of Engel's Law. (1) The shelling of Iraq with DU increases, contaminating the entire infrastructure with chemical and radiation poisoning. *Ecocide becomes official policy.* (2) The fantasms become more fervent in their affirmation the more they prove false to reality. Bush proclaims "Democracy is on the march." Quantity has, as Engels argued, become quality, bringing about a fundamental psychological change. Before Iraq, neocon fantasy was a dream that longed for projection in the belief that it could be realized in reality. It is now a delusion that can be sustained only by denying reality. The fantasmatic has become a psychosis. There is, accordingly, no way it can refer to or be corrected by reality. Only one solution is now possible: reality must be eradicated. The conditions of psychotic certitude have been met. The *infra* and *eco* structure of an entire country is destroyed in order to sustain the fantasy that one will be embraced as a liberator for destroying it. Because psychotic certitude has been attained, otherness cannot exist. Any challenge to Belief activates what has now become an underlying paranoia. Failure to conform to fantasy can only be the product of conspiracy. Patriot acts become necessary as a way to hypnotize oneself by systematically seeking out and eliminating any and all signs of dissent from the fantasy. It must become omniscient and omnipotent. Consequently, everything fantasmatic becomes hyperreal in a blind rush to global realization because with the onset of psychosis the mad know, in the evanescence of a consciousness they cannot sustain, the actual function that all their beliefs have played from the beginning. They are the ways one flees the void within, the catastrophic condition into which one would plunge should they ever collapse. Such is the inner state of those who throw themselves into the arms of the Lord, into absolute belief systems, in order to deliver themselves from themselves. The final solution that constitutes the inner condition of the paranoid psychotic has been reached: the necessity of continued, increased explosions in order to avoid a psychological implosion.

We are now in a position to describe the Amerikan psyche—a void defined by a panic anxiety that is relieved by conversion to an absolute faith: Jesus for Bush and Ashcroft, Leo Strauss for neocon ideologues, Kapital for Dick Cheney. Because the faith must bring total salvation, its reach must be global. That's what Technoscientific Rationality is: the obliteration of any logic other than its development and thereby a progressive estrangement from any other way of being. That's what capitalism is: the abolition of any moral restraint against imposing on the world what conditions will maximize profits. After all, people are nothing but consumers consuming. And it's what Christian fundamentalism Amerikan-style is: the need to establish an allegory in which as Good one is empowered to undertake an apocalyptic effort to rid the world of Evil. By turning Iraq into a vast Thanatopolis all three imperatives achieve simultaneous fulfillment.

Karl Marx, at a far more innocent time in history, saw the task of philosophy as one of extracting the rational kernel from the mystical shell of Hegelianism. That kernel was the proletariat and the materialist understanding of History the new guarantee. Living at a later stage of things, shorn of all guarantees, we face a very different task: *to extract the psychotic kernel from the fantasmatic shell.*

And thereby to understand its objective correlative. For the fantasmatic process traced above has a mundane corollary. Converting DU into a WMD that we could deploy throughout Iraq fulfilled another fantasy dear to the dream logic that informs capitalism. DU is pure waste. And like surplus products and the falling rate of profit, waste keeps piling up with no way to get rid of it. It's one thing when we only killed the poor bastards who had the bad luck to live downward of our reactors or the black inner-city children to whom we shipped radioactively contaminated milk. But now things have gotten out of hand. We've got over 10 million tons of radioactive waste. Eventually it'll seep into everything, turning even our paradisiacal estates into nuclear cesspools. Unless we can find a way to rid ourselves of it. Any solution, however, must derive from the logic that informs the system and fulfill the unconscious needs that fuel it. And then *voilà!* in answer to our prayers, one day we see a way to turn our waste products to gold. Nothing is ever lost. The deepest article of capitalist faith is fulfilled. There will be no bad, unintended consequences from our lengthy romance with the atom. We've found our own cunning of reason. Even our waste can be redeemed once we've developed the appropriate technology. With its discovery we seize a way to turn waste to profit while fulfilling an even deeper need: to dump our waste on everything that impedes the progress of global capitalism. Iraq is perfect. After all, the oil is the only thing there that has value. The rest of that landscape is nothing but a toilet. By dumping our waste products on it we get the true macho pleasure that comes from a good defecation: the feeling that we're releasing all of our toxic matter on the other—in this case those people of color committed to a religion that Samuel Huntington and others remind us stands unalterably opposed to the forward march of civilization. In short, the clash of civilizations and the making of the new world order require no less than the storm of depleted uranium being rained down over Iraq.

The maximization of death under the reign of Thanatos finds in Iraq one of its ghostliest embodiments. Another end to a desultory history. War in the twentieth century witnesses the progressive erosion of all distinctions between combatants and non-combatants, military and civilian targets. Inflicting the greatest possible physical and *psychological* damage to "the enemy" becomes the object of military strategy. Hiroshima was the first realization of that logic as a pure and unrestrained expression of Thanatos as global terror. Iraq now serves to advance that logic in a new, and qualitatively different, way. Thanks to DU Thanatos finds release from all restrictions and extension over time in a way that promises to advance its agenda through a silent, unseen, inner working on all that lives. Death is everywhere now: in the air they breathe, the food they eat, the water they drink, the shards radiating up at them from the DU debris that litters their cities, the sperm they transmit in the act of love, the coming cancers and birth defects, the violence to the DNA, in all the leukemias of body and of soul that will turn Iraq into one vast Thanatopolis, the city of the future, an *oidos* where all that lives will come to bear Death as its sole meaning, the visible and invisible sign that is present everywhere.

## A BILLET FOR DUBYA

"The man has a branch office in our brain called the ego and its mission is bad shit. We know exactly what they're doing and do nothing about it."

Thomas Pynchon, *Gravity's Rainbow*

Here, then, is a picture of our true historical situation, what we'd know if we looked at our world without the guarantees. The categorical imperative of the historian is to know the horror of a situation by apprehending the madness behind it. One name for that madness is *nuclearism*. A proper definition of it is now possible: nuclearism is the assertion of the right to unlimited power over nature through the overcoming of anything in the psyche that would resist that assertion. To put it concretely, there is no peaceful atom and there never was. Nuclearism has only one logic, implicit in it from the beginning. Ecocide. Another name for the madness is *capitalism*. It too is wedded to a deadly imperative: the extinction of everything in the human being that opposes the logic of acquisition and consumption. The ideal condition it seeks is one where there is nothing but consumers consuming. Everything else must be purged from the psyche.

When a belief becomes dominant in American psychological circles one thing is certain: that belief refers to something that no longer exists. Such is the case today with self, subject, identity, and the ego. The same goes for the countless guarantees that are invented to support that belief: as in the current emphasis on attachment theory (the perfect theory of mothering for the age of child beauty pageants) and relationality (the warm fuzzy of "adult" life) to provide new guarantees that healthy, normal development is in the cards. In its rush to be the mental health wing of the guarantees, contemporary American psychoanalysis has become a primary barrier to the truth. There is no self in Amerika today, only a void producing panic anxiety in the rush to compulsive consumption as the momentary way to fill what thereby becomes progressively empty of everything save one necessity. Malignant envy. That psychological disorder, brilliantly described by Melanie Klein,[10] has become the only motive that remains: the desire not to attain but to destroy anything and everything that excites one's envy. Iago triumphant disguised as progress. Only Thanatos matters. The envy that nuclearism projects onto nature, capitalism projects onto all human relations. The whole world must come to gorge itself under the golden arches. No moral restraint, no residual humanity can intrude on the necessity to reduce everything and everyone to the conditions that benefit capitalism. It's no accident that Dick Cheney's wife Lynne's time as head of the National Endowment for the Humanities was a watershed of reactionary ideology.

The History of the U.S. since 1945 constitutes a stunning refutation of our most cherished ideological beliefs. Events dance to a very different logic, which is not hidden. It's out in the open now as Thanatos takes the steps needed to gain control over all sources of potential resistance. That is why the principles expressed overseas must perforce inform actions in the homeland. The result under Dubya is an Amerika that can be defined by three interconnected developments: (1) an apocalyptic christo-fascism wedded to sadomasochism as the only pleasure capable of keeping the masses at a fever pitch of resentment; (2) a corporate capitalism in control of all economic decisions and political alternatives, thereby assuring the system's reproduction and extension; (3) a police state developing through the series of patriot acts required to create, even in the privacy of the home, a condition of generalized surveillance dedicated to the eventual extinction of any trace of otherness or resistance. To use Hegelian language, through these measures Thanatos as "Absolute Spirit In and For Itself" attains the form it requires.[11]

In Amerika today the condition Dostoyevsky described in the legend of the Grand Inquisitor slouches toward its final realization. *Miracle*, *Mystery*, and *Authority* find in Bush, Cheney, and Ashcroft the three functionaries needed to create a lasting, impermeable collective psyche that offers its subjects deliverance from freedom and the anxiety that can never be uttered or allowed to enter consciousness—that we exist without any guarantees. *Bush or miracle*: the theocratic allegorization of politics and international relations in order to assure us that we are good and everything other than us evil. (For those who can't find their way to God, the neocons offer a secular version of the same faith: progressive Western civilization v. reactionary Islamic fundamentalism.) *Cheney or mystery*: capitalism is the ultimate truth of economic reality; whatever we must do to secure its Empire is therefore good and ultimately of benefit to the entire world. Put money in thy purse: the hidden hand is the cunning of reason assuring future benefit to all. *Aschcroft or authority*: surveillance working in all subjects will complete what the Grand Inquisitor called "the happiness of man" in a condition of total obedience. Thereby Abu Ghraib will become the inner condition that defines the mass subject's relation to the State. At the same time that these structures of power extend their sway, the psychotic need to deny reality continues to take on new forms, each further removed from the possibility of correction. Thus, in the latest efforts to affirm that we were right all along—even if there aren't any WMD in Iraq—we get the following sequence: we couldn't know then what we know now; "Saddam aspired to making nuclear weapons" (Bush/Cheney); "Once out from under the sanctions, he would have developed them" (Powell); "Saddam Hussein is himself a Weapon of Mass Destruction" (Guliani). (From which follows the reason for Dubya's desire to revive the space program and go to Mars: that's where Saddam hid the WMDs.)

The above sections describe a collective psyche. Such a use of psychoanalysis is a far cry from the justly discredited "psychohistory," which I'll indulge briefly here for purposes of an important theoretical contrast. Thus: Bush had the hots for Saddam from the day he took office because deposing him would enable Dubya both to avenge and to replace his father. Recall, in this connection, his statement that if we'd had the courage and determination we'd have finished the work we (i.e. his father) began in 1991. Fortinbras replaces Hamlet in Dubya's imaginary. No wonder he couldn't wait to dress himself in borrowed garb (a military uniform such as his father wore as a pilot in the Second World War) pulled in as tight across the crotch as he could bear, and stride across the decks of the *Abraham Lincoln*. He finally had a dick and had to trumpet it to the world. But having found it, he can't stop shaking it ... All of this is of course obvious, irrelevant—and pernicious whenever it functions as an ideological blinder to deflect our attention from the real psychological forces that shape history. Bush is but a part of that psyche. At times its farcicalia and village idiot, at others its fundamentalist believer and "great communicator" who conveys the tidings to the masses in a way sure to reinforce their fascination with their own fascization. Dubya is a way to deflect attention so we won't see the puppetmaster Cheney pulling the strings. Nor, of more importance, the part that both play in the constitution of the collective psyche I've described. *That psyche is the proper object of psychoanalytic cultural and political theory.*

My effort here has been to offer us a new way to think about the possibility that there is a collective Amerikan psyche ruled by a Nuclear Unconscious that has a history which can be described in rigorous psychoanalytic terms. The principles whereby that psyche operates are a question not so much of the conscious intentions of particular individuals as of the role that different individuals and institutions play in securing the hegemony of the whole. That whole finds at each key place the man or woman it needs (from Groves and Oppenheimer to Colonel Tibbets, from Cheney and Rice to Private England) because the decision to do what the System wants derives from ideological choices that each individual has made long before the call comes. The end result in each and all is today the hegemony of a way of being in which Thanatos not Reason directs History. Such is the age we live in. An Age of Terrorism. State Terrorism. Everything else is a reaction.

## FINAL JEOPARDY

"'Personal density' is directly proportional to temporal bandwith ... 'Temporal bandwith' is the width of your present, your Now."

Thomas Pynchon, *Gravity's Rainbow*

To know this situation for what it is challenges what is finally the deepest and most fundamental of the guarantees. The principle of Hope. To appropriate Eliot: "After such knowledge, what forgiveness?" There is perhaps nothing that can be done to change the situation I've described. But then what is the purpose of knowing such things if they only produce meaningless suffering? Is despair the end result of a life shorn of the guarantees? Or are we finally like the drunks in O'Neill's *The Iceman Cometh*, knowing that in order to sustain the illusions required to go on living they must pronounce Hickey mad and reject everything he revealed to them about their lives as a product of that madness?

Perhaps it's time to admit what the need for Hope really signifies. Denial of responsibility for certain situations under the assumption that knowing them correctly would lead to despair. Raising that specter is, of course, the rhetorical ploy invoked to prematurely terminate inquiry lest it impinge on emotional and psychological needs. Despair thus remains an empty concept. We don't know what it is and never will as long as we use the need for hope to prevent discovery of our capacities to endure. Whether despair is what we will find on the other side of hope is something we can't know. For all hope really signifies is a testament to our weakness and our fears. Perhaps we are called to something beyond it. What Shakespeare called tragic readiness. For in opening ourselves to the possibility of despair we also open ourselves to the possibility of self-overcoming and through it the discovery of a *praxis* that lies on the other side of the conceptual and existential paralyses created by the guarantees. We can't know "what is to be done?" as long as we continue to respond to our situation by invoking ahistorical values and guarantees that are grounded in an essentialistic and ahistorical theory of human nature. (I take up the ethical implications of this idea in Chapter 10.)

"Is there anything more evil than shooting children in a school yard or flying planes into buildings?" One hears this rhetorical question often today. Getting it firmly implanted in our minds seems to be one of the current ideological functions of the media. A correct response requires careful reflection on the circumstance that underlies the knee-jerk response thanks to the power of the image it conjures up. The promise inherent in Technoscientificrationality is deliverance from images. Killing for it, like everything else, occurs at a distance. In the inaugural moment: Tibbets in the cockpit of the *Enola Gay* unable to imagine what he has just done as a human act. "It was all impersonal."[12] And today: in the silent, secret, midnight ways that radiation poisoning works from within, like a deed without a doer, separated in space and time from its absent cause. Perhaps killing at a distance is the greater evil precisely because it abrogates the image and the human connection between slayer and slain. If I kill another man with my bare hands my deed is immediate to my embodied consciousness. To kill that way you have to feel hate, fear, anguish, remorse, etc. whereas to kill from a distance or through an invisible contamination is to render the whole thing impersonal. With the desired result: the ability, for example, of the man who dropped the bomb on Hiroshima, incinerating 600,000 people in a second and condemning another 300,000 to the condition of *hibakusha*, the walking dead, to boast for over 59 years now that he has never felt a moment of regret or remorse. Tibbets' lack of moral imagination is one with his representative status as precursor. For now it's easy to litter a landscape with DU while denying that the stuff has any long-term medical or environmental effects.[13] The evil of killing at a distance is that it makes death unreal. Protected from the image, all who participate in the deed are delivered over to a pure and impersonal calculus. (An aside: if we really want to support our troops we must achieve for them a new Bill of Rights. No one should ever be ordered to use weapons without being given a full knowledge of the long-term human and environmental consequences of those weapons. To do otherwise is to deprive our soldiers of the choice that makes them human.)

The powers that be learned one lesson from Vietnam. No more images. The mistake was to let us see the carnage up close every night on TV. The news as image entered our consciousness at the register where genuine change begins. Where horror is felt, free of the tyranny of the concept and the hypnotic power of the guarantees. Desert Storm was the corrective: the Nintendo war, a war broadcast to look just like one of the video games we'd been programmed to love. Prohibition of the image is now a fundamental article of faith. No images are allowed to come back to us from Iraq II. (Michael Moore's real crime was to give us a brief glimpse at what the mainstream media proscribe.)

Abolition of the image is one of the primary conditions of ecocide. Everything must be rendered abstract, invisible, unreal. No image can be allowed to trouble our sleep, to lacerate our soul. For then we might begin to know that there is indeed an evil far worse than shooting children in schoolyards or flying airplanes into buildings. To move us toward that knowledge let me end with the forbidden, which I must here attempt to convey solely through the more abstract medium of words since I've not yet gained permission to reproduce a photograph I saw not long ago. *It's the picture of an Iraqi baby, a victim of DU, who was born with no nose, mouth, eyes, anus or genitals and with flipper limbs, a common result of radiation exposure in utero. That child's body, full of red open ulcers, is twisted in knots, its ulcerated face contorted in a look of unspeakable suffering. An authentic image of the sacredness of human life. Of the preciousness of every breath.* To look at that child is to realize one's duty to mourn it, to give voice to its right to invade our consciousness and expose the evil of those who prate on about being pro-life while refusing to let us see what they've reduced life to. *Luke, 17:1–2.* The image of that child must become the force in our minds that motivates us to deracinate all guarantees that shield us from the reality of that child's situation. Or to put it another way: every time one demands catharsis, resolution, and renewal that child is born again, condemned to its writhing.

That is why its image must embolden us to question the most hallowed of the guarantees, the one I've refrained from discussing until now. In the face of such evil what is to be done? Is resistance ever justified in resorting to violence? No, we are told, because "if we do so we become just like them." This ethical principle supposedly applies universally and atemporally. It does so, however, because it assures the guarantee that no matter what happens we'll never get our hands dirty. History can't intrude on the categorical imperative. Whatever action one takes one must maintain one's ethical purity. Even if that means there is nothing one can do and after it's been demonstrated that there are no non-violent ways to change the situation. Perhaps we can no longer allow ourselves the luxury of such an ethic. Bush did the moral imagination one favor. His pre-emptive unilateralism made official what has been clear for so long but denied due to its implications. There is no body to which we can turn for Justice: not the U.N., the World Court, or any other framework of international law. The U.S. will flaunt its contempt for such bodies whenever it suits its purpose. And thus another mode of peaceful, non-violent *praxis* is deprived of its guarantee.

But then what is to be done? I can't offer an answer. Because I don't have one? Because to do so would drive the last nail into the coffin of Hope? Because any answer would only serve to displace the trauma we have perhaps only begun to experience? Because doing so would minimize the psychological terrorism of this chapter? Or, for a final hypothetical reason—which I included in an earlier oral version presented to a Conference on Depleted Uranium—because to do so would legally open everyone who *hears* it to the charge of taking part in a conspiracy? But surely such warnings need not be attached to what we read. Surely we can preserve that guarantee. But of course we can't. Thanks to the Patriot Act, the same warning must now accompany the written word.

# 5

# A Humanistic Response to 9-11: Robert Jay Lifton, or the Nostalgia for Guarantees

My purpose in this chapter and the next is to offer a critique of the two paradigms that currently control the use of psychoanalytic thought in political and cultural criticism. As I'll show, for all their differences, they share a common error: the superimposition upon traumatic historical events of the very guarantees that those events shatter. Such is the inherent problem of thinking about history. History outdistances the frameworks we use to render it intelligible. Our frameworks, however, define for us the very possibility of intelligibility, establishing the philosophic assumptions and concepts apart from which thought appears impossible and life devoid of meaning. That's why the critique of frameworks is the necessary step toward a true radicalism. To be radical is, as Marx asserts, to go to the roots, but the only way to get there is by exposing the pull of guarantees. A correct appropriation of our historical situation only becomes possible through a systematic knowledge of the ways in which we blind ourselves to it.

## HISTORY WITH AND WITHOUT GUARANTEES

Robert Jay Lifton's *Superpower Syndrome: America's Apocalyptic Confrontation With the World* (2003) represents the credentials of one such framework as a way to help us understand the response of the Bush administration to 9-11.[1] We all owe a great debt to Robert Jay Lifton. In a remarkable series of books, Lifton has made the most horrifying events of the past century his subject. Death, indeed, is always on his mind and in the tradition of his mentor, Erik Erikson, he has brought to that study a spirit that is courageous, compassionate, and deeply humane. Lifton has often been the conscience of his society, especially in his work on Hiroshima and My Lai and with Vietnam veterans. Psychohistory in Lifton's hands isn't the reductive game of explaining Nazism (say) in terms of Hitler's relationship to his mother. It is an effort to comprehend collective traumas in terms of a psychological paradigm that affirms the continuity of life in terms of the quest for "symbolic immortality" and the power of the "self" (or what Lifton now calls "the protean self") to overcome the disorders of its time through a tolerant appreciation of ambiguity and limitations. This is the ability that enables us to respond to traumatic events in a way that is creative and ultimately transformative. Such is the grand system of guarantees in which Lifton casts his attempt to address what he sees as the apocalyptic currents of the present.

Within Lifton's oeuvre *Superpower Syndrome* is not a particularly good book. Much of it is hasty and undeveloped. Lifton's stated goal is to help us understand Bush's "war on terror" as an alarming development of what he terms "superpower syndrome," which may be defined as the desire of the United States to unilaterally impose its will on the entire world in order to attain an omnipotent control over history and thereby an exorcism of all our fears of vulnerability. There is much that can be said on behalf of this thesis. Unfortunately *Superpower Syndrome* presents it in a rambling and oblique way. We are more than halfway through the book before we turn to America, the Bush administration, and superpower syndrome. As extended preface to that subject we get a cook's tour of what Lifton calls *apocalyptic contagion*: a diffuse survey of various apocalyptic movements including Nazism, Mao's China, Aum Shinrikyo in Japan, McVeigh and *The Turner Diaries*, Bin Laden and the terrorist dynamic sweeping the Middle East. The point Lifton thereby makes is not particularly new but well worth repeating. Terrorism, he contends, derives from the fanaticism of the apocalyptic belief that mass destruction alone will purify and renew the world by bringing a cataclysmic end to History through a complete transformation of the existing order. The apocalyptic imagination is thus characterized by paranoid and grandiose ideation and wedded to the lure of martyrdom as what binds individuals together in extreme actions taken in the name of ridding the world of evil.

No one is immune from this contagion. We were drawn into it once before, when we bombed Hiroshima and Nagasaki, and we are in danger of giving in to it again. Note the assumption here (of which more shortly) that the source of evil is outside us and our participation in it a momentary aberration. Armed with this guarantee Lifton is finally able, more than halfway through the book, to approach the Bush administration as an American equivalent of the "evangelical apocalypticism" found in Bin Laden and other fanatics. The second half of the book develops this unexceptional thesis. As Lifton points out, the policies of the Bush administration—foreign and domestic—make perfect sense when seen as an unchecked expression of the imperative that defines superpower syndrome: the need to attain "exclusive control" over everything that threatens a megalomaniacal drive for omnipotence that can rest only when it has brought about a new world order.

As a primer for a mass audience seeking a quick handle on terrorism and the evangelical dreams of the Bush administration all of this is useful. But there's nothing new here, nor does Lifton develop any of his points in depth. One will not find here the kind of complex and nuanced sociological and historical understanding of fundamentalism developed in Almond, Appleby, and Sivan's *Strong Religion* (2003). Nor will one find the kind of in-depth study of the apocalyptic psyche that one finds in Dostoyevsky's *The Possessed*, a book that has again become required reading for any psychohistorian who wants to understand the present. Reading *Superpower Syndrome* I often wondered what function the discussion of *The Turner Diaries* or Aum Shinrikyo or Mao's China had in a book purportedly devoted to an analysis of Bush's America until I realized that this long detour is absolutely essential to Lifton's purpose for three reasons. It enables him to imply that the primary source of disorder is not finally something deeply ingrained in American society or the American psyche. The Bush administration, accordingly, can be seen as a temporary aberration. Lifton can therefore assure us that we can regain "our moral compass" by reaffirming our faith in traditional liberal verities and values.

The procedure of the book is thus a necessary function of the system of guarantees that have informed Lifton's *oeuvre*.[2] Everything is grounded for Lifton in a ontological guarantee that is supposedly provided by biology. As he outlines it in one of his finest books—*The Broken Connection* (1979)—we come into the world with an innate *self* endowed with an indestructible desire to experience the continuity of life as a meaningful process which is capped by the quest for symbolic immortality. Indeed, according to Lifton "there is evidence that by the time of birth the quest is well under way." Biological essentialism thus grounds a psychological paradigm that enables Lifton to view the horrors of history through the lens provided by a transcendental humanistic vision. Briefly, the paradigm asserts that there is a creative, life-affirming continuity to collective life. I.e., to history. This continuity can be broken but it cannot be destroyed. As Lifton puts it in the grandest reach of his thesis, there is "a humane symbolization of immortality inherent in the collective life of culture and history."[3] That being so, traumatic events can disrupt humanistic ideals, but they cannot effect their prior ontological assurance in what Lifton calls the "self." ("Self" is the code word American psychology uses to reassure us regarding the "essence" of what used to be called "human nature," which is the most powerful myth that has yet been devised for denying the force of History.)

All of this bears a strong resemblance to the system of guarantees elaborated by Lifton's mentor, Erik Erikson. There also essentialism reigns: *basic trust* creates ego identity issuing in the developmental process of a life cycle devoted to generativity. All Lifton has done is extend this paradigm (following clear precedents in Erikson) to the collective identity and life of nations. Thanks to this extension we can rest assured that renewal is programmed in us far deeper than death, discontinuity, psychic numbing, and self-fragmentation which are the great dangers of our times. Lifton, in short, has been able to immerse himself in the most horrifying events of the past 75 years because he has an *a priori* solution to every historical trauma. Evil is aberrant not primary. History, however painful, does not touch us to the quick. Lifton is the compassionate witness of its horrors, but he can never become the tragic sufferer because, in psychoanalytic terms, he is unable to *internalize* the events he studies. For to internalize is to take events into those places in the psyche where there are no ego defenses to protect us from them. To internalize is to suffer the power of an event to eradicate a guarantee. Only then is it possible in experiencing the destructive force of history to situate one's thinking existentially in it. In contrast, the only thing that madness and horror can *signify* for Lifton is the need to reclaim and reaffirm the *a priori* system of humanistic guarantees without which History would prove unbearable because it would impinge on the two beliefs on which Lifton's project rests: a belief in a humanistic "self" and a belief in a continuity of history that is progressive, quasi-Hegelian, and ultimately messianic.

Lifton must preserve these two guarantees because otherwise an antithetical problematic arises as the meaning of 9-11 and its aftermath. That problematic reveals Lifton's protean self as a last desperate effort to recycle, under the guise of flexibility, pluralistic openness, and ambiguity-tolerance, a litany of liberal, humanistic commonplaces that were exposed in their hollowness and their irrelevancy by 9-11. In his book devoted to the subject, *The Protean Self*, Lifton even argues the postmodern credentials of this "self."

As anyone who has read Lacan or Derrida (or Sartre for that matter) knows, nothing could be further from the case. The protean self is little more than a nostalgic belief that the postmodern deconstruction of the self and the system of concepts on which it depends is a passing fashion that we can apparently put to rest through the reassertion of what is really the last gasp of a resistance: the reduction of the "self" to a rhetoric of humanistic commonplaces.

### THE END OF HUMANISM

9-11 did not reveal that a period of psychic numbing after a terrible trauma enabled Bushian evangelism to gain a momentary hold over us. It revealed that we were already numb. That's why any feeling other than revenge proved beyond our capabilities. The inability to mourn revealed a prior deadening of affect that America had been living—under the sign of mandatory "happiness"—for a long time. (Date it, if you will, to August 6, 1945.) But this is a story Lifton can't tell because it reveals a radical *discontinuity* in history and with it the disintegration of the essentialistic guarantees on which his thought rests. Our inner condition remains the story Lifton must repress. One way to move toward its liberation is by outlining a series of contrasts with Lifton that will enable us to extend the valuable insights he gives us into apocalypticism and superpower syndrome *in the right direction*. Or, to put it another way, these contributions offer us ways of locating ourselves not outside or above contemporary history but as *subjects of* and *in* it.

(1) For Lifton death is always seen in the context of guarantees that reassure us about life and the fundamental health of the "self." The twentieth century is thereby contained. For the one thing we should have learned is that nothing limits death and its power within the psyche. The twentieth century gave psychology a new imperative: to rethink Thanatos not as something opposed to life, but as a force with a prior and more powerful rootedness in the psyche. Rather than a *dualism* of life and death, which assures the ontological stability of the former, we must construct a *dialectical* understanding of the psyche that acknowledges the priority and primacy of death in its inner constitution with life no more than the possibility of overcoming that power. Nothing, in short, assures the continuity or persistence of life in the psyche. That possibility rests on nothing but the existential situatedness of the subject within traumatic conditions that must be internalized in ways that permanently shatter the guarantees.

(2) For Lifton the psyche is not defined by excess or disorder. It's defined by normalcy, health, ego-identity, and a natural desire for meaning that is fulfilled by natural development within the life cycle. Disruption always comes, as a result, from outside, when some catastrophic event violates our "essence." In this connection, I note in passing the virtual absence of sexuality in Lifton's thought. That suppression, on which ego and self-psychology depend, is of a piece with the need to marginalize those intrapsychic conflicts where the destructive actions of the other persist as a force of Thanatos within the psyche. The ego and its defenses are the neurotic structure through which the vigorous denial of inner reality trumpets itself through the construction of a world it labels creative, generative, even protean. No psychiatrist has spent as much time studying the horrors of our late rebarbative century than Lifton. But if death haunts Lifton's thought, it haunts it from outside. Death for Lifton is not a force within the psyche, a power attacking it from within. It's the external event that resists the symbolizations through which we will eventually transform and overcome it.

(3) Belief in the self is *the* American ideology. Next to surplus value the self is our most important product: the thing we constantly proclaim and reassure ourselves about in order to cover over the emptiness of that concept and the void it conceals. Nothing is shallower than the inwardness of the average American, a subjectivity composed of little but the incessant mimicking of "signs" of success and affects that through ceaseless happy talk confer no more than a phantom substantiality. Beneath that chatter the truth of its inner condition continues to work on the American psyche: the death of affect, the deepening of psychic numbing, and a collective flight from anything that causes the least anxiety. There is nothing protean about the American character. If anything we represent Nietzsche's last man.

(4) Discontinuity is the primary fact of history. There is no principle in history, guaranteeing progress, continuity, or renewal. Historicity, contingency, and existence are the only *realities*. Save bad faith; i.e., the attempt to find some way to escape or deny them. Perhaps the most revealing example of that condition is the desire to picture Bush and his crowd as aberrations rather than representative figures who are engaged in the great work of assuring the dead that the peace they seek will be attained only when the entire world has become a haven of psychological infants. Bush is not an aberration, he's our high priest—a smug school-yard bully who is incapable of

nuance or restraint because anything less than the global terrorism he practices threatens the collapse of our born-again dependence on fundamentalist projection to deliver the Amerikan "self" from the void that defines it.

9-11 and its aftermath signal a crisis for the left, the crisis we've perpetually deferred. That crisis is defined by the need to purge ourselves of all guarantees, especially those that suggest we can renew ourselves by reaffirming humanistic beliefs and values that have become progressively abstract and empty of content because they never respond to history except by imposing themselves upon it. That's the bite of history. Everything we think and feel is submitted to it. That's why an answer to the question "what is to be done?" begins only when we know what is no longer possible. Otherwise we approach history with gloves on, refusing whatever in it we find too difficult to bear. What we lose thereby is the only option that is concretely creative. Nietzsche called it "a pessimism of strength," a call to exist tragically. Such existence is precisely what the guarantees have always been called on to marginalize—and then exorcise. To recapture that way of being our first task is to systematically refuse the pull of the guarantees so that we can experience all that they make it impossible for us to know—and be.

Guarantees come in many forms however. The next chapter will examine how a very different system of guarantees operates in a thinker very different from Lifton—Slavoj Žižek. Thanks to Žižek our task will become clear. To get to the left of the left by seeing that postmodernism is as rife with guarantees as the humanistic modernism it would replace. Moreover, the guarantees it draws on perform the same function—to shield the thinker from that which remains the Medusa for the postmodernist also: History. To see the dead end to which Lifton's essentialistic way of thinking—both about the psyche and about politics—leads one need look no further than to the work of the current luminary of the Democratic Party, George Lakoff. *Moral Politics: How Liberals and Conservatives Think* is an extended exercise in the intellectual vacuity that results when the psyche is reduced to moralistic ideological commonplaces and the circulation of those commonplaces becomes the defining political act. The application of what Lakoff calls *framing* (i.e., the construction of a story or myth that gives members of a group in fusion a personal and collective identity) to those commonplaces results in the new sound bites—Liberals follow the loving father model and conservatives the punitive father model—that are certain to *interpellate* or persuade large blocks of voters by telling the future constituents of a renascent Democratic Party (drawn from that vast middle that yawns open to those like Hillary Clinton who know that in order to seize it all one has to do is compromise whatever principles one once stood for) the nice bedtime stories they want to hear about what loving beings liberal democrats are and why this fact confirms their right to rule. The widespread commitment of self-proclaimed leftists to yet another simplistic exercise in identity politics as the yellow brick road to election in 2006 removes any lingering doubts about the bankruptcy of the Democratic Party.[4]

# 6

# A Postmodernist Response to 9-11: Slavoj Žižek, or the Jouissance of an Abstract Hegelian

*Persons attempting to find a thesis in it will be shot.*
After Mark Twain

## THE PLEASURES OF IDEOLOGICAL CRITICISM

If Lifton represents the liberal *modernist* left secure in the humanistic ethical guarantees from which it views history, Slavoj Žižek represents the new *postmodernist* left in all the energy and conceptual audacity of its effort to formulate strikingly new concepts and boldly go where we could not as long as our thought was hedged in by the need to preserve the guarantees. Žižek is (arguably) the most important theorist on the left today. And the most prolific. Books come from him faster than articles do from the rest of us. And every one of them is dazzling in its insights, both in the dense theoretical formulations that come at particularly charged moments of each text with stunning amalgamations of Hegel, Kant, Lacan, and Marx and in the continuous stream of insights into popular culture, the media, and the topics of the day that drip from his pen like sap from a tree in Maine in May. That latter accounts for Žižek's immense popularity. Here is a theorist who understands all the difficult thinkers from the inside but who is also a good read, a writer of great wit who peppers discussion of even the most abstruse philosophic issues with examples drawn from the latest film or the latest monstrosity of popular culture.[1] Even those readers who doze off when Žižek turns to Hegel on the logic of the retroactive or Lacan on the *sinthome* read on under the spell of *enjoyment*, unconcerned whether it all adds up to anything or whether a coherent position could be abstracted from it. The value of the text is sufficient unto the pleasure of minds delighted by the *performative* nature of Žižek's style, by a high-wire performance that is always dazzling even if it always arrives at conclusions that have now become predictable and formulaic. So what, the thrill of the ride is all that matters, the random insights, not the abstract frame? To read Žižek is to be reminded of Hegel's discussion of *Rameau's Nephew*. Here is the manic dance of an intellect on fire with its own energetics. To ask Žižek to confine himself to the development of a coherent argument would be like asking Al Pacino to play Hamlet reducing the part to the single note of affectless melancholy. The easiest conclusion one can reach about Žižek, and the easiest way to read him, is that his books offer a rambling hodgepodge of isolated insights, some dazzling, others preposterous, some heartfelt, others dashed off to amaze, startle, court controversy ... anything just to keep the discourse moving in its metonymic stream as if in Žižek we have the Jack Kerouac of philosophy, an *écriture* unable to arrest the flow of digressions within digressions, a writing not in search of a thesis but in an effort to perpetually delay the melancholy moment when mania is asked to collect its results. To demand coherent development of a thesis is to kill the play of thought, to rob it of the dynamic from which all insights come, even the ones that Žižek probably dismissed as he wrote them but that he can't bother to re-examine at a later hour. This is a reasonable approach to take to Žižek's work but a flawed one, I'll show, because for all his diffuseness Žižek is a rigorously systematic thinker.

*Welcome to the Desert of the Real* is no exception, though the surface diffuseness of the text makes this book one of Žižek's most maddening performances. Written in the immediate aftermath of 9-11, it is as if the text itself embodies the shock of that trauma, mimicking the general condition of all of us in our inability to put our discourse into some frame and not clutch wildly at the random thought of the moment in the hope of finding some relief, the bare beginnings of some comprehension. Closer scrutiny, however, reveals a coherent argument of great originality and power. My purpose will be to articulate that argument in order later to identify the contradictions of the theory from which it derives. The key to such a reading is simple. Like Kristeva's subject *in process/on trial* Žižek's is a thought in motion, available to us—and one suspects to Žižek—only at the end of each chapter where he always ties things down in a way that enables us to go through the chapter again and, as Eliot says of experience, know it for the first time. To illustrate this thesis I will follow the discussion of each chapter of the book with a summary statement of the theses it develops. That sequence will reveal the unity of the argument that *Desert* develops.

The book begins with a brief introduction. There Žižek sets forth the thesis he promises the book will develop. If we are to attain a genuinely *antagonistic* relationship to ideology we must reject the false choice that has been imposed on us in the wake of 9-11: the choice between terror and democracy.

## 9-11 and/as Independence Day

> "Let's face it, we've always been at the movies"
> Pynchon, *Gravity's Rainbow*

Chapter 1 then develops a new wrinkle on an utterly predictable occurrence. Namely, that the reigning commonplaces of postmodernism would become the wisdom that many so-called leftists of the academy would proclaim as the true meaning of 9-11. *Everything has become a spectacle. Reality is fantastically textual.* This is the inviting prospect of joining a glib thinker like Baudrillard in the assertion that nothing happened on 9-11.[2] Everything's a simulation of a simulation. Žižek has been accused of endorsing precisely that view in this chapter. Actually he's after something far more complex. As any student of popular culture can testify, we had dreamed of this event for a long time. How else account for a blockbuster film such as *Independence Day*. Long available on DVD one can only imagine its frequent screening in the caves of Tora Bora. But as Žižek knows there's also something that stands in a dialectical relation to endless simulation: our passion for the Real and our incessant search for it. My favorite example, a middle-aged woman interviewed on TV who said she'd come all from way from Florida on her vacation to eat at the Mezzaluna restaurant and visit the place where Ron and Nicole were killed because "I want to be where Reality is." 9-11 was supposedly the coming of that rough beast on a global scale. Žižek's insight is that this claim exemplifies the primary error that ideology has imposed on us with respect to 9-11. To put it in Lacanian terms—and mark this as the first entry of the theoretical superstructure into Žižek's argument—on 9-11 the traumatic Real didn't enter our world. What entered instead was *the image that was already at work structuring the fantasy whereby we protected ourselves from reality.* The reality, of course, is capitalism. For all the intellectual pyrotechnics Žižek is never coy when it comes to church dogmatics. Every time he risks interpretive closure he does so by citing a Marxist commonplace. These assertions are so pat that they remind one of the canonical ending of Lukác's essays where he reminds the reader how everything he's said squares with the thought (sic) of Josef Stalin. As Žižek sees, massive assaults on our country are the mainstay of popular movies like *Independence Day* because they both reveal and conceal capitalism's just desserts: the chickens coming home to roost. The pleasure of such films is the pleasure that comes from letting the guilt of the system suffer just punishment as prelude to its triumphant reassertion.

There's nothing new about the foregoing, as Žižek would be the first to admit. What's significant is the thesis he derives from it. Popular collective fantasies reveal the obscene underside, the unacknowledged dirty truths, on which the system depends and which everyone acknowledges at some level of their consciousness before evolving the ideological blinders that enable one to deny what is thereby propagated. Žižek's best example of this is the long-standing relationship of the Catholic Church to its pedophile clergy. The obscene underside of the system is fully acknowledged, protected, and extended by official policies.

What's new here is the central thesis Žižek derives from such observations. The task of ideological examination and critique is to formulate the entire body of *obscene unwritten rules of the system*. This is a magnificent project. I hasten to add that (sadly) Žižek makes no effort in *Desert* to carry it out. It should also be noted that the only thing that distinguishes this from the long tradition of Marxist ideological critique is the addition of the word *obscene*. The task here proposed is paramount Žižek contends because ideology cannot be combated directly since such discussions are controlled *a priori* by underlying ideological assumptions and beliefs, those who attempt to engage ideology in this way are inevitably lead into the deadlock of a forced choice, as in the option of terror or democracy that provided Žižek's starting point. To secure the possibility of *antagonism* a radical break with the system is required. Many of Žižek's finest moments in the book come from showing how so many on the left are trapped in the positions he demystifies.

Chapter 1 thus constitutes a rigorous sequence of thought in support of an ambitious program. To summarize its theses:

(1)   9-11 was not the entry of the traumatic Real into our world. It was the arrival of the fantasy that protected us from admitting the truth about capitalism.

(2)   That fantasy points to our task: to formulate the entire body of obscene unwritten rules of the system.

(3)  Doing so is the only way to combat ideology. Otherwise one falls into the trap of those who don't realize how ideology controls the assumptions and ideas that structure discussion.

(4)  Antagonism thus requires stepping totally outside the system.

Doing so is imperative, moreover, because otherwise what may be the rich possibility of our historical situation will be lost. Žižek is well aware that 9-11 happened. He is also aware of the essential fact: that event only exists through the discourses developed in its wake. Here there is no choice. Unless we can develop a discourse outside the parameters set by ideology mystification will seize the day.

### The media made me do it

> "Paranoia is the ability to make connections."
> Thomas Pynchon, *Gravity's Rainbow*

Chapter 2 begins by showing how the "paranoiac perspective" assumed so readily after 9-11 performed its ideological function in making a historical examination impossible. Any effort to inquire into the social circumstances behind the attacks opened one to the charge of justifying them. The same function was performed by invoking evil as the only term of (non-) explanation. The deadlock was then in place when deep thinkers like George Will, William Bennett and a host of less well-known academics joined chorus in proclaiming that 9-11 put an end to the Age of Postmodern Irony. The recovery of reference and a new seriousness beckoned. Seriousness, we quickly learned, required embracing not only the claim that "nothing will ever be the same" after 9-11 but with it the empirically false idea, even within its proximate time frame, that 9-11 is an act of horror unlike all others. With the ideological space of discourse thus defined everything moved to what Žižek correctly cites as the perfect example of the *forced choice*, the first of three that the chapter identifies and submits, I think, to withering critique. If one condemns the attacks one justifies American global capitalism. If one dares talk about the causes behind Bin Laden's ire one blames the victim. As a way out of this trap and thus an example of how to step outside ideology and toward antagonism, Žižek invokes the Hegelian category of *totality*. (Mark this as the second appearance of the underlying theoretical framework.) "Adopt both positions simultaneously." Doing so leads to the first of many eloquent ethical gestures in the book. To the horrified "how could this happen here?" totalization brings the ethically transcendent yet densely historical question, "how could this happen anywhere?"

That perspective enables Žižek to show how easily many on the left were led by the *forced choice* of being *for* or *against* terror into the trap Cheney, Ashcroft, and others were quick to capitalize on by claiming *to question this choice is to support terror.* Thereby a discourse was rendered impossible and with it the chance to see that the real choice we face is not between democracy (American) or fundamentalism (Islamic)[3] but between capitalism and its other. This, the second invocation by Žižek of doctrinaire Marxism is marked, however, by a historical problem; namely, how to locate this vanishing other? (Žižek will later make a series of unsuccessful and increasingly bizarre efforts to constitute this term.) The more immediate task, however, is to underscore the ethical gains of the chapter by advancing two ideas that seem to me hardly new, though the mystifications imposed on us after 9-11 probably make their reassertion mandatory. (1) Employing the category of Justice after 9-11 requires the recognition that there is no innocent gaze.[4] (2) Critical thinking requires the rooting out of all ideological mystifications. The latter is, as Žižek will soon show, a lesson that the left desperately needs, since it remains blind to all the ways in which it is manipulated by the ruling ideology.

The Chapter thus adds five planks to the developing thesis of the book.

(5)  Being trapped in false choices is what prevents the move outside ideology necessary for antagonism.

(6)  The Hegelian category of totality offers a way out of this deadlock.

(7)  Following it gives birth to a radical ethic.

(8)  It also uncovers history. For forced choices blind us to the real choice. It alone addresses the truth of our historical situation.

(9)  Getting to it by overcoming all ideological mystifications is our primary duty.

## On not being politically correct

> "Boys and girls, all I want is for you to be happy."
> Hickey in *The Iceman Cometh*

Chapter 3 offers concrete training in that task through a castigation of the left for sacrificing *desire* to Happiness. (The Lacanian term desire marks the third appearance of Žižek's underlying theoretical framework.) For now think of it as an absolute dialectical unrest. The betrayal of desire for Happiness is the *bad faith* of left, liberal, democratic thought. That bad faith takes the form of the repeated gestures of tolerance, openness and pluralism and the endorsement of policies that one knows have no chance of being enacted and to which one is actually opposed, since their passage would affect one's privileged position, but which one supports because they make one feel morally righteous.

Developing this theme enables Žižek to wreak havoc on the world of the Politically correct left. The need to extend Happiness to everyone is the underlying principle to which all other principles are sacrificed. (On this point Žižek has some telling remarks on Jurgen Habermas' fidelity to the Enlightenment.) The result is the co-opting of every possibility of antagonism into a reinforcement of the system. The particularly apt example Žižek cites here is multiculturalism, which turns all cultures into commodities and curiosities lumped together under the umbrella of a tolerant pluralism that does away with the primary fact of history: antagonism. Žižek's argument here is reminiscent of the earlier and more incisive concept of "repressive tolerance" developed by Herbert Marcuse (1969).[5] As Marcuse showed, the system is supremely tolerant. It tolerates whatever contributes to the maintenance of the system. Tolerance has a limit, however, and one quickly discovers it the moment one says anything authentically subversive. The cry "be reasonable" then silences the voice of dissent.

Democracy for Žižek is the master signifier for all such practices. Žižek has little interest in defining this term historically or seeing all the ways in which it is internally contested.[6] For him it functions as a call to arms. The left must formulate an alternative to democracy. That necessity becomes the only choice open to us once we see that "rightist populism and liberal political correctness" are not opposed positions but "two sides of the same coin."[7]

The way out of that bind lies, for Žižek, in "remaining true as to one's desire"; i.e., by realizing that desire, unlike Happiness, is radically disruptive. The concept of desire thus complements the Hegelian concept of totality that broke the deadlock of the previous chapter. Desire is dialectic incarnate, that which overturns all ossified concepts. And such is his adherence to it that Žižek endorses as central to the *ethic* it generates—and as the antithesis to tolerance—a willingness to embrace excess in any and all forms. Mania is not just a property of Žižek's style; it frequently generates his content. In that spirit the chapter concludes its overture to the ethical with this revealing image: against the Fascist with a human face (an image that for Žižek includes both the right and liberals on the left) we need the freedom fighter with an inhuman face.

To summarize, the chapter offers the following developments of Zizek's thesis.

(10)  Liberal political correctness is the primary mystification we must overcome.

(11)  To do so we must expose the category of Happiness and all the ways our investment in it makes antagonism impossible.

(12)  Desire, in contrast, is the radically disruptive principle that we must constitute as a political force.

(13)  An *a priori* blessing is thus bestowed on any act that can be analogized to the dynamics of desire. (He wasn't there, but Žižek would have been at home in the Southern California of the 1960s.)

### The gospel according to John Ashcroft

> "*You must make a friend of horror … horror and moral terror.*"
>
> Kurtz in *Apocalypse Now*

Chapter 4 clears the way for Žižek's radical ethic by connecting, in a single critique, the two things that stand in the way.

(1) Liberal democratic gradualism blinds us to the void at the center of the system. The truth of American society is the absence of any genuine subjectivity. *Interpassivity* not intersubjectivity defines us. This concept, which is one of Žižek's most original contributions to modern thought, is illustrated by phenomena such as canned laughter; the machine both cues us and does the job of responding for us.[8] The popular film *The Matrix* thus for Žižek grasps the truth of contemporary history: "in our innermost being we are the instruments of the Other's (Matrix's) *jouissance*."[9] This idea is anathema to liberal democratic thinkers because it violates all the humanistic pieties. The result of allegiance to such essentialistic, ahistorical ideas is, Žižek argues, a consistent misappropriation of radical European thinkers, the most recent example being Agamben's *Homo Sacer*. The same mistake occurs repeatedly. A European thought emphasizing "the closure of every democratic emancipatory project" is "reinscribed"

into the belief in a "gradual and partial widening of democratic space."[10] Such space, Žižek argues, is a mystification.

(2) No better proof of this contention exists than "The War on Terror," which Žižek proceeds to examine with great insight. As Voltaire might have put it, if 9-11 did not exist it would be necessary to invent it so perfectly does it fill the void left by the end of the Cold War. To conceal its contradictions every system must create an Enemy on whom all discontents can be projected in order to justify any repressive action deemed necessary; as in Ashcroft's argument that in order to fight terror we must give him a blank check to limit our freedoms. To nail down this point Žižek repeats what is perhaps the most important lesson he learned from Lacan, a lesson on which his breakthrough book *The Sublime Object of Ideology* (1989) was based. The Enemy is the *point de caption* required for the unification of ideology. The Jew performed that function for Hitler; the terrorist does the same for Bush and Co. Terror is elevated as "the hidden universal equivalent of all social evils."[11] Nothing else need or can be said about it or anything associated with it. The telling example Žižek cites is the 2002 ad campaign that propounded the superegoic reason to say no to drugs: those who buy drugs provide money for terrorists. (Also to the banking system, the CIA, and the government but we won't go into that.)[12] Fixated on terror as an englobing abstraction, every other historical cause vanishes like mist on a golf course at dawn.

This is the dilemma—or opportunity—Žižek sees for the left. There is no way to work within the system. And no way to get out of it save through radical disruptive actions. Such acts are what is needed more than anything, even if they involve "a gesture of radical and violent simplification"[13] as well as the considerable nostalgia that Žižek here invests in those romantic currents within Marxism that were criticized by the very Lenin Žižek recently claimed as a model.

In moving toward the radical act Chapter 4 adds the following essential steps to Žižek's argument.

(14) The liberal idea of a gradual widening of democratic space is a myth and a bankrupt model for radical politics.

(15) It fails to address where we must begin: with the contradictions of the system as they are made evident by ideology and, specifically, by the *point de caption*.

(16) For its function is to force us to locate all evil outside the system. The War on Terror is a perfect illustration.

**But who knows where or when?**

> "And what rough beast, its hour come round at last"
>
> W.B. Yeats

Chapter 5 is devoted to Žižek's radical ethic. He begins with an example that sets forth the basic requirement of this ethic with great clarity. In 2002 hundreds of Israeli reservists (some highly decorated) organized a refusal to serve in the occupied territories. That action illustrates two primary criteria for the ethic Žižek seeks. It must be (1) a moment of true Justice that (2) interrupts the cycle in which everyone is trapped. Žižek then proposes a method to assure such events. Take something like "the war on terror" and universalize it. One thereby exposes the nationalism behind it, thereby changing "the very co-ordinates of a conflict" in a way that moves us from the deadlock of false positions toward the liberation of something else, which I deliberately leave vague for the moment. To cite one of Žižek's best examples, here are two false positions on the Israel–Palestinian conflict: (1) liberal Israelis who support Sharon and (2) Western liberal intellectuals who support Hamas. Resisting the trap of such forced choices leads us, Žižek argues, to a position outside the conflict. Rather than offering a radically new program of action, however, sustaining this possibility quickly becomes the assertion of the oldest truth of doctrinaire Marxism. Once the parties to such conflicts realize that their shared enemy is capitalism they'll move to the solidarity of the only solution. Žižek calls it "Islamic socialism," though its not clear whether the term is meant to shock with its preposterousness or whether it indicates the desperate and Utopian nature of Žižek's thinking. But things get worse. Examining actual political movements within the Middle East would lead Žižek far deeper into the empirical and concretely historical than he ever cares to go. Refusing such discipline tips the hand of the *a priori* deductive necessity that controls Žižek's thought, leading to a preposterous proposition. "Islamic socialism," Žižek argues, is a reality that may emerge "precisely because Islam harbours the 'worst' potentials of the Fascist answer to our present predicament. That's why it could also turn out to be the site for the 'best.'"[14] Žižek can, however, cite nothing concrete in support of this flight into magical thinking. As we'll see below, he doesn't have to. Historical possibility derives for him from somewhere else.

Despite several flights of fancy the chapter does, however, contribute an important plank to the argument.

(17)  A radical ethic must break the cycle in which everyone is trapped by changing the very co-ordinates of the conflict.

### Did Anyone Say Praxis?

"Dancing in the dark, til the tune ends, we're dancing in the dark."
Howard Dietz

The concluding chapter returns to 9-11 in order to show how the radical political ethic developed in the book applies to its subject.

There are, Žižek argues, two ways to react to traumatic events. One is the way of the superego, which exploits them to fill gaps in the system, as the Bush administration did in declaring a global war on "terror." The other way is the ethical response. As a final example of it Žižek cites the beautiful and powerful act of the Jewish ballerina who agreed to dance for her captors in Auschwitz only to use the occasion to seize a machine gun and kill several of them before herself perishing. Such an example is salutary, though how it translates into the terms of organized political action remains glaringly unspecified. Casting around in search of an equivalent resistance to Bush's pre-emptive unilateralism all Žižek can find is absence in the place from which he thinks resistance should come: Europe. Perhaps "Wachtet Europa" is the true purpose of the chapter, and its real function not to offer us examples of the radical act but to show, with due apologies to Bob Dylan, that we don't need a Weatherman because there's no Wind. Except, Žižek reminds us, from the radical right, which he correctly sees as the only serious political force today. Liberal democracy co-opted in its thinking by the very system it would oppose offers us only one insight: that nothing will happen as long as we think along the lines it maps. Longing for an alternative Žižek continues to dream of the radical act. He may not be able to point to it, but he knows what it would be: a break with the system that would lack all guarantees, including a guarantee against its own excesses. This is both the inescapable danger and the sublime exhilaration of the act. Sworn foe to mystification, in proposing this solution Žižek indulges in a striking mystification of his own. Some of us spent the 1960s in unsuccessful devotion to this one.

But whatever its defects in terms of *praxis*, the chapter provides the final steps of Žižek's argument.

(18)  Applying the Lacanian logic developed in the book to 9-11 reveals that there are two responses to trauma: the superego one that reinforces the system and the ethical one that shatters it.

(19)  The latter is the call Žižek issues to Europe in hopes of awakening it to its role as the foe of U.S. imperialism.

(20)  The radical act is also a call to each of us individually: to imagine acts that would break with the system, shatter the liberal-democratic consensus, and move us into a realm of new possibilities.

Every reader will, I think, concur from the summary offered here that *Desert* is one of the most important analyses yet developed of 9-11. It is also, I will show, an analysis severely limited by the method that underlies it.

Calling for the radical act is, as Žižek knows and would be the first to admit, a far cry from having it. Those who are quick to point out the unexceptional and even nostalgic nature of Žižek's solution miss the most important point. This solution is a function of Žižek's own deadlock, a direct result of the brand of Hegelian–Lacanian theorizing he's developed. To demonstrate this I turn from *Desert* to a brief sketch of Žižek's general theoretical framework. Despite the manic intensity of his procedure, everything Žižek does derives with deductive, logical necessity from a rigorous framework. That is perhaps the irony of Žižek's position in contemporary thought. The manic play of an intellect that consistently dazzles with the discovery of new insights conceals the fact that everything Žižek says is deduced from a few fixed, *a priori* and dialectically related concepts.

Those readers uninterested in philosophic issues can skip the rest of this chapter. Or wait to read it until after finishing chapters 7–10 where I lay out the way of thinking about the psyche and history that underlies this critique.

## HOW TO BECOME A CRITICAL CRITIC

"I operate on things, not in them; you won't see me getting caught up in it."
The philosopher Teddy, in Harold Pinter's *The Homecoming*

Here's a brief primer on how with Žižek to know everything *a priori*. Follow the Magna Carta of twentieth-century philosophy. Begin with language. Everything we experience is structured by it. Indeed, who we are as subjects is a function of our inscription in it. It speaks us. Existential inwardness is the grand illusion. Going inside in search of myself all I'll ever find is language, writing me, determining me, creating in what I mistakenly regard as my most personal feelings and intimate experiences nothing but an illustration of its laws. The task of thought is to map this prison-house. To develop a systematic theory of the structure of language and then show how that structure informs all the other structures whereby we think and make sense of the world. Thus, if language is binary so will the world be, with social, political and cultural structures so many instances of that linguistic condition. The same applies to thought in all its forms. The logic of language is the meaning of meaning. Categorical thought is merely, in fact, the most advanced development of this logic, the point where it can become aware of itself as a total system of possibilities that can now be comprehended in terms of its inherent dynamic and its basic contradictions. The payoff of thinking along these lines is considerable. One knows *a priori* how to explain any event—such as 9-11—as well as the discourses to which it gives birth.

Providing such a guarantee is, for Žižek, the achievement of Hegel's *Logic* and the reason why it provides one of the two foundations of his thought.[15] In the *Logic* Hegel provides a method for attaining an *a priori* standpoint that is beyond mystification, one that reveals the limitations and contradictions of all other positions while comprehending them as moments in the movement to the perspective that it alone attains.[16] As Žižek sees it, thanks to Hegel we know the laws to which all thinking is bound.[17] As a result, we can enter any controversy, such as responses to 9-11, and assimilate all partial positions to a perspective that transcends and corrects phenomena. And that's just a beginning. Hegel offers the possibility of something far more grandiose. For the *Logic* maps the possibilities of experience itself. All that human beings do and suffer cannot only be explained by the *Logic*, it can be *deduced* from it. All that's needed is someone bold enough to map this logic unto the corpus of Freudian thought and *voilà*, we'll have it, a synoptic understanding of the psyche itself in terms of structures (indeed, finally, mathemes) that pre-exist and determine each individual psyche within a range of variations that are also determined *a priori*. Providing that articulation is the achievement of Jacques Lacan and the source of his appeal as the other thinker on whom Žižek bases his thought. Lacan, in effect, offers a way to make the later Hegel finally appear concrete again. Using Hegel's dialectical logic Lacan generates a series of categories (*object a*, the sinthome, Das Ding, the Three Registers as borromean knot) that do for the psyche—and for psychoanalysis—what the *Logic* did for thought in general: an *a priori* mapping or schematization of its structures and laws. This possibility depends on a single assumption, which grounds Lacan's project. Psyche, like language, must be conceived as a signifying system. By teaching us how to so understand it Lacan provides what minds in love with the *a priori* crave. In treating a particular patient one already knows all that one needs to know; for once someone speaks (and Lacan never tires reminding us that Freud called analysis "the talking cure") they reveal in their language—its slips, its fixations, its overdeterminations, its prime signifiers—the key to their psyche; i.e., to what they too could know if they made the linguistic turn away from experience with all its emotional confusions toward an understanding of the ways in which language speaks us.

Once we master Hegel and Lacan all intellectual work is essentially done. Culture, history, politics, the newest film, the latest fad are but opportunities for application. Or what amounts to *deduction*. Since all phenomena in the human cultural order are translations of *a priori* laws into temporal terms, any topic one considers—including 9-11—will be but an occasion to put the System into play in order to demonstrate that it alone explains what no one else has been able to fathom. Such performances can be opaque and self-consciously surreal as they often are in Lacan's writings and *séminaire* or dazzling in the manic energy of their apparent embrace of all phenomena as in Žižek, but in both cases the same operation maintains. Faced with the messy world of particulars nothing will suffice but a fit of abstraction. That's the discreet charm of this program, the seductive lure of the siren song it brings to the study of history and culture.

What is true for the psyche must also be true for history. It too must be something we can understand once we map the correct dialectical coordinates onto it. What Marx did for the economic laws of history in *Kapital* can thus be extended to all the operations that define the socio-political system. This is, in fact, the goal of a theory of *ideology*: to formulate the general laws underlying all the particular operations whereby ideology maintains its control over collective consciousness. The marriage of Hegel and Lacan is precisely what this project requires since the task is *to formulate a psycho-logic of the social*.[18] Not just the laws that bind the mass of interpellated subjects to the social order, but that order itself as a Collective Subject determined by laws which, as good Marxists, we will show point to its inevitable collapse. This is the purpose in each application of Hegel–Lacan to Society or what Žižek calls the Symbolic Order: to show that the *hole* in the Symbolic defines it, making *The* Trauma of *The* Real the destiny to which it is repeatedly delivered. Constructing such a theory of ideology is the considerable achievement of *The Sublime Object of Ideology* and the many subsequent books in which Žižek has refined a program which offers critics of ideology a strikingly new focus. The task is to identify then analyze the *fantasies* or *fantasms* that underlie and support ideology. The long sought marriage of Marx and Freud is thereby finally ours through the ministrations of Lacan and Hegel. A Lacanian examination of fantasms takes us to the heart of the political Unconscious. In the fantasms that underlie the Symbolic order one can discern the psychological needs and disorders of the whole. The high priori road is thereby complete. And it turns out that it's what we always hoped it would be: the yellow brick road that enables us to claim we've mastered every trauma, every contingency of existence. In Lacan the project of the Enlightenment is recovered. The dream of reason is realized: we now know *a priori* all that is possible and, of more importance, that nothing can exceed or escape the framework we've constructed. Any phenomena will but serve to illustrate what is already known. The effort of chapters 1–4, in contrast, was to get from fantasms to deeper underlying conflicts in order to show how those psychotic pressures interact with specific historical events to give a new historical direction to a collective psyche that is tied to specific economic forces.

Before proceeding let me stand back for a moment from the postmodern fixation on language (of which Žižek's theorizing is but one instance) and "tease out" an ironic reflection on this linguistic theme of infinite variations, all of which happily move within the confines of the same hermetic circle, which is drawn the moment one decides that *Language is all there is.* For then wherever one turns the same condition maintains. We might "experience" something but until we put it into language it remains evanescent. Once we do, language imposes its rules on what we may have thought was outside it. On reflection, in fact, the apparent difference vanishes. We always experience through language. The very stream of consciousness is a verbal process. There is no immediacy of lived experience. The philosophy of language holds the key to everything. Its history, however, is like all philosophic histories. Each thinker (deSassure, Chomsky, Austin) claims to reveal its essence, determining and therefore limiting what *makes sense* only to be overturned by the next theorist, with the one who deconstructs all who went before crowned heavyweight champion in the academy of pure mind.[19] Which may suggest that philosophy is an ouroboros eager for its own tail. Or, to formulate a heretical hypothesis that could free us from the deductive rigidity of *a priori* theories, maybe inquiry into the structure of language should end with a question not a program. What is language? Perhaps it's that which remains open to fundamental transformations that are determined by conditions that are in fact beyond it. Why privilege rational, categorical conceptions of language? Why relegate Literature to "semi-grammatical utterance" (Chomsky) or non-serious speech (Searle)? Maybe James Joyce is the one who reveals what language is and can do, and what experience can be if we are rich in our *use* of language and not reductive: for when we are *tropped head* and *bare falls witless* in our *seemetery* of *impassible abjects alcoherently* joined in a *notional gullery* where each phrase yields *two thinks at a time* (and where to euphemize is to euthanize), the effort *to idendefine the individione* will come to the one end that is always present: *Whoevery heard of such a think?*

In terms of method we now know that what happens to 9-11 in a book like *Desert* is the same thing that happens to everything Žižek touches. For Žižek events such as 9-11 exist only when they've been transformed into abstract categories. Real historical traumas must become The Trauma of the Real. Which is always the same it turns out. It's that momentary experience we have whenever our signifying system breaks down. Yet such is the anxiety this "experience" creates that we must perforce rush to complete the circle of our thought and name this thing in what amounts to a Cratylean pointing in which speech is rendered speechless. It's come again, as we knew it would—The Trauma of The Real. That is all ye know on earth, and all ye need to know. And having said it we rush quickly to another examination of another phenomenon in order to come again to this same conclusion, as we must, since that's what our methodology enables us to do.

The program Žižek derives from Lacan–Hegel is thus both systematic and fairly simple. The signifying system is defined by its effort to give us the illusion of a fullness of meaning. It does so, however, by excluding something. That something comes whenever we're struck speechless by an event, by something that can't be incorporated within the smoothly running terms of the Symbolic. But rather than make that experience the overture to a concrete thinking that would enter into the traumatic and sustain it by finding the psychoanalytic method needed to constitute its meaning, all Žižek can say is that we've again run up against that *excess* before which meaning collapses. Because he's moving in a circle there is for Žižek something uniquely satisfying in that moment. It's the *jouissance* of the critical critic. It comes whenever knowledge corresponds to the *lethal jouissance* of the world. Or, to put it more concretely, whenever Žižek can seize the chance, to the delight of his non-theoretical readers, to make large ethical claims for any form of excess, just as long as it inverts the dominant order.[20]

By dialectical necessity Žižek's thought always moves to the same abstract end. Every analysis discovers again The Trauma of the Real; once it is invoked nothing more needs to be or can be said. The Trauma of The Real is the noumena, the transcendental signified. All particular traumas—whether of the individual or the collectivity—serve but to illustrate its overpowering "presence." Such a system works perfectly because the one thing that could challenge and reverse it has been eliminated *a priori*. That thing is the thing Kierkegaard reclaimed the first time the System announced its completion: *the inwardness of individual agents in their existential struggle to engage the concrete conflicts of their situation in order, to put it in Hegelian terms, to discover what happens when existence becomes the medium in which one moves so that in constituting a trauma (not resolving it or abstractly invoking it) one discovers both history and one's situatedness in it.* The high priori road is of no help in this endeavor because *existence* is precisely what the fixation on language eliminates. The disappearance of existential subjectivity is perhaps the deepest way to read the movement of thought from structuralism through post-structuralism. It also indicates the irony of its irony. For such a movement constitutes a repetition *in reverse* of the most famous passage in the dialectical progression of Hegel's *Phenomenology*—the movement from stoicism and skepticism to the unsublatable reality of Unhappy Consciousness—or existence. Thanks to Lévi-Strauss (and others) that principle was banished in a reversion to stoicism. Derrida (and others) then returned us to skepticism, but without being able to complete the passage back to existence because fixation on language entails dependence on a trope that must be hypostatized. Irony. Irony is that which needs must ironize itself and thereby everything else. In Lacan and Žižek one finds another permutation of that necessity.

But then that's the lure of such thought. It offers a way to transcend the messy business of existence while claiming that one has revealed its laws.[21] Kierkegaard and the existential pathos are put back in their place by those who have mastered the cynical truth of things. Human beings aren't tragic existential agents. They're props in a comedy they can't comprehend. The only meaningful attitude toward it is irony. Irony—the way of becoming demystified by specifying the ways in which everyone else is of necessity mystified. One can't overcome the *aporias* of signification; one can only acquiesce in the superior awareness that comes from knowing that none of it could be otherwise. For to know that assures the one thing that's necessary. One will never get caught up in it. One will always operate on it, not in it. And whenever anxiety supervenes, one will find in the signifying system a deliverance more powerful than the appeal of older religions. As Chapter 7 will show, this connection identifies the contradiction shared by the right and the left: the persistence of a religious search for that master discourse that will overcome historical contingency.

Adherents to the postmodernist faith find in Jacques Lacan another ultimate master who has triumphed over existence itself by formulating the laws that control all those who never grasp the truth: that their existence is never theirs. Like everything else, existence is, Lacan informs us, nothing but the translation of pure logic into temporal terms.

> If I am a psychoanalyst I am also a man, and as a man my experience has shown me that the principle characteristic of my own human life and, I am sure, that of the people who are here—and if anybody is not of this opinion I hope that he will raise his hand—is that life is something that goes, as we say in French, *a la derive*. Life goes down the river, from time to time touching a bank, staying for a while here and there, without understanding anything—and it is the principle of analysis that nobody understand anything of what happens. The idea of the unifying unity of the human condition has always had on me the effect of a scandalous lie.[22]

Having invoked concrete experience throughout this critique, my duty is to develop it as a concrete alternative to the model that Lacan and Žižek offer. Moreover, to show that it is precisely what we've lacked in our efforts to fathom 9-11 and its ideological aftermath in the Amerikan collective historical unconscious.

## THE MISSED ENCOUNTER

"Organs Without Bodies is not a "dialogue" between these two theories [Lacan–Žižek and Deleuze] but something quite different: an attempt to trace the contours of an encounter between two incompatible fields. An encounter cannot be reduced to symbolic exchange: what resonates in it, over and above the symbolic exchange, is the echo of a traumatic impact. While dialogues are commonplace, encounters are rare."

Slavoj Žižek

### Who thinks abstractly?[23]

What follows constitutes an attempt to establish a systematic contrast between Lacanian thought and another way to think about the psyche. (Both, I should add, share a critique of the ego and the subsequent attempts of American psychoanalysts to put that old essentialistic wine in new bottles.) The contrast developed here, unlike the one with Lifton, occurs within an area of considerable agreement. What I'll try to show, however, is that each of Lacan's central ideas stops short precisely because, like Hegel, the only kind of mediation he can conceive is rational mediation: i.e., that mediation permitted by the logic of language, which, as Lacan like other postmodernists shows, is in effect the impossibility of mediation with the consequent arresting of the psyche in certain *aporias* of signification. There is, however, another kind of mediation and in terms of the psyche it is the one that counts. I term it *agonistic* or *dramatic self-mediation*. As we'll see, it enables us to restore the movement of Lacan's categories to an understanding that supercedes them. To put it in quasi-Hegelian terms, Lacan's formulas *arrest* the psyche at what is merely its first moment. The contrasting formulations I will offer restore its progression toward something they cannot contain. That thing, as we'll see, is existential subjectivity concretely *mediating* the very *formulations* through which Lacan seeks to dissolve it.

One way to think of this contrast is in terms of a shared effort to sustain what is most radical in the traditions on which Žižek and I both base our thought. Lacan and Žižek offer a radical reorientation of thought based on the application of Hegelian dialectics to psychoanalysis. My effort will be to show, in contrast, that there is another Hegel and another Freud who can serve as models for a thought that will become concrete precisely where Lacan and Žižek are necessarily abstract. Bear with me reader. The contrast is not merely theoretical. On it turns the possibility of recovering both experience and history.

Through his reading of the *Logic* Žižek offers us one Hegel. There is another Hegel, however, who ironically Žižek might have discovered had he pushed his reading one step further. This is the Hegel recovered when one moves from the *Logic* back to the *Phenomenology*.[24] and then *repeats* the problematic of that work by reading Hegel against Hegel. For the *Phenomenology* offers more than the first appearance of the great existential experiences and themes that would haunt subsequent thinkers (desire, master-slave, recognition, Unhappy Consciousness). It also indicates the need to reject the *foreclosure* Hegel imposes on these experiences so that he can assure a rational march to Absolute Knowledge. Repeatedly in the *Phenomenology* Hegel opens a tragic dimension of existential experience which he then refuses to sustain because his sole concern is to show its contribution to the development of Reason. Rational mediation thus consistently imposes itself on the more concrete dynamics of existential self-mediation. This is the flaw and the limit of the *Phenomenology*, its failure to sustain the concreteness Hegel claims as the goal of his thought. One proof of this is what emerges when a genuinely phenomenological thinker such as Sartre renews Hegelian themes in the great, tragic explorations of experience developed in *Being and Nothingness*. Another is provided by Hegel himself in the notorious problem of transitions. Hegel claims that every transition in the *Phenomenology* is one of necessity in keeping with the stated purpose of the work to trace the necessary movement of experience from the simplest position to the absolute standpoint. Commentators have uniformly agreed, however, that many of Hegel's transitions are "transitions of sentiment"; or what amounts to the same thing, ones of logical and rational rather than experiential necessity. The threat to Hegel's project is that the phenomenological investigations will get bogged down in the concrete dramas of existence. The experience of Unhappy Consciousness may, for example, be inexhaustible and unsublatable. That's why whenever experience is in danger of becoming too complex, Hegel abruptly transcends upward to the next stage of rationality. What's left behind is what must be recovered, a field of exploration into the dynamics of subjectivity that Hegel deserves credit for having opened but which we can constitute only if we resist the *desire* to impose rational, *a priori* methods of mediation upon it. Overcoming the phenomenal is, of course, the rationale behind the shift to *Logic* that fascinates both Hegel and Žižek. That desire is already far too present in the *Phenomenology*. Often termed a *panlogicism*, the truth of everything vital in the work points instead toward what may be termed a *pantragicism*. To immerse oneself in the experiences Hegel opens up is to immerse oneself in the tragic or, in terms of the critique of Žižek, in *traumatic experiences* that can and must be sustained and deepened through agonistic self-mediations. That, as we'll see, is the true route to the concrete. It begins with the recognition that one's true anxiety is not over one's situatedness in language, but over the concrete awareness that one's existence is irretrievably *at issue* in the inner disorders that bind one's psyche to very personal conflicts that must be engaged and that can't be transcended by convincing oneself that all anxiety is about The Trauma of The Real.

A similar reorientation applies to the effort I share with Lacan to preserve what is most radical and disruptive in Freud against all attempts to domesticate his thought. The following system of contrasts will show, however, that the existential position I'll articulate becomes concrete at precisely the point where Lacan necessarily remains abstract. In effect what follows forms a series of *concretizations* which restore the *dialectical movement* of experience by liberating the existing subject from the brilliance of Lacan's effort to dissolve it. Lacanian thought, as we'll see, constitutes a systematic attempt to displace a tragic understanding of the psyche. Its contradictions, however, retain the traces of the displaced experience it thereby points us toward.[25]

Here, then, a brief survey and critique of Lacan's thought in terms of its most basic *categories*. These categories, which are arranged in a dialectical progression, interconnect in numerous ways, but for reasons of space I leave that argument implicit in order to keep the focus on the contrast between Lacan's concepts and the ones I advance. For it is here that the issue of the concrete is engaged in a way that will enable us to move from fixed postmodernist dogmas back to a way of thinking about the psyche that we must recover if we're to comprehend what has happened historically since 9-11.

## A Critique of Lacanian Psychoanalysis

### The Unconscious

*The Unconscious is structured like a language.* This is perhaps Lacan's most important formulation, the one from which he has drawn the most radical implications through his deft use of deSassure and his unbridled effort to write in a manner that is gnomic, equivocal, and surreal as befits a *style* that endeavors to mimic the operations of the unconscious; if, that is, the unconscious is that self-deconstructing linguistic process that frustrates all attempts to arrest its energetics.[26] But what if it isn't? What if a better theory might be stated thus: *the Unconscious is structured like a tragic drama that has been arrested* in media res. This contrast is crucial because it turns on the difference between ironic understanding and existential self-mediation. Lacan's definition of the Unconscious resolves the psyche into the passive by-product of a language that "speaks us" and that prosecutes its desires independent of all efforts to mediate them. The second definition establishes agonistic self-mediation as the basis of a subjectivity that lives out the bitter truth of experience: conflict deferred proceeds inevitably to a traumatic breakdown; what we refuse to know about ourselves is what we do—to the other; anxiety is thus the *signal* that opens the subject to its inner world and not the force that mandates flight from it.

This difference rests on a philosophic one: that between symbolic mediation, which is the only kind possible in Lacan's linguistic world, and dramatic self-mediation. In the former everything derives deductively from the logic of signification, the mapping of that logic being the object of thought. Dramatic self-mediation, in contrast, takes up the conflicts and emotions that define one's actual relationship to oneself and others and submits them to an *agon* of change through *action*. That process counters Lacan's assertion that "*desire is the desire of the other*" with the reply that existentializes it: *desire is the internalization of the contradictions and conflicts of the other's desire as the barrier to and origin of the effort to attain independent agency by overcoming the "voices" (both pre-oedipal and superegoic) that assault one from within.* This contrast entails two radically different theories—and experiences—of subjectivity. In Lacan, subject is the discourse of the other; i.e., our subjection to the *impasses* to which signification condemns us and the neurotic fixations that result from every attempt to defy Symbolic Law. For me, in contrast, subjectivity is an inwardness defined by experiential conflicts that must be mediated because they constitute our existential and interpersonal situatedness as agents who through action give determination to our being.

## The Three Registers

The best way to illustrate this pivotal difference is through a contrast with the three categories that structure Lacan's thought: the Imaginary, the Symbolic, and the Real. Lacan's *Imaginary* is a world of narcissism and aggression, of subjects condemned to the impossible effort to comprehend, let alone satisfy, the other's desire; subjects who thus mirror the conditions of their paralysis in a circle of violence that cannot be broken. Because it is a world lacking the possibility of existential mediation, all mediation must come from somewhere else. Enter the structuralist Lacan, the theorist of the *Symbolic Order*, for whom Language and its hypostatization provide the only structure of mediation that can deliver the thereby Oedipalized subjects from both the Imaginary and the threat of psychosis. The iron laws of Language have the additional value of providing a new way to secure the central dogmas of classical Freudianism—castration, the Oedipus complex, sexual difference—by making them structures that derive *a priori* from the laws of signification. After mapping this order, Lacan undertakes a revolution within his own thought. The transformation comes once the Symbolic receives its proper name— Ideology. Lacanian structuralism then emerges as a way station on the road to something that exceeds structuralism. The Symbolic Order, it turns out, is defined by the attempt to conceal a void at its center. Enter the *Real* as the traumatic kernel that exceeds symbolization, the force of *jouissance* before which all linguistic attempts to fix meaning collapse. Despite its romantic aura, the Real functions as the final abstraction that completes the circle of Lacanian thought in the only way that an abstract dialectic can achieve completion: through the production of an entire new system of concepts—*objet a*, the sinthome, the drive, agalma, etc.—which are generated *deductively* through the simple inversion of the system of concepts that defines the Symbolic Order.

Lacan is at pains to argue that his categories stand in a dialectical relationship of mutual complication.[27] I think it can be shown, however, that they actually trace the circularity of a progressively abstract series of displacements. The basic error occurs at the beginning in the deliberate swerve of Lacan's thought away from its considerable initial debt to Melanie Klein. The Lacanian Imaginary is a frozen structure incapable of mediation because its entire rationale is flight from a prior order of experience which Lacan, unlike Klein, refuses to explore. As Klein shows, pre-Oedipal conflicts are ones in which one's existence is at issue. Though she has her own way of displacing the primary implication of her discoveries, the pre-Oedipal world Klein describes is one of humiliation and cruelty that turn on what happens when the internalization of the other's destructiveness generates emotional conflicts that make the struggle to avoid inner deadening the primary organizer of the psyche.[28] Lacan's *mirror-stage* is a flight from the emotional turbulence and agonistics of that situation through a displacement of its aggressivity into the frustrations of a paralysis. If one recovers all that Lacan thereby displaces the result is the discovery of a *dynamic existential unconscious*, as opposed to Lacan's linguistic one, an unconscious defined by pre-oedipal conflicts and anxieties that must be confronted because the very possibility of life or death, of psychic integration or psychotic dissolution, hangs in the balance. The Lacanian Imaginary is an effort to resolve that *agon* in a frozen realization of one of its possibilities. It is as if, without knowing it, Lacan is saying "if I can mirror the other and realize their desire I can escape the specter of their destructiveness and the anxiety of my own conflicted feelings toward the other and toward myself." From this perspective the Lacanian Symbolic emerges, in turn, not as the Imaginary's mediation through linguistic *intervention* but as its reification through the enforcement as cultural Law of the rigid conventions of meaning that bind socialized subjects to one another in collective flight from existential anxieties. Such beings are, of course, haunted by a return of the repressed. They get the one they deserve in the Lacanian Real. For romantic proclamations notwithstanding, the Real constitutes a return of all that one has failed to confront in one's inner world now rendered massive, impersonal, and overwhelming as a result of one's persistent flight from it.

The actual relationship of the three categories that structure Lacan's thought is therefore not a dialectical one (as Lacan and Žižek claim) but, rather, the process of displacement whereby flight from dramatic self-mediation begets a formalism of pure linguistic relationships from which all experiential possibilities are derived through *deductions* that are void of any meaning other than their linguistic self-reference. The system forms, in short, a vast and impersonal tautology. Actual anxiety is thereby silenced. A language of anxiety is replaced by anxiety over language. Little wonder that the final condition to which Lacanian thought aspires is the superior irony of those who are demystified of all illusions about human subjectivity and human agency; and yet who claim to liberate and remain true to a desire that has itself been reduced to a sheer energetics devoid of agency and fatally tied via the *objet a* (of which more shortly) to the reification of an initial condition that cannot be mediated.

To this way of thinking I offer the alternative of tragic self-mediation. Recognition and reversal (though not I hasten to point out in their Aristotelian meaning) are the prime movers in this process because it is defined by the two moments that constitute the movement of a genuine psychoanalysis: (1) the recognition of how the conflicts one refuses to face structure one's life and (2) the effort to act within the *agon* that is thereby recovered in a way that will bring about a complete reversal in the very structure of one's psyche. If anxiety is for Lacan the force that motivates a system of displacements, anxiety is, for a tragic sensibility, what Keats called "the wakeful anguish of the soul."[29] As such it is the overture to the dialectic process that defines the inwardness of what I term the *melancholic subject*. Anxiety is the signal not to flee but to attend to one's inner world. One can only do so, however, if one is willing to suffer the burden of depression, which is no less than the burden of confronting the truth about the feelings toward the other and oneself that define one's inner world. (The great example, of course, is the transformation Hamlet goes through from the false piety of his original vow of fealty to the paternal superego to the process of existential individuation that overturns everything he once believed—especially about himself.) The possibility of self-mediation depends on the ability of the human being to live within and thereby deepen the revelatory power of depression. This contrast to Lacan's thought may be the most revealing because the greatest lacunae in the Lacanian edifice is the absence of any theory, let alone consideration, of depression. In Lacan's nosology (his classification of neuroses and their etiologies) there are only five possibilities or subject positions: the hysteric, the obsessional, the pervert, the phobic, and the psychotic. This is so because those possibilities are the ones that can be deduced from the laws of signification. Having no standing in that logic, depression is ushered from the stage and with it the possibility of an inwardness capable of sustaining those emotions and conflicts that light up the true conditions of our inner world. In the attempt to displace this dynamic of the psyche, Lacan's thought oscillates between obsessional and hysteric mechanisms. Obsessional mentation tries to get everything pinned down, fixed forever in a system of clear and distinct structural concepts and mathemes, but then the whole edifice falls apart in the return of a hysteria that must be displaced in a renewed effort to fashion a "world in the head," a world of "words words words" as verbal magic promising conceptual deliverance from a situation that cannot be faced. Here too Žižek is Lacan's true son. Or, to put it in terms of the missed encounter, Žižek and I have the same subject—traumatic anxiety—but while my effort is to constitute its experiential meaning, everything Žižek does is an attempt to flee that prospect. This is the true source of the mania that defines his procedure. If one keeps moving, constantly showing how much one can say about whatever topic comes to mind, one can forever forestall the day when everything stops and all that one has refused to know about oneself knocks on the door. To displace the anxiety of that prospect—in fact to keep anxiety confined to its most immediate form—Žižek, like Lacan, alternates between obsessional and hysterical mentation. Obsessional: the need to reassert the same set of abstract *a priori* truths (i.e., The Trauma of the Real) at the end of each discussion. Hysteria: the need to immediately begin again and keep the dance of intellect moving at a fantastic clip. For the secret that drives and haunts obsessionalism is the attempt to deny something that one already knows. That's why the moment one proves to oneself beyond the shadow of a doubt that one has triumphed over the thing one wants to deny the whole process begins again. Fortunately one thereby escapes the fear that haunts one. For to confront what one knows yet needs to deny is to open oneself to the necessity of depression, which is that experience where all displacements cease and one is overwhelmed by the actual emotional burdens of one's inner world.

### Desire

"The paradox is this: when we fall in love we are seeking to refind all or some of the people to whom we were attached; on the other hand, we ask our beloved to correct all of the wrongs that these earlier parents or siblings inflicted on us. So that love contains within it the contradiction: the attempt to return to the past and the attempt to undo the past."

Lewis Levy (Martin Bergmann) in Woody Allen's<br>*Crimes and Misdemeanors*[30]

There are two ways to constitute the dynamic of desire that Hegel uncovered in the *Phenomenology*. Desire, as Hegel shows, is the dialectical unrest that informs subjectivity. For desire is defined by a dissatisfaction that demands progressive self-overcoming. I desire this. I achieve it only to realize "that's not it." I desire something else, something more. I'm defined by perpetual dissatisfaction, and contra the capitalist commodification of this condition, reflecting on desire leads to one inevitable conclusion: "self-consciousness achieves its satisfaction only in another self-consciousness."[31] That conclusion, in turn, establishes the fundamental dilemma of human relations, since dissatisfaction with commodities is nothing to the dissatisfactions that love activates. Concrete relations with others are marked by perpetual struggle.[32]

There are two ways to think about the origin of the psyche. For Lacan, desire always produces dissatisfaction because desire is and remains the desire of the other. My desire thus proves my continuing subjection to the other. Subjection is how desire is formed and how it operates. I am what I represent for another signifier; how I am signified by them as an expression of their desire. A double trap results. I can never fulfill the other's demand nor fathom the enigma of their desire. Nor can I ever break free of it and constitute an independent desire of my own. It is impossible to give the other what would complete them or to stop trying to do so.[33] (It's worth noting that the other is in the same trap with respect to their desire. Enigma and infinite regress are here two sides of the same coin.)

But what if desire isn't the bedrock Hegel and Lacan claim, but itself the displacement of a darker and more exacting condition? That possibility offers another way to look at the origin of the psyche. The projection of the mother's conscious and unconscious conflicts is the founding condition that delivers the psyche over to the necessity of self-mediation. The effort to fulfill the m/other's desire is an attempt to avoid confronting the conflicted feelings that are the deep and lasting impact of that experience. The psyche is defined by *primary emotions*. These, the true issue of our earliest experiences, deliver us over to existing as a subject threatened with self-dissolution. Love one learns is not unqualified; like a Greek bearing gifts, it comes with a host of messages defining what one must do and become to prove worthy of it—and what will happen if one doesn't. The depressive's fear—that hate will prove stronger than love—is the defining experience of childhood. What the other desires that one *be* is a function of their unconscious conflicts. "Be what I need you to be so that my emotional needs are fulfilled." This message is communicated to the child in a number of ways: the approval given and the approval withheld; the use of humiliation and cruelty as tools of instruction; the terror of an abandonment that would prove destructive—the withdrawal of love; the persecution internalized that assaults one whenever one tries to say No to parental demand. The internalization of such experiences creates the clash of primary emotions that define the child's inner world, a world of conflict that turns on feelings of desperate love and violent hatred—and beneath both a struggle to persist in being as a subject by overcoming the destructiveness one has internalized. To be a subject is to suffer nameless dread, catastrophic anxiety, and a *wound* that goes to the heart of one's being. This is the reality that is prior to desire: the existential vulnerability of a subject at issue to itself as a result of experiencing a violent appropriation by the other. To be a subject is to exist as a *who* posing the question *why* in response to the cruelty of the other. But because the feelings connected to such experiences are overpowering we build a crypt around the *wound* that defines the psyche and atop that crypt we erect the world of desire. Desire is a displacement of the terror of humiliation and cruelty. It is how a subject flees itself, not how it confronts or expresses itself. In fact, both of the options it offers are traps. One can try to fulfill the other's desire, but only at the cost of the *resentment* one then feels. Or one can lose oneself by making oneself the stark inversion of the other's expectations. Either way entails flight from the actual existential task. Contra Lacan, the fact of the matter is that one can know the conflicts of the m/other's Unconscious as well as how one's own conflicts derive from one's insertion in that drama. And armed with that knowledge one can take up the task of reversal. But only if one is willing to endure the trauma that such an effort unleashes in one's psyche. Failure to do so, however, also reveals the inadequacy of the Lacanian paradigm. For one only remains fixated on the repetition of an attempt to fulfill an enigmatic desire when one fears or refuses to confront the actual feelings and conflicts that define one's relationship to the other. Or, to put it in even more concrete terms, one only remains bound to a frustrating and impossible desire as long as one refuses to confront one's complicity in the perpetuation of that frustration. Doing so, moreover, is not something one can escape by terming it impossible because from its inception desire is dialectical. It is both the desire of the other and the desire to liberate oneself from that desire. That is what one feels *immediately* the first time one experiences those questions that are only experienced in unspeakable pain. Why does my mother recoil whenever I hug her? What is it about my crying that terrifies her? Why does my father try to humiliate me? What is it about me that makes him hate me? Is there any cause in nature that makes these hard hearts? No, the child doesn't pose these questions in these terms. It does so far more deeply and concretely. It lives them as traumatic experiences that will inform one's later response to the conflict.

## Subjectivity: As Subjection or as Existentialization

Anticipating the predictable charge from doctrinaire Lacanians that conflict is just another word for desire, the contrast developed above (though slight in terms of shared Hegelian principles) indicates a fundamental difference. It can be brought out most readily by contrasting the view of subjectivity articulated in the graphs developed in Lacan's greatest essay—"Subversion of the Subject and the Dialectic of Desire"[34]—with the order of subjectivity that those graphs render impossible. Both views, I should add, share the effort to liberate the subject from the substantialism and essentialism of ego psychology and all subsequent attempts within psychoanalysis to posit a stable self and self-identity.

For purposes of brevity I confine discussion of the four graphs to their conceptual meaning. The graphs trace a progressive decentering of the subject. The position I present articulates, in contrast, the bases of existential liberation.

*Graph 1*: I am subjected to the other and to what the other signifies me as. Hegel's mistake was to posit the autonomy of desire. Desire is the desire of the other. When I desire I desire what the other has determined me to desire. I think my desires are mine—the result of personal choices—when they are really the other's. This is the primary subjection of the subject. Narcissism, the belief in the ego and the search for identity are the ways we try to deny this condition. And thereby illustrate it. For the ego, as Lacan demonstrates, is the illusory coherence of a being totally dependent on adapting itself to the demands of the other. Qua subject, I am bound to a Signifier ("you're a good boy who would never shame your mother") which the other imposed on me or which I latched onto in an attempt to become the embodiment of their desire.

*Contra*: Desire is a displacement of the terror of confronting the emotions that define one's true relationship to the other and the conflicts that are engaged the moment one tries to say No to the superego, which is the true voice or presence of the other in the psyche. Resistance to its demands delivers one over to the threat of psychic dissolution, which is only engaged if one manages to sustain an anxiety that begins on the other side of the fear of abandonment and the loss of the other's love. Desire is a relief from the dread that this prospect brings; and a way to displace the conflicts it engages. The wound at the heart of the psyche is prior to desire. If liberation is to become possible, it is there that one must begin.

*Graph 2*: The condition established in the first graph is played out in the larger world of Symbolic Identification or what Lacan terms the Big Other. The ideal ego seeks the approval of the ego-ideal. This involves a double subjection. The ideal ego is the self we try to become so that we'll be likeable; that is, so that we'll embody the signifiers that attract and realize the desire of others. This further alienation from the possibility of any independent desire introduces permanent insecurity. We view ourselves through the gaze of the other, but we can never be sure we've received it. The alienation of the *mirror stage* in which I first fell under the spell of the other is thus repeated in the attempt to fashion an identity that will appeal to the Big Other. The result is a further decentering in which I become utterly dependent on others, on social recognition. The Hegelian dream of recognition thus devolves to the kind of thing one finds in academic careerism: the pursuit of a professional reputation—and with it an identity—through the incessant advertisement of one's name recognition to others engaged in a similar pursuit. There's no way to arrest this activity nor to see the void at its center because everything is controlled by a question one dare not ask: when you enact a role—and try with all your heart to be it—who are you enacting it for?

*Contra*: The second graph is an incisive charting of the fundamental trap that subjects fall into as long as they remain dependent on others for their "self-worth." The reason people cling desperately to this project, however, is the deliverance it offers from the dread of existence. It returns in the anxiety that comes whenever one finds oneself alone, alienated from the group or threatened with exclusion. We seek safety and security in the They because we live in terror of representing or pursuing anything that doesn't have the blessing of consensual validation and reflected appraisals. The social determination of the subject that is given schematic articulation in Lacan's second graph is for the most part the truth about human beings only because it displaces a prior problematic of existence.

*Graph 3*: The condition articulated in the second graph reveals its binding power whenever the subject attempts to go inward. That act is defined for Lacan by the question *che voui?* That is, what does the Big Other really want of me? Why am I what you (the Big O) say that I am? Those questions haunt the subject, bringing with them a freight of doubt and anxiety. Have I fathomed the other's desire? Do I know what the Other really wants from me? Subjection to otherness has delivered the subject over to two intolerable questions. *Fantasy* is an attempt to provide an answer by filling up the gap that desire opens. We think of our fantasies as private and individualistic, but Lacan shows how completely this inwardness dances to no different drummer. Fantasy is not about what we desire, but about what the O/other desires and how we offer ourselves as the object that will fill that desire. I am what is lacking in you. I will complete you. And thereby attain the illusion of fulfilling myself. The effort entails, however, a fundamental contradiction. All fantasy is a response to "the unbearable enigma of the other's desire." *The fundamental fantasy*—the core one we repeat in endless variations—is an attempt to represent one's identity in terms of who one is for the other. But one can never be sure one's got it right. The irony of the situation is that in this we meet at least, though as ships in the night. For the other never knows either. I keep thinking the other has a desire that can be fulfilled when like me they're defined by a lack they're desperately trying to fill by becoming the lure to another's desire. The comedy of human relations derives from this fact. As does the lure of Hollywood, the dream factory of collective fantasy. Without the movies most people wouldn't have the slightest idea what they want or what kind of woman or man embodies the object of their desire.

*Contra*: We remain fixated on the world of public collective fantasies because it delivers us from confronting the actual anxieties and conflicts of our inner world. Fantasy is a text we refuse to submit to the very interrogation that it makes possible. For the deepest fantasies reveal not only *who* we are for the other, but what it costs to be a function of the other's desire. One sits at the window awaiting the long overdue return of one's wife or husband indulging again the fantasy of the accidental death that will deliver one magically into the bliss of one's freedom. Such a fantasy represents the frustrations of one's inner world as contradictions that demand *drama*. In fantasies of this order the question *who am I?* reveals the possibilities one dreads. Lacan neglects such fantasies because they point to an ongoing act of existential self-reference at the heart of the psyche, with fantasy the way of enacting the very problems that Lacan consigns to silence. Fantasy reveals a subject defined by problems such as: how expel the bad object, not how secure the good one? How survive under the pressure of Thanatos in the psyche? How deal with the self-lacerations of a heart that feels a depth both of love and hate toward the same others? How overcome the staging within fantasy of one's death as something that has already occurred? Such fantasies are attempts by the psyche to represent to itself the conflicts it must engage in order to free itself from all the ways it is dead and dying within. Fantasy, so understood, is the attempt to call oneself to account, to identify the actions that one must take within oneself.

*Graph 4*: As the furthest reach of Lacan's dialectic the fourth graph schematizes the difference between the Law of the Big Other and *jouissance* or *enjoyment*. The quickest way to get at the great complexity of this graph, to which I can't do fully justice here, is also the most concrete. Castration as Symbolic Law—of one's subjection to signifiers, most notably those that determine one's destiny as sexed being—establishes in us an opposition between the Big Other and *enjoyment*. The latter comes whenever the field of signifiers is permeated by a pre-symbolic stream of enjoyment or *jouissance*. Within the vast ocean of the Symbolic there are such islands. The erogenous zones for example. Those able to *traverse the fantasy* and experience *subjective destitution* attain a liberation that enables them to enter a realm of pure Drive that is beyond desire. Drive, however, has no human coordinates. It is not the experience of a subject. It is, rather, what one is transported into whenever the delays and detours of desire collapse and one experiences the pleasure of a pure pulsation of raw energy that is in excess of all symbolizing frames and that expends itself in a discharge or expenditure without reserve. As Žižek shows in *Desert*, many claims can be made for such an experience, primary among them the notion that one thereby recovers what one was alienated from by one's entry into the Symbolic.

*Contra*: In Lacan the pursuit of enjoyment or *jouissance* becomes the ultimate goal of the psyche because it delivers it from the tragic burdens that define it. For those subjects who take them up, enjoyment is always secondary to the duties one bears to oneself. Primary among them is the need to engage the conflicts of one's inner world in situations that will put one *at issue* and *at risk*. That task involves reversing the displacements of desire in order to tunnel into the crypt of one's deepest wounds. Life and death then hang in the balance, engaged in an *agon* that can end in self-dissolution.

That *agon* is the situation most worth having, however, because it establishes an ethic grounded in a principle or "drive" that is beyond both the pleasure and reality principles. Existence, like *jouissance*, gets at something absolute in us that is defined by excess. The freedom of the human subject is grounded in the refusal to compromise the demands one places on oneself.

## Trauma

There are two ways to conceive of and respond to traumatic experiences. Trauma is for Lacan that experience which is incessantly fled and always returns. That's the secret of signification. And its destiny: to repeatedly collapse all symbolic systems before the return of The Trauma of The Real. Trauma is by definition that which cannot be signified. In a sense that's all one can say about it. But the collapse of speech is mere prologue to the swelling act of "experiencing" what trauma reveals: the emptiness of the other. The game of desire ends. One is thus able to traverse the fantasy and experience the ultimate truth about subjectivity: *subjective destitution*. One then enters the impersonal world of the Drive and achieves the long sought, infinitely deferred *jouissance*. The collapse of the subject becomes the triumph of the impersonal. One co-exists with an absolute expenditure of pent up energies, an explosion of pure force beyond all signification. But this lasts only for a brief time. One has made contact with the *traumatic kernel* of one's being. But trauma, Lacan contends, cannot be confronted. It can only be "suffered." The minute we begin to speak we lose it again. Our speech, however, has now become the demystified consciousness of one who knows the *aporias* of the Symbolic and, of greater importance, what they conceal. Speech will now be (as in Lacan's writings) an ironic playing with something that one knows is empty.

My effort is to develop an antithetical understanding of trauma as the experience that reveals to the subject the deepest truths about its inner world. That formula formulates the fundamental difference with Lacan. There is no Trauma of the Real. There are only particular traumas and what they reveal is always radically concrete. Trauma is the experience that tears away all the lies that hide the subject from the truth about itself. In trauma the displacements that sustain the ego collapse. One is delivered over to what I term *primary emotions*. Such emotions engage the psyche in an *agon* with itself. The conflicts that define one's being return in all their intensity. The other is present again in its true visage. One is assaulted within by emotions in which one is at issue and at risk because there is now no inner distance between what one feels and *who* one is. The wound that defines the psyche is present as the demand to do what traumatic experience alone makes possible: not just know the truth of one's situation but act within in an effort to reverse it. For example, a sexually abused child whenever that trauma returns experiences again both the horror of the original betrayal and violation and the equally violent protest of one's outraged reaction to it. All the defenses that have softened that trauma—including the most terrifying one, that of justifying the abuser and blaming oneself—collapse. The drama that defines one's psyche is re-engaged or fled once again, depending on what one is able to summon oneself to do within the traumatic space. Those subjects able to sustain it (and one should never underestimate the terror accompanying that effort) recover the possibility of taking action within themselves and thereby reversing the traumatic condition of the psyche in the only way one can: by bringing the clash of raw conflicted feelings to white heat, engaging the destructiveness one has internalized in a struggle to the death.

Engaging trauma in this way depends on making concrete precisely what is rendered impossible in Lacan's theory. The register of one's psyche that he argues can never be confronted (the traumatic kernel) is precisely where action begins. Trauma is the opportunity to take action within the crypt—i.e., at the deepest layer of the Unconscious—by engaging suffering in its actual moment. By sustaining the trauma one recovers those existential choices one made when one's being was first assaulted, but now within the possibility of a new edition. *For if and when, within trauma, one finds a new way to feel one creates a new way to be.* There are things we must tear out of our hearts in order to be free. When it is so engaged trauma becomes existentializing process. To anticipate a predictable objection, none of this entails a return to the Symbolic and its limits. On the contrary, a subject taking action within itself within the space of trauma has entered into another way of being. Think, for example, of the kind of drama Artaud calls for, an art that exceeds the Symbolic by creating images that "are true insofar as" they are "violent."[35] Whenever one creates such an image or, more concretely, when in trauma one suffers again the internal eruption of the images that epiphanize the wounds that define one's psyche, one exists in an order of experience that is outside the Symbolic. The traumatic process is the immersion of one's being in such an effort. So understood, trauma is not that which must be resolved by a return to the ego and its defenses, as the American mental health industry tells us. Nor is it what one transcends through an abstract articulation of its defining structures as in Lacan. It is that which is entered into, even welcomed, as the process through which a thereby existentialized psyche gives itself determination. The contrast formulated here turns, of course, on two distinct ways of experiencing and responding to anxiety.

## Anxiety

By his own reckoning it is on the topic of anxiety that Lacan makes his fundamental contribution to psychoanalysis. Anxiety is the ur-emotion and through its displacement the source of all other emotions.[36] Its return, moreover, reveals the truth about the subject. We experience anxiety Lacan says whenever what he calls the *objet a* or *o(a)* approaches.[37] That is, whenever one experiences something that returns one to one's original experience, but with the unsolvable enigma of the other's desire now experienced as the *lack* in the other, that lack one is impelled to try to fill but with no way to do so. In anxiety one "knows" this yet also knows that there is no way to get free of the effort. Anxiety thereby reveals the truth of the Unconscious. *Wherever I say I, I am o.* What I think of as most my own is precisely where one finds the overpowering presence of the other. Desire tries to escape that recognition only to be repeatedly delivered over to the truth desire strives to deny. "Desire is loving where one isn't wanted."[38] Anxiety reveals the truth underlying that folly. For in anxiety one comes face to face with the *lack* in the other as the thing one can't address to which nonetheless one is bound. In a sense, Lacan's effort is to restore one category from the forgotten legacy of existentialism: the absurd. Anxiety is what Sisyphus experiences when he realizes the utter futility of it all. In Lacan's hands that experience is not the source of a heroism of endurance. It's the beginning of the *fading of the subject* before the insistence of a demand that one is powerless to resist whenever a *part object* sets desire in motion. Anxiety is the momentary recognition that one would arrest that process if one could. Only there is no I to do so. That's the significance of the part object as *cause* of desire. The founding act of subjection defining the psyche binds it to certain part objects and signifiers that have their way with us whenever we find ourselves in their presence. The power of arresting this or understanding it is as remote as the chance that Swann can arrest all that is foreordained to happen to him (and similarly to Marcel, Saint-Loup, Charlus in the Proustian representation of the universal structures of desire) the moment he associates a vulgarian named Odette to Vinteuil's sonata and sees in her face an uncanny resemblance to Boticelli's painting of *Jethro's Daughter*. Anxiety is the fading of the subject under the pull of forces that remain forever beyond mediation.

Lacan's theory of anxiety brilliantly arrests its inherent dialectic, resolving into one term what I will show are two terms locked in the conflict that defines them. Lacan's position depends on substituting a secondary question for the primary one that anxiety poses. That question is: *Will I remain stillborn or can I come to life by reversing the power that the other has over me?* Anxiety is the signal that this drama has been joined in some way. For all anxiety derives from a single condition: *it is what happens whenever we violate the demands of the superego and it responds by assaulting us*. Most people collapse under that assault, which is why anxiety usually serves as the motive for reinstituting ego defenses. Those who are able to sustain anxiety, however, create the possibility of activating the *agon* that defines the psyche's inner condition. For each time we refuse to capitulate to the superego we activate a greater aggression in response and with it the movement toward a situation in which the superego will reveal its true visage. Anxiety is not the overpowering presence of a single force—o(a). It's the simultaneity of two forces met in the conflict that defines them. The truth of both is what emerges when that *agon* is sustained.

The superego one then learns is that force in us that has the power to annihilate us. One also learns that the only viable response is to meet that aggression with an equal and greater aggression. Compromise is but another form of capitulation. There is only one way to deal with the superego. Agonistically. This is the possibility that anxiety joins, however briefly. *Anxiety is the psyche in conflict with itself at the inner register where everything is decided.* When this drama is sustained the superego drops all pretenses of being loving and beloved, revealing itself as a force of internalized destructiveness that attacks every effort to move out from under the shadow of its demands. To put the contrast in Lacanian terms, anxiety is the overture not to capitulation but to deracination. That is the action one must perform in order to *be* or exist where "I am o."

Anxiety, to conclude, can be the signal of the subject's dissolution or the possibility of its reconstitution. The same is true of sexuality.

## Sexuality

It is on this topic, of course, that the reader will most likely question the political relevance of the discussion. Chapter 7 will show concretely that understanding the radical Republican right is impossible apart from a disciplined psychoanalytic understanding of sexuality. The fixation of the right on sexuality is well known. What we lack is an understanding of what this fixation signifies and, consequently, what the stakes of sexuality are for an understanding both of history and the task of resistance. The discussion that follows attempts to fill that void by replacing the abstract understanding of sexuality developed by Lacan with a concrete one that will show why the marriage of Marx and Freud that was first attempted by the Frankfurt School remains the synthesis that is needed if we are to understand how ideology roots itself in individual psyches in a way that assures mass collective allegiance to political movements, as in the current alignment of Christian fundamentalism and right-wing Republican capitalism. A libidinal politics depends on a concrete and not an abstract understanding of how the sexual is the register of our psyche that we must grapple with in order to liberate ourselves. This is a task that far too many on the left refuse to undertake, even though failure to do so leaves one prey to ideological manipulation (and not only by the right). The personal is the political and that fact is never more true than with respect to human sexuality. What follows offers each reader the possibility of discovering that fact in intimate ways. With Lacan, however, we have a thinker who restores sexuality to the center of psychoanalysis only to dissolve it in abstract formulae. In his hands it becomes a theory of the subject positions in which men and women are trapped by the Law of the Signifier, the Law of the Father. That law articulates for Lacan the truth of sex. Men are condemned by it to inhabiting the logic of *exclusion*: i.e., no man can represent the phallic function, though it seems all must try, which is why male relations so often fixate on attempts to psychologically castrate one another. The phallic logic assigns women a subtler position: that of the *not all* for whom the phallic function is not valid and who therefore always exist somehow outside its determinations.

The upshot of all this is the absence of any comfort either from the kindness of strangers or the effort of long-term relationships, since with respect to intimacy we are never more than ships passing in the night. As Lacan puts it in another one of his shocking statements which aren't all that shocking once one understands them, "there is no sexual relation." The logic that the formulae of sexuation impose on men and women condemns them to the frustration of trying to effect the impossible, to establishing a relationship where there can only be an antagonism. As Joan Copjec puts it near the end of the seminal examination of Lacan's thought on this issue: "Sexuality is the effect on the living being of impasses that emerge when it gets entangled in the symbolic order."[39] Not surprisingly, Žižek gleefully deduces the glibbest conclusion from this line of thought. We never touch. When we "make love" all we experience is our fantasm. Even if we achieve orgasm together we're always on different tracks, each individual running the solipsistic tape that plays on in the mind. In a curiously Cartesian way, that is all that sex is for Lacan. At a poignant moment in Edward Albee's *A Delicate Balance*, the character Edna offers one realization of the wisdom that comes with age: "to know … that the one body you've wrapped your arms around … the only skin you've ever known … is your own."[40] What Edna doesn't know is that for Lacan she remains a prisoner to the last mystification; for the cold kiss flesh bestows on itself is but another illusion of a touch that never occurs. Even here the only correct response to our condition is demystification and the grandiose pleasure that comes when one can draw conclusions that mock the travail in which the unenlightened labor, especially those who believe in the flesh as a form of intersubjective experience that is uniquely revelatory, even existentializing. For the consolation of being demystified is especially keen when it enables one to achieve a conceptual triumph over whatever anxieties one may have experienced sexually, with the added benefit of being able to mock those who continue to regard sex as something dangerous and inaugural when a proper understanding of its centrality shows it to be just another example of our paralysis.

There is, however, another approach that also restores sexuality to the center of psychoanalysis and in a far more concrete way. For reasons of length I must condense that phenomenological and existential approach here to a series of theses, which are arranged in a dialectical order of increasing complexity in order to show thereby how the experience that defines each is sustained and concretized in the one that follows. The sequence offers each reader a very personal understanding as well as a framework (as Chapter 7 will show) for the analysis of historical, cultural phenomena.

(1) Sexuality is the most traumatic experience because it is the one in which we incarnate the psychological conflicts that define us in the terms of an existential immediacy. The sexual body is the expression of our psycho-sexual "identity."

(2) Sexuality has its origin in our experience of the way in which our being is affirmed yet appropriated in that prolonged sensual symbiosis with another's psyche that constitutes our first love relationship. This is the original experience that establishes the possibility of our most intimate experiences. For sexual intimacy is the act in which the internalization of the m/other's unconscious creates the conflicts that are necessarily incarnated whenever we make love.

(3) Personal history is sexual history. The key developments that shape the psyche turn on experiences where the original conflicts of intimacy either worsen because one capitulates to the superego or are reversed because one sustains a break with it. Sex is always disruptive because it touches, however momentarily, on the possibility of a relatedness that transcends mutual cruelty and Sartrean struggle.

(4) A theoretical understanding of sex thus derives from one of the few things that experience enables us to know with a Cartesian certainty. Sex is that area of human life where we are psychologically most vulnerable and can be hurt in ways that will prove irreversible. Perhaps that's the real motive behind theoretical efforts to gain conceptual mastery over it. Sex reveals to us things about ourselves we don't want to know. Recognizing that fact implies a Kantian question: what must the psyche be in its inner constitution for sex to have this power?

(5) Here then some implications of a drama that we cannot escape insofar as we are sexual beings:

- Sex is existentially dangerous. One can be wounded here in a way that effects one's power to be. Or affirmed in a way that addresses and perhaps heals that wound. This is why feeling desired is the greatest turn on and also the greatest threat. Defenses disappear.
- In sex the ego and rationality give way to a more concrete drama. In it we come to know ourselves in a way that goes beyond their range of disclosure.
- Sex is often peremptory—during key periods of life (adolescence, young adulthood, mid-life) and especially

after a traumatic experience—because it is a primary way that human beings restore an old "identity" or pursue a new one. In pursuing sex we're after something that is always beyond satisfaction. The ungraspable phantom of erotic life is the psyche itself concretely engaging the conditions of its own self-overcoming.

- Touch is the inherent terror of sex. There is perhaps no experience more terrifying than to be touched in tenderness by someone one loves. For then there are no defenses to prevent what opens in one's psyche.

(6) There are three ways to experience one's sexuality: (a) *unconsciously*, when inhibitions, dysfunctions, symptoms, etc. manifest our allegiance to the superego; (b) *traumatically*, when there's a break with this and one is flooded with the conflicts that define one's sexuality; and (c) toward *active reversal*, when one sustains those conflicts in a body struggling to free itself sexually from a superego that now assaults it in the body, revealing its true identity: that of an erotic or libidinal tie that has become destructive and self-punitive.

(7) Sex is self-revelatory. One can say all sorts of fine things about oneself, play out the full range of multiple narrative identities, but in bed we give ourselves away. The way we make love tells the other who we are. Our desire isn't enigmatic or unfulfillable: it's immediately present. Dysfunctions, such as premature ejaculation and impotence, frigidity or vaginismus, aren't bodily behaviors; they're ways in which the anxieties of the unconscious conflicts that sex activates express themselves. The real terror of sex isn't Lacan's "there is no sexual relation." The terror is that relating here is utterly revealing. Though we devise innumerable ways to disguise or fake it sex is one of the acts in which it is impossible not to ooze betrayal. Sex necessarily engages our deepest feelings and conflicts. The effort to prevent its doing so is but one way in which the truth of this proposition is illustrated.

(8) Sexuality realizes the precise terms of our perpetual frustration as subjects or engages us in the possibility of fundamental reversal. The first project describes the ways in which the conditions of object choice conform to the dictates of the superego. Perfect couples from this point of view are ones where the disorder of one person finds its perfect match in the disorders of the other.

Falling in love happens, in short, when the unconscious finds someone who assures the repetition of the pattern to which one is wedded because it conforms to the disorder one refuses to confront. The second project is grounded in a radically different *relationship* to the other. Here love is not the effort to feed each other's disorder; or what amounts to the same thing, to try to provide what the other lacks so that as couple we can flee self-knowledge together by creating the illusion that we've completed each other. We are only worthy of love when we break with this pattern. Contra Lacan, *relating* then becomes the mutual effort to open the wound in the other and sustain that condition as that which enables us to relate most deeply to one another when we make love. Sex is then the effort of two subjects to root out everything that is inauthentic within them. Such an effort is the antithesis of the hatred and fear of sex that, as we'll see, drives the fundamentalist right. Our countervailing task is to recover for our sexuality the full legacy of Romanticism's understanding of passion and wed it to a renewal and transformation of Freud's dialectic of Eros and Thanatos so that this dialectic, having shed all traces of the essentialistic, the cosmological, and the ahistorical, will become the fundamental and radically historicized categories for understanding our historical situation. Constituting that dialectic is the overarching project of this book.[41]

## The goal of a psychoanalytic politics: the ironic and the tragic

> "This is the end, my friend, of all your plans, the end ..."
>
> Jim Morrison, The Doors

Lacan defines the end and ethic of analysis as the possibility of "remaining true to one's desire."[42] This sounds good until one realizes that it amounts to persisting in an absurd quest that one did not determine and which cannot be fulfilled. The experience of subjective destitution—the pivotal experience to which analysis supposedly leads—is also a dead end. All it liberates one into is the blind, impersonal, repetitive circuit of the Drive: the *sinthome* as a pure *jouissance* addressed to no one in contrast to the *symptom* as a *ciphered message* addressed to the other; sheer excess as an experience that destroys all boundaries in a pure *enjoyment* that has no purpose but its own persistence. Contra the opinion of some, the Lacanian subject is not existentialized at the end of analysis. It's dissolved in the blind embrace of impersonal Drive or transcended in the superior irony of one who looks on human phenomena from the perspective of a God who is "indifferent, paring his fingernails."[43] Lacanian thought produces the fading of the subject, the dissolution of drama in that which cannot be mediated. A psyche committed to the possibility of existential self-mediation engages a far different task. That task is to reverse the force of Thanatos, the destructiveness of the superego, by making *deracination* the relationship one lives to oneself. The *act* that defines the psyche is the effort to engage in self-overcoming within the *crypt* of one's most deeply buried conflicts and anxieties. This is the traumatic place one must get to in oneself and then sustain at the cost of whatever suffering it brings. For it is only through this effort that an existential subjectivity uncovers and engages that *agon* in which one can lose the thing that is more important than one's life—one's reason for living. The condition that makes us human is that we can die within; and that we come to life only through the effort to reverse a Thanatos that is at work in us long before there's anything there to oppose it. Existence is the upsurge of that opposition, the no to death that can only be lived concretely by immersing oneself in those experiences where one finds one's very being *at issue*.

I visited Prague in the spring of 1970. While there I met a cab driver who had previously been employed as chief chemist in a high-ranking government office. Shortly after the tanks rolled in he quit the Communist party in protest. His new job was his reward. We spent an evening talking, largely about life in Prague and the forced jocularity of a populace busily engaged in trying to put a happy face on things. "One only has one choice now," he said, "to suffer tragically or to live life as a comedy." Lacan and Žižek represent the most eloquent examples of the latter choice. Like the Heideggerian forgetting of being, we've so lost contact with the other way that it strikes us as a nostalgic and no doubt sentimental regression to an archaic humanism naively blind to the truths of postmodernism. I would suggest that is so because we've lost contact with the tragic and everything in ourselves on which this possibility depends. There was a game that used to be played in the early days of *Saturday Night Live* called "Mas Macho." The repeated question asked contestants with respect to the qualities of two actors was "Who is mas macho, Fernando Lamas or Ricardo Montalban?" Academic intellectuals have their own version of this game. It centers on the topic "who is most demystified?" That is, who has dispensed with the metaphysical illusion that one can demonstrate all other contenders for the title still depend upon. Though this game is a poor substitute for philosophy and for living it does provide a keen insight into what ideas will be accorded a hearing in the groves of academe. The criterion is simple: those ideas that can be turned into glib commonplaces capable of providing academic careerists the thing they most need: a chance to craft careers based on nothing but the demonstration of how clever one is in applying the latest dogma in order to confer the sense of intellectual superiority—over existence itself—that comes from this practice. The irony of irony is the god term to which all gravitate without suspecting that victory in this game is foreordained to whoever fashions the latest proof that one can't step in the same river once. "Nobody does it better" than Slavoj Žižek, with more *élan* and with a greater sense that demystifying play is the route to what Adrian Leverkuhn in Mann's *Doctor Faustus* termed the *break-through*, into something beyond irony and exacting in a way it can never be. But whenever he gets close to this prospect Žižek quickly retreats; whereas *for us* the sovereign act in the life of the psyche begins only when one sustains the plunge into that which *measures* us because sustaining trauma is the way we struggle to realize our innermost possibility. It is along this path that one recovers the tragic and with it the movement into the depths of those realms of experience into which, as Rilke saw, "irony never descends."[44] "Spirit is the life that cuts back into life; with its suffering it increases its knowledge."[45] This is the way of being we must regain if we're to explore again our truest and deepest experiences rather than continuing to place a supreme value on those ways of thinking and being that deliver us from them.

# Part Two
# To the Left of the Left

# 7

# Bible Says: The Psychology
# of Christian Fundamentalism

"I know you're a Christian, but what are you a Christian against."

Kenneth Burke

"The Constitution guarantees Americans freedom of Religion, not freedom from Religion."

Senator Joe Lieberman

In *Apocalypse*, a study of Christian fundamentalism based on extensive interviews over a five-year period with members of apocalyptic communities, Charles Strozier identifies four beliefs as fundamental to Christian fundamentalism. (1) Inerrancy or biblical literalism, the belief that every word of the Bible is to be taken literally as the word of God; (2) conversion or the experience of being reborn in Christ; (3) evangelicalism or the duty of the saved to spread the gospel; and (4) apocalypticism or endism, the belief that the book of Revelation describes the events that must come to pass for God's plan to be fulfilled.[1] Revelation thus becomes an object of longing as well as the key to understanding contemporary history. Each of these categories, Strozier adds, must be understood not doctrinally but psychologically. What follows attempts to constitute such an understanding by analyzing each category as a step in the *progression* of a disorder that finds the end it seeks in apocalyptic destructiveness.

Before undertaking that examination a note on method. My goal is not to number the streaks of the tulip with respect to Christian fundamentalism[2] but to get to the essence of the thing by offering a psychoanalytic version of the method Hegel formulated in the *Phenomenology of Mind*. My effort, that is, will be to describe the inner structure of the fundamentalist psyche by examining those beliefs in terms of the psychological needs they fulfill. The examination of each belief will thus reveal its function in an evolving logic tracing the sequence of internal operations required for the fundamentalist psyche to achieve the form required to resolve the conflicts that define it. The difference between my method and Hegel's is this: Hegel's effort was to describe the sequence of rational self-mediations required for the attainment of absolute knowledge. Mine is to record the sequence of psychological transformations that must take place for another kind of certainty to be achieved: one where, as we'll see, Thanatos (and not Hegelian Reason) attains an absolute status, freed of anything within the psyche that could oppose it. In effect, my goal is to offer fundamentalists a self-knowledge they cannot have, since it is precisely the function of the belief structure we shall examine to render it unconscious. What, after all, is religion but a desire displacing itself into dogmas all the better to assure the flock that what they desire is writ into the nature of things?

Who does the structure we'll examine describe? George W. Bush and some of those closest to him? The 42 percent to 51 percent of those Americans who now identify themselves as fundamentalists? Or perhaps something larger: the over 1 billion viewers worldwide who found Mel Gibson's *The Passion of the Christ* a singularly compelling expression of their faith and who are thus already far more fundamentalist in their hearts than they realize? The power of any religious belief system derives from how deeply it taps into collective needs and discontents. In this regard we may already be living in a fundamentalist *Zeitgeist* with the collective American psyche now characterized (even among those who seldom or never see the inside of a church) by the emotional needs and psychological principles of operation that find their most seductive realization in fundamentalism. We may even find the same kind of "faith" informing a project that initially appears to have nothing to do with fundamentalism—global capitalism.

Though he does not share their beliefs, Strozier comments often on the charity and gentleness of his interviewees, seeing in them a sign that we should temper any criticism of fundamentalism by acknowledging the good things it does for people, many of whom would be lost or miserable without it. Be that as it may, in terms of the psyche a far different condition might maintain, involving a pronounced dissonance between the blithe sincerity of the surface and the depths where something quite different has taken hold of the psyche. Moreover, to comprehend a belief system the primary concern must be not with the sheep but with the Grand Inquisitors who give them their marching orders; or, in more psychoanalytic terms, who plant in them the superego that holds them in thrall to its commands. Our concern, in short, must be not with fundamentalism as a pathetic phenomenon, a halfway house for drug addicts and a panacea for those who find in it the infantilization they seek, but with it as what Nietzsche would call (though with horror) a strong valuation; an effort to take up the fundamental problems of the psyche and fashion a will to power out of *resentment* by developing a system of beliefs that will make one strong and righteous in that resentment, like Falwell, smug in its smug certitudes like Dubya, confident in the right to rule over those it reduces to the status of sheep, blissful in their blind obedience to a Will that has been collectively imposed on them.

Religion remains of course the one topic we are enjoined to treat with kid gloves; indeed, the one area where critique is *verboten*. Violating this rule is the quickest way to lose what current statistics indicate will be the 93 percent of one's audience who believe in God. It's thus incumbent on me to state up front that this is not a rhetorical contract I can honor. Like Freud,[3] I think it can be demonstrated that religion is a collective neurosis. One implication of the following examination, in fact, is that Freud didn't go far enough. But let me reformulate this hypothesis in a more convivial spirit. Let's bracket the whole question of whether religion has an object. On second thought, let me concede it, the ontological truth of all the basic beliefs, every each one. Only then perhaps can we focus on the question that constitutes the inherent and lasting fascination of religion. *Not what people believe, but why.* Considering religion as a psychological phenomenon contains, perhaps, an additional value: the discovery that religion is invaluable because it offers the deepest insight into the nature of the psyche and its needs.

## LITERALISM

"I don't do nuance."
George W. Bush

Literalism is the linchpin of fundamentalism; the literalization, if you will, of the founding psychological need. That need is for an absolute certitude that can be established at the level of facts that admit of no ambiguity or interpretation. (Fundamentalists, ironically, are the true positivists.) To eliminate ambiguity and confusion one must attack their source. Figurative language. That is the danger that must be avoided because in place of the literal, figurative language introduces the play of meaning and with it the need to sustain complex connections at the level of thought (not fact) through the evolution of mental abilities that are necessarily connected with developing the metaphoric resources of language. The literal in contrast puts an end to thought. It offers the mind a way to shut down, to reify itself. It thereby exorcises the greatest fear: interpretation and its inevitable result, the conflict of interpretations and thereby a world forever bereft of dogmatic certitudes. A metaphor is the lighting flash of an intelligence that sees, as Aristotle asserted, connections that can only be sustained by liberating thought from the immediate.

Literalism is the attempt to arrest all of this before it takes hold. Its innermost necessity is the resistance to metaphor. For with metaphor one enters a world that has the power to unravel the literal mind. Let me offer one example. "There is no God and Mary is his mother." In this great aphorism Santayana asserts an ontological impossibility that is also a psychological necessity. I once tried the statement out on some fundamentalist acquaintances. They were at first puzzled by its unintelligibility, then amazed that Santayana and I were so dumb we couldn't see the contradiction. Finally the light went on. Almost in chorus they enacted the literalist equivalent of deconstructionism: "If he wasn't God how could she be a mother?" All attempts to suggest that the statement wasn't meant to be taken literally only produced further confusion then frustration then anger. Santayana's statement made no sense to them precisely because it was a paradox intended to produce reflection, even introspection. It was there I suggested one would find the key to its meaning; not in their assertion that its meaninglessness constituted evidence that Santayana was perverse or mentally unbalanced. We were, of course, talking at irretrievable cross purposes with no way to bridge the gulf between us. This was, of course, the point of the exercise.

Literalism is the first line of defense of a mind that wants to put itself to sleep. Through it one creates the sensibility of Nietzsche's last man who can only blink in blank incomprehension at anything that can't be immediately understood. Literalism is the great protection against a world teeming with complexities. It offers a way to keep the mind fixed and fixated at its first condition. The way: the refusal to comprehend anything that exceeds the limits of the simple declarative sentence. Two reductions thereby feed on one another: the world is reduced to facts and simples; the mind to a permanently blank slate.

Fundamentalism fosters this reduction of the mind to the conditions of the immediate. For in fundamentalism literalism is raised to the status of a categorical imperative, the law that assures deliverance from all confusion. There is a single text, the Holy Bible. It contains clear, simple, direct messages—proclamations—that establish immutable Truth. All of life's questions and contingencies are thus resolved by statements that are beyond change and interpretation. In literalism reading and interpretation realize the Cratylean dream: one need only point to the appropriate passage and "pouf" all doubt and ambiguity about what one should think, believe, or desire with regard to any situation vanish. One need no longer wrack one's brain or one's heart or confront the complexity of a world that exceeds one's grasp. The Book's unequivocal meaning and Life are adequated to one another in a relationship of stark and simple imposition. You see, God has a plan for us and unlike secularists and post-structuralists He speaks in clear and unmistakable terms.

When approached literally, the Book necessarily takes on a number of other characteristics. Everything in it must be factual and nothing outside the Book can contradict those facts. The very possibility of scientific investigation is sacrificed *a priori* to the need to proclaim the text's inerrancy. Every word of it must be the unalterable and unchanging word of God, which of course can contain no contradictions. One irony of fundamentalist reading is the rather considerable constraints it places on the deity. He proclaimeth and what He says remains so forever, beyond development, change, revision. Whatever abomination of sex hatred one unearths from Leviticus must remain gospel today. The Book cannot be read progressively or retroactively, despite the repeated claims of Jesus to cancel the old law. An eye for an eye remains true for all time however repugnant to the law of charity. After all, "It's in the Bible." That repeated assertion expresses the essence and fundamental paralysis of the literal mind. The idea of reading the Book along the pop-Hegelian lines pursued by Jack Miles as the story of how as He develops God changes his mind, softening his prematurely hardened heart, is anathema. God's role is set by the limitations of the literal "imagination." His job is to lay down the Law, once and for all, and in no uncertain terms; to be that superego who operates by the only *logic* that literalism permits—*binary opposition.* All conflicts and confusions must be resolved into a simple and comprehensive opposition between good and evil. Else comes again the fit of contingency and ambiguity. Binarism is the realization in logic of the literalist attitude toward language, the reduction of language to the declarative statement wedded to a logic that turns everything into an abstract allegory.

The most interesting reach of literalism comes, however, in the interpretation of the prophetic writings, especially Revelation. Here confronting what even it must see as image and metaphor, literalism performs the only operation that to it makes sense. *The metaphoric is literalized.* Armageddon must take place on the plain of Jezreel near the ancient military fortification of Megiddo (35 miles southeast of Haifa), even though this patch of land is not large enough to bury the vast multitudes who will perish there. Gorbachev must be the Beast (how else account for that red swath on his forehead); Saddam Hussein must be the Antichrist—or Yasser Arafat or Bill Clinton ... Anything and everything that happens in the Middle East must be scanned as a sign that we are, indeed, moving toward the Tribulation. When he speaks prophetically God is playing a little game with us, to activate what in fundamentalism passes as the exercise of imagination. To make sense of the text thus requires the precise matching of its ornate and expressionist images to persons, places, and events which are thereby assigned the only meaning they can have. Mapped onto history the Bible offers us an absolute certitude about history, thereby vanquishing the greatest contingency. In dealing with the Middle East, for example, a fundamentalist presidency need not confuse itself with the messy details of political history or develop a *nuanced* appreciation of Islam. Such things only breed confusion. All one need do is literally match a prophecy to a contingency and *voilà!* literal certitude is attained; or what amounts to the same thing, the fantasmatic imposition upon reality of what one wants to believe.[4]

In all these operations sustaining a literal interpretation of the Bible is a desperate necessity. For once let go of that and the Book slips into the hands of those who eventually will find anything in it—liberation theology, Bonhoeffer's religionless Christianity, a searing message of love—since reading and interpretation will now be guided by nothing other than the attempt of a heart in conflict with itself to use the Book to pry open the most conflicted registers of its own interiority. Who can tell, perhaps this approach could even lead to the discovery that the Book hates the simple minded; that it is, indeed, Kafkaesque in presenting parables and prophecies that only deepen our burden by demanding of us an intelligence equal to the convoluted chambers of the human heart.

Literalism is a cardinal necessity of the fundamentalist because it *guarantees* the primary psychological need. For a certitude that in its simplicity puts an end to all doubt, even to the possibility of doubt. That is what one must have and, once attained, what nothing can be permitted to alter. The literal meaning of words one need only point to for their meaning to be established once and for all must be imposed on the world without a blink of hesitation, a shadow of doubt, and, when necessary, beyond any appeal to the claims of our humanity. Two examples. Perhaps the most chilling moment in a recent CNN special on fundamentalism occurs at the end of an interview with a young girl—between eight and ten years old—who her mother tells the interviewer was saved at age three and who is now so firm in every article of the faith that she no longer needs doctrinal help from her parents or teachers. (Earlier when her mother was asked if she'd ever let the children watch *South Park*, the young girl intervened before her mother could reply: "I wouldn't want to watch a program like that.") The interview ends with the all-important question: "what happens to those who don't believe?" Like a trumpet call, in the blinking of an eye, even less, without batting an eyelash, the child answers: "they go to hell." What makes this statement so chilling is the absence of the slightest sign of doubt or pity. If there's an innocence left here, it lies in the possibility that, unlike her parents, the child has not yet started to feast on images of the damned. She is, however, already in league with where fundamentalism will take her because she's attained the correct posture: the assumption of an absolute certitude in which there is and can be no conflict of the heart with what it is told to believe, no questioning of a God who is capable of the titanic condemnation she's just asserted as an absolute article of faith. Nor, of course, is there any longer alive in her the possibility of the only legitimate choice such a "truth" would demand—the rejection of such a God. 2+2=5. Whatever one is told the Book says becomes the truth one clutches to one's bosom, locking oneself in step to its every command, *Kadavergehorsamkeit*. My second example comes from poor Mel Gibson, who judging from a TV interview accepts with apparent indifference the belief that barring conversion to Catholicism his own wife (mother of his seven Catholic children) will suffer eternal damnation. Such is the literal nature of his faith, and the power of that literalism to seal off everything else in him, so that we need not fear Gibson will ever find himself in the place of Milton's Adam, who chose death because he couldn't bear the thought of an eternity apart from the woman he loves. Literalism protects the heart from everything, even its own deepest urgings.

There is something terrifying in our first example; something appalling in our second. Together they reveal the emotion in which the literalist passion is grounded. Hatred—of all complexities. And the need to impose that hatred upon the world in a totalizing way. It is sometimes alleged that fundamentalists are just like the rest of us, confused by the world and seeking something to hang onto as a portal in the storm. This view is invalidated by the kind of answers that the fundamentalist finds: answers that annihilate the problem, turn the desire for knowledge into a farce, and make confusion the motive for self-infantilization. (By their answers ye shall know them.) Literalism is the way, but hatred is the through-line. That is why fundamentalist certitude always becomes rectitude; and the Bible mined for all the things one can label abomination. Thereby a sensibility that wants to have nothing to do with the world takes revenge upon it. On the surface, literalism looks like something free of psychological motives; on investigation it reveals itself as one of the clearest signs of the psychological need in which the fundamentalist project is grounded; the first realization, in fact, of the informing fear and hatred of all the contingencies that constitute being in the world. That is the first threat fundamentalism must vanquish. The second, we'll find, lies at a more intimate register.

## CONVERSION

"But if a man is to become not merely *legally* but *morally* a good man ... *this* cannot be brought about through gradual *reformation* ... but must be effected through a revolution in the man's disposition...He can become a new man only by a kind of rebirth, as it were a new creation."

Immanuel Kant, *Religion Within the Bounds of Reason Alone*

This category is best approached through narrative. Fundamentalism is in love with a single and common story it never tires of telling. This story is the key to the transformation it celebrates and the absolute split that transformation produces.[5] A subject finds itself lost in a world of sin, prey to all the evils that have taken control of a life. A despair seizes the soul. One is powerless to deal with life's problems or heal oneself because there is nothing within the self that one can draw on to make that project possible. The inner world is a foul and pestilent congregation of sin and sinfulness. And there's no way out. One has hit rock bottom and totters on the brink of suicide. And then in darkest night one lets Him into one's life. And all is transformed.

Changed utterly. A terrible beauty is born. Before one was a sinner doing the bidding of Satan. Now one is saved and does the work of the Lord. The old self is extinguished. Utterly. One has achieved a new identity, a oneness with Christ that persists as long as one follows one condition: one must let Him take over one's life. Totally. All decisions are now in Jesus' hands. He tells one what to do and one's fealty to his plan must be absolute. There can be no questioning, no doubt. For that could be the sign of only one thing—the voice of Satan and with it the danger of slipping back into those ways of being that one has banished forever. The self one once was is no more. Such is the power of conversion. A psyche has been delivered from itself. And it's all so simple finally, a matter of delivering oneself into His will, following His plan as set forth in the Book, and letting nothing exist within one's consciousness but the voice of Jesus spreading peace and love throughout one's being.

The most striking thing about this narrative is the transparent nature of the psychological defense mechanism from which it derives and the rigidity with which it employs that mechanism. *Splitting*— which as Freud and Klein show is the most primitive mechanism of defense employed by a psyche terrified of its inner world. *The conversion story raises that mechanism to the status of a theological pathos.* Though the story depends on recounting how sinful one's life once was (often in great, even "loving" detail), the psychological meaning of conversion is its power to wipe all of that away. Magically one attains a totally new psyche, cleansed, pristine, and impermeable. One has, in fact, attained a totally new self-reference. For the self now is a function of one's total *identification* with Jesus. Consciousness is bathed in his presence. It has become a scene in which his love expresses itself in the beatific smile that fills one's face whenever one thinks of one's redemption, the tears that flood one's blessed cheeks, the saccharine tone that raises the voice to an eerie self-hypnotizing pitch whenever one finds another opportunity to express the joyous emotions that must be pumped up at every opportunity in keeping with the hyperconsciousness required to sustain the assurance of one's redemption. The whole process is a monument to the power of *magical thinking* to blow away inner reality, and as such a further sign of the primitive nature of the psychological mechanisms on which conversion depends.

The power of conversion to produce a saved self makes the Catholic confessional the operation of rank amateurs. There, through forgiveness, one gets temporary relief from sins that in all likelihood both priest and penitent know will be committed again. One gets a momentarily cleansed psyche, but not a lasting transformation. Through conversion, however, one achieves an absolutely new beginning. One's life is divided in half. Split between B.C. and A.D. Everything one once was is washed away. Everything one now is becomes its antithesis. Such was the miracle that descended on Dubya by the end of his walk along the beach with Billy Graham. The man George W. Bush was was no more. That person was but the stuff that the dream of conversion was built on; and now all that once characterized that person's life has vanished leaving not a rack behind. Dubya is reborn to the very depths of his being. Everything that follows thus becomes a pure expression of the new self he now has. Thanks to Jesus. For that's the key both to conversion and its aftermath. The individual is powerless to effect this transformation. Agency is the Lord's. He enters one's psyche and performs precisely what the psyche could not do for itself. Moreover, the new agency that results from conversion is also His. Everything one now does derives from His Will. One has become the medium through which the Diety achieves its Purpose. Individual will finally has nothing to do with it. One is the servant of His Will, doing what He tells one to do as He makes His purpose known. That's also why error is inconceivable, why, when asked, Dubya was unable to discover any mistake he'd made as President. That incapacity serves a deeper exigency. His Will put one in the position of the most powerful man in the world and He must have done so because He had something special in mind.

Such for the fundamentalist is what it means to have a self. To live an abstract allegory. Devil before, God after, with the self dissolved under the force of the one or the other. And never the twain shall meet. Except as absolute antagonists. One could say that conversion transforms the self, but it would be more appropriate to say that it annihilates it. That is in fact its function. For salvation to occur the self is precisely what must be rendered powerless then transcended through a transformation that can only come from without. That transformation produces accordingly a split that is absolute and must be maintained at all costs. That split is what the psyche depends on to deliver it from everything disruptive and unstable in itself. Even if at times one finds oneself again a sinner, that sinfulness is the work of the Big Other, Satan. Salvation is deliverance and such is fundamentalist despair over the self that deliverance must be total.

Conversion thus presents the antithesis of what happens in an authentic psychoanalysis. A contrast between the two will bring out what happens within a converted psyche. The key to an authentic analysis is the assumption of full responsibility for who one is through the attainment of a concrete and intimate knowledge of one's psyche, of the unconscious desires and conflicts that have structured the history of one's life. Attaining such knowledge entails three steps. (1) Recognition that one is the author of one's condition; not Satan, not the parents, not demon rum in its effects on a pre-existing physiological condition. The psyche in its bankruptcy is the function and fruition of a desire. That is why Freud insisted that one listen to the details of one's illness because it is in the details that one will find the seeds of genuine change. (2) Through the second recognition: that the problem of the psyche is not to extinguish desire but to reclaim it by seeing that the destructive pattern of one's life is something that one has (like Oedipus) brought upon oneself through one's effort to avoid knowing oneself. The solution is not flight from oneself into the hands of a savior, but the recognition that inner conflict is and remains the burden and reality of the psyche. (3) This begets the third recognition: that change requires taking on a total responsibility for one's psyche. Rather than fleeing one's conflicts, one must engage them. Life is a process of becoming responsible for oneself by becoming aware of all that within oneself for which one must assume responsibility. A genuine analysis thus turns on the assumption of a tragic agency. One is not freed from one's disorder but delivered over to it.

Working through (*Durcharbeit*), the most important part of any analysis, is essentially an education in the process of assuming a tragic relationship to oneself by accepting the suffering that self-knowledge entails. Rather than seeking a magical solution to depression, one must sustain it as that melancholy that Keats called "the wakeful anguish of the soul." Becoming responsible for oneself depends on a single circumstance: the concrete and bitter immersion in the particulars of one's life in a recognition of one's responsibility as cause. No satanic agency produced one's condition and no messianic agency will come to blow it away. One must uncover those things in oneself that have shaped the self-lacerating history of one's heart. There is only one source of inner strength and the way to it is full acceptance of the suffering that is our deepest attunement to ourselves. Authentic self-analysis is based on the recognition that there is no deliverance from desire and inner conflict. Satan, in contrast, is the blank check that puts an end to that process before it can begin. Consider the contrast between two statements. "I was a lustful man and a fornicator who worshipped the Beast within me." "I was a man who hated women and used sex to injure them psychologically in order to act out the emotional conflicts of my relationship with my mother." The difference between the two statements is enormous. The first obliterates the need for further description, exorcising the possibility of self-knowledge. The second is but overture to the painful problem of probing and taking on responsibility for every word of it.

Conversion is flight from such action. The psyche is safely delivered into the hands of abstraction. No real responsibility exists because one was under Satan's power when one did all those terrible things. That's how He works. He invades a soul like a thief in the night and under his spell we do all sorts of things that are against our nature. But once we let Jesus in we are cleansed. Born again. All before was the work of an otherness that invaded us. It is now burnt and purged away. We can of course feel remorse, but at the same time those we harmed should know it wasn't really our doing. The cause is not in ourselves but in the virus that tried to destroy our soul. Psychoanalysis delivers the subject over to itself as a relationship that cannot be transcended. Conversion delivers the subject from itself. What one was is not a disorder one must plumb concretely in the full horror of all that one must come to know about oneself as author. It is, rather, all that conversion enables one to blow away. Such is the power and pleasure of splitting as a mechanism of defense. In its absolute reliance on that mechanism fundamentalism renders up its secret.

Here, then, is the real truth of conversion: fear and hatred of the psyche and a desperate desire to be rid of it. Any sign of its continued presence after conversion produces panic anxiety. That is why for conversion to work one must ever after maintain a carefully limited subjectivity preoccupied with the self-hypnotic iteration of all the signs and behaviors that proclaim one's salvation. The presence of anything else within fills the fundamentalist psyche with terror, loathing, and the need for a fresh exorcism. The psyche is the problem in fundamentalism not because it's sinful but because it's exacting and what it teaches is not things about the Devil but things about actual deeds one has done to the harm of others that one must admit as the price of remaining human. How perfect then to find a way to be done with the whole thing, to shed one's former life the way a snake sheds its skin and then be reborn with all one was consigned to the past. The only way to sustain that state, however, is by constantly pumping up all the positive emotions and happy talk that witness one's oneness with the Lord while guarding against the expression of any emotions that would suggest the opposite. Proclaiming one's salvation has become an obsessional necessity. Life comes down to a single thing. Proving at all times—especially to oneself—that one is on God's side.

To be saved is to enter a condition in which one only has positive, Christian emotions, which are always played "over the top" because the primary purpose of the performance is self-hypnosis. This is in keeping with a duty that cannot be shirked: one must become the walking embodiment of one's simplest version of the love that God has for us since any other kind of love would be exacting whereas this one offers the bliss of self-infantilization. That's the source of the monotonous sameness of fundamentalists: the aping and mimicking of one another in the identical smile of mindless bliss, the tearful displays, the saccharine tone in the proselytizing voice, the need to constantly proclaim how wonderful it feels to be saved and to bear witness to that fact by turning every possible occasion into a chance to inflict on others (even or especially strangers) a bevy of uplifting sentiments as if being a Christian amounted to becoming a walking Hallmark card. In all this the believer labors under a manic necessity. But it isn't enough. That mania must find a *practice* that will enable one to complete the circle in which one moves by re-enacting, as it were, the process and content of one's conversion.

## EVANGELICALISM

"this is deadly work." Samuel Beckett, *Endgame*

Evangelicalism is that act: the manic repetition whereby the split in the psyche created by conversion is projected onto the world. Thereby one confirms the identity one has attained through a fresh exorcism of the one that was vanquished. Evangelical activity offers the fundamentalist the only way to sustain the reborn self: by attempting to recreate the experience of one's conversion in others in order to re-enact an unending exorcism. In the other one locates the split-off self one once was, but now placed totally outside oneself. It becomes the fantasm through which one perceives the other. For those not saved must be wallowing in error and sin, their minds awash in the torrents of secularism, dumb to the clarity that comes from the Words through which one brings them enlightenment, could they but hear. This is the root cause of the frustration that quickly comes to those who make the mistake of bidding entry when the fundamentalist knocks on the door. In vain one offers discourse to those who are seized by a necessity. It's not just the repeated citation of biblical truism as absolute truth ("do you know that Satan was once an angel close to God; that's why he's so powerful"), or the repeated refrain that puts an end to every discussion ("well I believe the Bible and the Bible says ... "), or even the inability to hear any objection except as a sign that one's auditor has not yet grasped the truth that's galling. It's also the recognition that despite the charitable demeanor, evangelical activity is based on a total lack of respect for the minds of those who are being offered salvation.

That lack of respect is, however, necessary. Anything less would be a confession of doubt, which would make the other a threat rather than an image of what the world in its unregenerate condition represents; namely, the field for the projection of everything that conversion supposedly removed from one's psyche. That's the dirty little secret that must remain unconscious. Through evangelicalism one engages in a necessary *repetition compulsion*. The only way to prevent a return of the projections is through their continued projection. By locating evil, sin, and error outside oneself and waging an "attack" on them one is delivered from the specter that they might still exist within. Everything bad is now outside oneself and one must do everything to keep it there. One can share with one's auditors a confession in the abstract that one is a "sinner" too, but the discussion better shift quickly to the evils of the world: to homosexuals and abortion and the entertainment industry and, best of all, the imperiled state of a nation bereft of "moral values." One is well tuned then. Thereby the manic drive sweeps to a revenge upon anything that can be even remotely *associated* with one's former self. One has entered a dream state of desire primed for wrathful discharge upon a world drenched in sin. Evangelicalism thus offers the psyche a chance to be cleansed again of everything that may still fester within somewhere, longing to break out. Though splitting and projection produce denial, one is always in danger of slipping. One needs a ritual to reaffirm who one is by once again exorcising what one was. This is the function proselytizing has for the fundamentalist.

It should now be evident that what looks at first like the least important of the four characteristics of fundamentalism perhaps fulfills the deepest psychological necessity. Without evangelical activity the fundamentalist psyche would *implode*. The obsessional need to preach the gospel and to let every stranger one meets know as soon as possible that one is a born-again Christian derives not from a lack of social skills but from a manic necessity. For the saved there is and can be nothing but salvation as the master narrative to which all lives must conform, a tale told as often and as ardently as the Ancient Mariner tells his. Though for antithetical reasons. The Mariner tells his tale to relieve an inner suffering by injecting it into the consciousness of listeners who will be existentially individuated by the tale. Evangelists tell theirs to reassure themselves about their "identity" by trying to compel others to participate in it. Structurally and psychologically, however, both tellers labor under the same necessity. Repetition as the attempt to retain an identity in order to flee something else—in the Mariner's case a suicidal depression; in the fundamentalist perhaps the same thing—that is buried deep in the unconscious. One piece of evidence in support of this hypothesis: without the chance to engage in evangelical activity the fundamentalist psyche sinks into a state of empty boredom.

Thus the lassitude of Dubya before 9-11 and the hectic messianic energy that has defined him since. 9-11 gave him what he needed—the chance to transform a stalled presidency by adopting an evangelical stance toward the entire world. Pre-emptive unilateralism is not just a political credo. It's an evangelical necessity. The world must be divided into good and evil. And one must deliver that message to the world in the same way the fundamentalist does when visiting the doorsteps of the unconverted. If those one addresses—the United Nations, other countries, members of the Republican Party—aren't converted that can only be a sign of their error. Or worse. As Ashcroft never lost an opportunity to remind us, their complicity with the enemy. The whole world is either with us or against us. And nothing anyone says can have any other meaning. Our message cannot be tainted by saucy doubts or fears. The fundamentalist mind, closed off from discourse by its own certitude, can only project itself upon the global stage in a way that serves inner psychological necessity: *manic activity under the guise of rectitude as the proof that one has triumphed over all inner conflicts*. And thus a new necessity beckons. The opposition between good and evil must be extended as far as possible—from Afghanistan to Iraq to the Axis of Evil to the 60 nations identified as supporters of terror—because God has chosen one not just to convert the world but to wage war on whatever one labels evil. The only certainty here is that one will always find fresh targets because doing so is the projective necessity of a mania that can only achieve the *omnipotence* it requires by pushing the war on terror to some ultimate realization. Moreover, in waging this war what one does is justified beyond any appeal to conscience. In terms of policy this assurance results in another doctrinal innovation that distinguishes Dubya from all previous presidents: the assertion of the right to a first strike use of nuclear weapons and, accordingly, the developments now under way to create a host of new "tactical" nuclear weapons. To deliver the world from the specter of nuclear terror we must ready ourselves to wage a nuclear war on the world. Paranoia thus projects as policy an omnipotence drive beyond MAD. And so we should all indeed be trembling in our boots to know the mindset that now has its finger on the nuclear trigger. Happiness is a warm gun.

The war on terror has many meanings, not the least of which the blank check to disseminate an Orwellian fear whenever the administration desires. Its deepest meaning, however, is as the founding moment in which *politics in Amerika became inseparable from the projection of a religious ideology.* 9-11 told Dubya that the time was ripe for a mission that the Deity *elected* him to perform. A seamless transition thus exists from an evangelical presidency to the fourth characteristic of fundamentalism, the one that, as we'll see, informs and completes the others thereby taking us to the heart of the disorder, the innermost necessity that hallows all its dreams.

### APOCALYPSE NOW

"[D]evout believers are safeguarded in a high degree against the risk of certain neurotic illnesses; their acceptance of the universal neurosis spares them the task of constructing the personal one."

Sigmund Freud, *The Future of an Illusion*

Apocalypticism is the capstone that completes the process of fundamentalist self-fashioning. Without it, as we'll see, the entire edifice would crumble. In the apocalyptic moment the disorder at the core of the fundamentalist psyche achieves a final form, passing over to the register of the sublime. The sublime register is tapped when the desire that informs a psyche achieves an unbounded expression. All conflicts are then resolved in a release of tension that is total, bringing on what Lacan terms *jouissance*. As we'll see, each structure described in the previous sections requires apocalypticism and achieves completion in it. The apocalyptic fantasm gives ultimate expression to the conflicts that define the fundamentalist psyche by projecting the grand action needed to bring those conflicts to their only possible end.

The necessity of apocalypticism is a direct outgrowth of the psychological mechanism on which the fundamentalist relies to structure the world. *The only way to prevent a return of the projections is through a final evacuation.* Thus the need to picture a world beyond redemption held under the brand of an all-consuming wrath. That image finalizes the split that defines the fundamentalist psyche by giving sublime expression to the way the world must be viewed when seen from the standpoint of one's salvation. Apocalypticism thereby completes the psychological operation that has been employed *repeatedly* from the beginning. One cleanses oneself by projecting one's disowned desires onto the world. The resulting split must then be maintained rigorously with nothing allowed to fall outside its scope. The psyche must be voided of everything save the serenities of the saved. For that to happen, however, the world must become the object of a violent attack on all that one has externalized there. And this act must be endless lest the projections return. By its internal logic fundamentalism is thus driven ineluctably to a need for *quantitative* expansion through the discovery of greater, more insidious forms of evil. The mathematical sublime beckons, the need to produce greater and greater magnitudes. The world becomes the polluted chamber of one's foulest imaginings with no way to check the demands of that vision. Within the psyche an even greater transformation occurs. One craves constant expression of an emotion that one must just as strenuously disclaim. Hatred. Fresh supplies of it are as necessary to the inner world as is the need of Amerika to ransack the globe for fresh supplies of oil. No matter how loudly one proclaims that one has been purified in the blood of the lamb, hatred has become the innermost necessity to which one is wedded. Moreover, that hatred must break free of any containment. Hatred of one's former self is no longer sufficient. One now hates the world and is driven to seek out everything in it that one can claim caused or can cause an inner condition other than the purity of the saved. One hates, that is, everything that resists surrender and absolute obedience to the system of literalism and literal commands to which one has committed oneself. As the scope of what one hates grows apace it necessarily maximizes the *binary opposition* that is essential to it. Good and Evil divide the world in two, giving ontological form to the rigidity of the split that defines the fundamentalist psyche.

All differences, all particularities, all complexities must give way to the demands of a comprehensive abstraction. And the fury of that abstraction can brook no exceptions. Everything thus resolves itself into the ultimate necessity required by the informing hatred. One longs for and demands an end to all the contingencies that have from the beginning been sources of fear and confusion. One dreams apocalyptically of what one has always sought. To be done with all of it. With the contingency of the human. To be done with all ambiguity and complexity and confusion. Done with the feeling that history has no purpose other than chaos or meaningless repetition. Done with embodiment itself—and all the unwelcome desires it imposes on us. Done with the very source of all that one hates and fears. To locate it all ontologically in a single principle—evil—and then be rid of it all once and for all through sublime and triumphant expression of that hatred that has the power to extinguish it all.

Literalism tried to keep the world at bay by reducing everything to the simplest formulas and the mind itself to the most unproblematic blink of consciousness in stupefied adherence to the fixations needed to banish metaphor, ambiguity, and uncertainty. But it wasn't enough. The world kept seeping in. There must be a way to be done with it, once and for all. To find what one has craved from the beginning. The end. But a proper end—one that will give sublime expression to the true object of one's worship. Death. The longing for death transformed into a sublime celebration of death. Life in its complexity demands too much of us. *That in a nutshell is the fundamentalist message.* Only death can deliver one from the threat life poses. One is safe from a return of the projections and an eruption of the repressed only when life is done. One has always longed for deliverance into a realm free of desire and its temptations. Death alone offers the comfort one seeks. The resentment in which the psyche has centered itself demands no less. One must work one's hatred of the world into a frenzy and feed that hatred with sublime images of evil in order to bring it to a fevered pitch. Release and satisfaction then come with the deliverance of that world into the hands of an angry God expressing his wrath in an orgy of pure destructiveness. Thank God for the book of Revelation. For the only way both to satisfy and to purge one's hatred is to express it on a massive world-shattering scale. The death one seeks projected into the death one delivers. The self is thereby done with life, freed for transport of the saved split-off self to a realm of bliss freed from all cares. A psyche wedded to Thanatos has found in Thanatos the final solution. One's resentment against life has been turned into a righteous and of necessity cosmic attack upon it.

In *Transformations* (1965) Wilfred Bion tries to conceptualize a destructiveness "that goes on working after it destroys personality, time, and existence."[6] Such is the desire that feeds the fundamentalist fixation on the book of Revelation. A psyche wedded to Thanatos, seeking sublime expression of that desire, finds repeated satisfaction in Revelation, since its author, like the director of the next disaster movie, keeps seeking the perfect image to feed his rage or to bring it, with each repetition, closer to that sublime image in which destructiveness will find its objective correlative. One makes allowances, of course, for the author of Revelation, what with his people under genocidal persecution at the hands of the Roman Empire. But how account for the fixation on such images, as if they were the only real source of pleasure, of those whose greatest fear is that their wife will find the G spot or that Mommie's little darlings will see MTV before the V-chip is installed? How account for the persistent unscratchable itch for picturing the great Whore of Babylon while anticipating the delectable synesthesia of the golden cup "in her hand filled with abominable things and the filth of her fornications"? How account for the thrill that comes with each new reading of the incomparable description of all the plagues that will be visited upon the earth? And how account for the necessity of the grand crescendo to which everything moves as the enraptured reader approaches Armageddon and the final battle that will put an end to that folly, human history, thereby giving the reader the true pleasure of the text, since one has believed all along that history could have no purpose or meaning other than its destruction? One loves this book and longs to see all its prophecies come to pass so that one can see fulfilled on a cosmic stage the very process that has structured one's psyche, as if the apocalypse one suffered on the little stage were but a prefigurement meant to whet one's appetite for the Big One.

Here, then, a reading of the function that Revelation plays in the fundamentalist psyche. In the depths of its psyche, fundamentalism is ruled by catastrophic anxiety, the condition of a self tottering on the brink of a dissolution in which it will fragment imprisoned in a world that will impose all of its terrors and evils upon it. We fail to understand fundamentalism as long as we resist seeing how close it is to a psychosis. Fundamentalist rage is the attempt of that subject to hold itself together in the only way it can: by waging war on all that terrifies it. The psyche commits itself to destructiveness to allay a destruction that already threatens it from within. The result is a paradoxical situation that finds its only possible solution in Revelation. *Destructiveness must be given a full, unchecked expression and the psyche must somehow survive that act.* The drive toward death thus repeats itself in increasing magnitudes as it moves toward a final conflict that will obliterate all future conflict, transporting the self to a realm of unending bliss. The slight textual support (1 Thessalonians 4:17) notwithstanding, the Rapture is a psychological necessity. It embodies the magical thought that the coming of global destruction is also the coming of salvation. One has always dreamed that a feast of aggression would lift one to a condition free of the world. That is why when that moment comes it is impossible to prevent the surfacing of a long-suppressed and twisted sexual desire. Thus: as destruction approaches so too does ascent to a realm in which one is free to project a marriage consummated in the sky with Christ serving as Bride. The randy delights of that image should not prevent us from seeing what has happened here. The longing for death has been turned into an ecstatic embrace of it; a rapture so complete in its *jouissance* that one can no longer disguise the fact that all of one's libidinal energies have gone into the quest for such a complete and final unbinding, an extinction within consciousness of everything save the ecstatic recognition that one is saved and that all the connections that once bound one to the world have been severed once and for all. *The psychotic attack on linking finds its apotheosis in apocalypticism.*[7] The Rapture must be interpolated into Revelation at precisely this point because one's salvation corresponds of necessity with the arrival of something else—the dawning of the cataclysmic aggressions that must be vented in order to bring destruction upon the earth, ushering in the millennium. In the clouds, safe with Jesus, one can continue to rejoice, free of life, or cast a cold eye down upon it from time to time like one looking back on the moment just before one's conception but free now (an angelic Onan) to nip it in the bud. In either case one spends the 1,000 years millennium in bliss because one is assured that though peace reigns, destruction will come again, one last time, with the dead themselves resurrected so that they can be slain again in a greater destruction than has ever been visited upon the earth. Revelation 19–20. And then, as if that isn't enough, the evil are consigned to torment day and night—forever. Only then is the rage that informs John's text discharged. And only then can love be expressed without leading to a new burst of rage.[8] Only then can a new heaven and a new earth be celebrated in language admittedly of great beauty with God himself wiping away all tears, putting an end to death, pain, and sorrow, making all things new, delivering believers from those realities that they could never see as anything but arguments against life. Long before Nietzsche conceptualized it, Revelation revealed resentment as the essence of religion. A great love feast at the end. It's a pretty fantasy. As if once rage fashions its masterpiece the heart will open and what has been frozen for so long will become a warm and virgin spring.

Historically the great transformation in the use of apocalypticism to incite fundamentalist believers to political action came in the 1980s, during the Reagan years, when Jerry Falwell (to cite but one example) shifted from the pre-millenarian belief that the faithful can do nothing but spread the gospel and wait as the modernist evil that will bring about the Tribulation runs its course to the *activist* position that fundamentalism must become a political force, indeed take over the country if possible, and make it a Christian nation worthy of being spared as well as the one chosen to advance the movement toward that long-sought, long-delayed, deeply longed for and blessed apocalyptic event. George H.W. Bush was finally a man of restraint with a keen appreciation of the realities of global politics. Dubya labors under no such burdens. His is a mind unencumbered by any countervailing pressure that the world might offer to his singleness of vision. Thus there's no telling where the faith will lead now that Dubya has his mandate and must deliver to satisfy the grandiose conception of what God himself elected him to do ... Perhaps He wants Dubya to find a straight shining path from the cataclysmic future that defines that paranoiac present that constantly recedes before the fundamentalist unless, that is, the apocalyptic future can become the evangelical present? Under Dubya that is now one source for reading what is going on in the Middle East.

The contempt for life that informs fundamentalism is difficult to conceive. As a final example, however, a testimonial to the environmental policies of the Bush administration, consider the quaint piece of fundamentalist folklore known as "dominion theology."[9] This tenet of the faith was openly professed by former secretary of the interior James Watt, the mentor of the current Secretary, Gale Norton. Dominion theology holds that the Bible commands us to use up the earth's resources. We glut ourselves not just for capitalist greed but by biblical mandate. And as the end approaches it is our duty to do so globally, since there's little time remaining to complete that job and thereby bring that final day ever closer. Besides, why bother preserving the planet. After the Second Coming, none of it will matter. And so with each new success—the hole in the ozone, the melting of the ice caps, drilling in the national wildlife refuge, the Alaska pipeline—we give further proof that history is moving in the right direction. Since all is yellow to the jaundiced eye, the only thing the fundamentalist, like the capitalist, can see in nature is that which must be conquered, used up, then disposed of. The oft-chronicled battle of fundamentalists against environmentalism follows the demands of the manic triad. Triumph, contempt, dismissal. Thereby destructiveness is projected onto life itself. Sublimity for the fundamentalist is not found in the rain forest, but in its ravaging. Thereby another way is found to project hatred of life onto another object that has the power to deepen our love of it.

It is hard to know which is colder, crueler: the logic of fundamentalism or the logic of capitalism? But then that question assumes that they are different in some fundamental way. And let's face it we want to hang on to that difference because it offers reassurance, even a guarantee, that we can somehow play the two off against each other. The Bush crowd suffer from no such illusion. They know the secret we need to fathom if we're to *historicize* the connection that Max Weber saw between Christianity and capitalism and thereby learn that Christian fundamentalism and global capitalism correspond to one another because they feed on the same destructive violence.

In concluding I offer a summary of how Thanatos works in the fundamentalist psyche to bind everything to the search for a sublime discharge. Apocalypticism satisfies both the final *evacuation* needed to prevent a return of the projections and the *jouissance* required to bring about the complete unbinding that can come only by putting an *end* to everything. The hatred in which the psyche is grounded requires no less: the hatred that has total control over the inner world demands a matching totalization. In the images of destruction that warm the fundamentalist heart one sees externalized the process that has ravaged the inner world. In that sense, fundamentalism is the most extreme act of sadomasochism toward oneself that has yet been devised. As such it offers us perhaps the deepest insight into the superego as the force of death in the psyche; as an agency that is satisfied with no less than soul murder. Literal obedience to literal commands is merely the tip of that iceberg. It is within that the true process of soul murder operates through the willingness of the psyche to sacrifice everything in itself in order to placate an authority that is vindictively cruel in the wrath it directs on the slightest opposition to its will. In an attempt to achieve *identification* with that force, the psyche wages war first on itself and then upon the world. The former act reveals the destructive power of the superego; the latter act offers a way to confirm one's identification with it. By sacrificing everything in oneself to the superego, one attains the right to become the walking embodiment of its wrath. The fundamentalist can loudly proclaim his or her love of God, but the fact of the matter is that they fear Him because terror is the only relationship He permits. And such is His hold over the psyche that all transgression—or the mere thought of transgression—unleashes an overpowering guilt under which the psyche unravels. *Superego guilt is Thanatos in its immediacy ravaging the psyche by punishing it with the loss of a "love" that is indistinguishable from hate so absolute is the sacrifice it requires.*

But how does such an agency come into being? On what must it draw to create the enormous energy that gives it such power within the psyche. Could it be that this too has and must have its beginnings in love? We've traced the effects of the destructiveness to which the fundamentalist psyche is wedded, but we have not yet considered the cause. We have traced the dialectical progression of a disorder that we must now consider in its *genesis*. To do that we need to strike through the sound and fury of fundamentalist rage and get at what Ahab called "the little lower layer" by showing how *Thanatos* first takes root in a soul and why it continues to ulcer there until it finds fulfillment in apocalyptic expression.

Before turning to that examination a brief summary of the psychoanalytic understanding we've developed of the four characteristics that Charles Strozier isolates as fundamental to fundamentalism. (1) Inerrancy is the infantilizing need to reduce all complexities to the literal in order to confine the mind to its simplest operations; (2) conversion is the employment of the primitive psychological defense known as splitting to establish an absolute separation of the saved psyche from the damned; (3) evangelicalism is the manic activity needed to sustain and project that split; (4) Apocalypticism is Thanatos incarnate projecting the event that will satisfy the death drive that defines the fundamentalist psyche. In discussing these characteristics I deliberately withheld the issue of sexuality until now not in order to minimize its importance but to maximize it by creating a picture of fundamentalism's defining characteristics that only makes sense once we grasp the sexual disorder informing the whole. Fundamentalism will then emerge as one of the clearest examples of the old and oft forgotten Freudian insight that sexuality is at the center of the human psyche and the opposition of Eros and Thanatos at the center of culture. The previous sections describe a superego "morality" grounded in Thanatos. The following section will describe the sexual roots of that disorder, thereby offering an explanation of how Thanatos can assume complete control over the life of a psyche.

## SEXUAL ROOTS OF THE FUNDAMENTALIST PSYCHE

"Think of the depressing contrast between the radiant intelligence of a healthy child and the feeble intellectual powers of the average adult. Can we be quite certain that it is not precisely religious education which bears a large share of the blame for this relative atrophy?"

Sigmund Freud, *The Future of an Illusion*

My goal is to plumb the root cause of phenomena that are well-known. Fundamentalists live in a world obsessed with sexuality. Their favorite citations from the Bible fixate on it. It is also the prime referent of the fulminations against secularism, postmodernism, ethical relativism, feminism, etc. It's what the vaunted claim of "moral values" is all about. Morality for the fundamentalist is not about a life of charity or the pursuit of justice or the need to open oneself to the depth of human suffering. It's about avoiding certain sexual sins and fixating on that dimension of life to the virtual exclusion of everything else. Battling sex is apparently what life is all about, as if the primary plan of the creator is to put us on earth so that we'll be tempted by that in us that we must condemn in order to win salvation. By the same token, each new scandal reveals the consequences of sexual repression: the brutal abuse of young boys by a legion of pedophile priests; the sexual license of Jim Jones and David Koresh; the sadomasochistic bondage rituals that Jimmy Swaggart needed prostitutes in order to enact; the epidemic of physical, sexual, and psychological abuse that is the untold story of the fundamentalist family; the world-wide assault of Dubya's abstinence-only policies on the condom. Such events witness an old truth: the repression of sexuality has as a necessary consequence the brutalization of the other.[10]

The phenomena here are variations on the same tired story. Sexual repression breeds foul imaginings, which of necessity fixate on the sexual. What has been rendered foul within runs amuck in the world. Following the dictates of a punitive superego the psyche becomes obsessed with the attack on sexuality. The purpose is to render evil virtually everything connected with sex until life itself is reduced to an allegory in which the battle of good and evil is all about the temptations of the flesh, as if nothing else in life matters so complete is the vindictive fixation of the Deity on the human genitals.

The eroticization of Thanatos necessarily has a flip side: the demonization of Eros.[11] The libidinal economy on which fundamentalism rests is as simple as it is devastating. Eros must be turned into evil, sin, pollution so that all of one's desire can be channeled into Thanatos. Or vice versa. Once destructiveness has been eroticized all one's energies become fixated on the erotic, since it poses the greatest threat to the resentment one feels toward life in general. The chicken–egg question of temporal priority misses the necessary dialectical connection. The only way to triumph over Eros is by eroticizing death. And the only way to secure that eroticization is by projecting guilt, sin, resentment, and punishment into every aspect of human sexuality. Such is the basic logic to which the fundamentalist project is wedded.[12]

To understand why this is so requires, however, an answer to two questions. (1) What must sex be for it to assume such importance? (2) And what must happen to it for the fundamentalist mind set to gain control over the psyche? What is needed is an account of the *genesis* of fundamentalism through a description of the sequence of formative experiences through which Thanatos by invading and poisoning sexuality installs itself as the sole power in the psyche.

Fundamentalism fixates on sex not by accident or divine decree but by the exigencies of immediate experience. Eros is that force which binds us to life as a blessing that can be lived and loved as an end in itself. It is the spontaneity that weds the child to an innocent and unbridled curiosity; the vitality that resists the imposition of any restraints on the outpouring of an affective embrace of life in all its forms; the self-liberating ability to experience natural processes, prior to and free of the ethical, as matters of fascination and exploration. Eros is that in us which wants to incarnate itself fully, to expend oneself in investing all of one's energies into life. And when all of this becomes overtly sexual it discovers its innermost meaning: to open oneself to another, incarnating in the body the depth of feeling that two subjects can have toward each other. Sexual pleasure is the temple of a holiness that neither wants nor needs other worlds so completely has it found fulfillment in this one. Such an erotic valuation becomes in poets like Whitman and Blake the prime agent of all human perception; in Plato the source of noble laws and institutions; and in Freud that which pits itself against the forces of death. It is also, of course, that which rises up at puberty and at crucial crises throughout life in rebellion against the controls that those who hate and fear it have placed upon desire.

Because it poses a comprehensive threat to the fundamentalist project Eros must be poisoned as early as possible. Ironically there is only one way such a project can succeed. Through love. To summarize briefly a concept I've developed at length elsewhere, parenting is the act through which the parent's conscious and unconscious conflicts and desires become the psyche of the child. This transmission is the act through which the child's psyche is born. The child's unconditional love is the condition that makes it all possible. For fundamentalists this condition creates an incomparable opportunity. From an early age the child must be indoctrinated by those one trusts and loves in the primary lesson: that obedience is the price one must pay to retain love. So deep must become one's need for this love, moreover, that one becomes willing to make any sacrifice it requires. Thereby the condition is set for the greatest transformation. The energy from which the very life of the psyche springs has been invaded by a virus that attacks the subject from within. The process that will issue in the superego has taken root. In Lacanian terms, one's desire has become the desire of the other with that paralyzing bind set as the way one will experience both oneself and the world. Good and evil can now be bred into everything. The body has become the scene of ethical instruction. All natural functions are turned into matters of intense preoccupation. All innocent curiosities nipped in the bud. Spontaneity itself becomes a source of inhibition. The reign of the literal is born. That which most intimately attaches us to life becomes the thing upon which a ceaseless attack is waged. All natural instincts become evidence that the only way to experience the body is as a site of sinful desires. Embodiment itself must become something one hates and fears, a condition in which one finds something evil and disgusting always at work. Everything that desire opens up in the subject must be turned back against itself. Sin, shame, and guilt must come to define the relationship that the subject lives to itself. The goal of fundamentalist child-rearing is to create a subject preoccupied with waging war on itself, with battling against its own desires under the gaze of a judgmental, punitive superego.

The superego maintains this power because internally a fundamental transformation has occurred. All of one's desire has been channeled into one's service to the superego. It is thereby empowered to wage an unrelenting attack on anything in the subject that would oppose or threaten its reign. The superego is, as Freud noted, harsher than the actual parents. It is so because *it fuses prohibition with the quest for love.* What is the first and perhaps the deepest attachment of one's life becomes bound to a force opposed to the very thing from which it draws its energy. Sexuality of necessity brings this conflict to a head. For in it one experiences at its greatest intensity the clash of the two principles that constitute the psyche: (1) that in us that would break free of the superego and constitute a desire independent of it and (2) the power of the superego, as a result of the love one has invested in it, to crush that effort. This conflict is inescapable for the simplest of reasons. Operating upon sexuality was precisely how the superego was formed. It is in one's sexuality, accordingly, that one experiences the true virulence of a force that has the power to turn the inner world into a place of self-torture. All one has to do is desire what it forbids. One then learns the truth. *Capitulation under the unrelenting pressure of internal self-torture is the triumph of a fundamentalist education.* In the war on sex, the process of fundamentalist formation completes itself. Its product: a subject living a relationship to itself defined by self-contempt, self-punishment, and self-unraveling. Any attempt to break with the superego only serves to increase its power. Appearances to the contrary, the superego isn't about morality. It's about power— and the irresistible privilege that comes with power: to torture, in fact to erect torture as the relationship the subject lives to itself.

How could it be otherwise? What else could child-rearing be for the parents but the chance to prove themselves to the Lord by taking whatever measures are required to assure that His commands assume total control over the child's psyche. Getting the child to internalize a superego that makes guilt over one's desires the primary relationship the subject has to itself takes on in fundamentalism the status of a categorical imperative. Life must be filled up with inhibitions and prohibitions in order to assure that sexuality will always be experienced as a fall into sin. Internally that sinfulness is guaranteed by the condition that lays in wait to assault the transgressive psyche, even when the transgression is only in thought or fantasy. Transgression, one discovers, floods the psyche with guilt, shame, and the conviction of a fundamental badness that can only be purged by an attack on oneself. *That attack is the nuptial offering that seals one's marriage to the superego.* Through it one restores one's communion with the superego. In punishing oneself one experiences the libidinal pleasure of a union that feeds on destructiveness. Thereby one reveals the truth: that Thanatos has taken control of the psyche. A subject at war with itself has been created, one that will experience desire itself as a sign of guilt and will loathe it as that within oneself that one must strive to extinguish. Thanatos has created a psyche dedicated to soul murder—to the murder of one's own soul. The power that death work has assumed in the psyche now ravages it. In three interconnected ways. (1) So great is the power guilt has assumed that any opposition to the superego unleashes an attack that threatens the psyche with self-dissolution. That's the truth of this relationship: unending torment with no exit save suicide or psychotic self-fragmentation. (2) To guard against that threat, *ego identity* thus becomes the active, constant effort to spy out and combat everything in oneself that could be labeled a source or occasion of sin. (3) In the *body*, consequently, a condition now maintains in which every desire becomes the overture to a war that must be waged until the very sources of desire have been conquered; until everything that might once have been natural has been rendered thoroughly unnatural. *Sado-masochism has come to define the subject's relationship to itself.* The only pleasure lies in the coldness and cruelty of an unrelenting attack upon one's sinfulness and the pleasure one gets from making oneself the abject object of that wrath. A world of perfect self-hatred has been created. A culture of pure Thanatos has been installed as the unity of a psyche that must project good and evil, sin and punishment, damnation and salvation into everything until life itself becomes the doleful and guilty passage of a shriveled and shrunken (but saved!) subjectivity toward the only thing it can desire. The End—the death of desire itself and of the unending struggle against it and the ever-present danger that one will slip and find oneself in the clutches of the damned. The apocalyptic project is born.

Sexuality has been transformed into the festering wound out of which *resentment* is born. Because every time desire rises up one experiences again one's powerlessness to break the stranglehold the superego has over one's sexuality. A jaundiced eye then casts its gaze on all who have succeeded where one failed. Malevolent envy rises up, offering one the only exit from inner conflict—hatred of the sexual and unending war upon it. That war has become one's deepest necessity. Envy begets hatred begets rage. The only way to relieve that rage is by projecting it onto the world. That act has an added charm: through it one achieves *identification* with that superego that has never stopped assaulting one from within. *As avenging angel damning a sinful world one reclaims as resentment what one has had to sacrifice as desire.* The transformation is complete. One is no longer a child tortured into submission by a punitive superego. One has become an adult projecting that destructiveness upon the world. A psyche so bound to hatred requires a constant supply of fresh objects and occasions on which to vent itself. It is wedded to the search for a sublime fulfillment of the rage that defines it. And because everything within the psyche opposed to this project has been killed there is no way to halt it. Death has become absolute and craves that total unbinding that can come only with a totalizing apocalyptic projection. (The destructiveness analyzed in the above discussion of apocalypticicism is the necessary outgrowth of the sexual condition described here. This inversion is the circle confining the fundamentalist psyche to a room identical to the one occupied by Count Ugolino in Dante.)

The process I've just described is not a disorder restricted to the reddest neck in the reddest state. It's a portrait drawn from what typified a Roman Catholic childhood in the 1950s—and many times before and since. What Freud struggled to comprehend, Roman Catholicism throughout its history has known instinctively and with a thoroughness that enabled it to raise the whole thing to the level of a system based on the most fundamental of recognitions: that working upon human sexuality is the way to attain dominance over the psyche. The systematic perfection of that labor depends on a single insight: wounding someone in their "soul" is the way one gains the greatest power over them; and one does it best when one takes what is most open, vulnerable, and loving in a child and exploits it to forge the bonds that will enslave that psyche, perhaps forever. The superego draws its force from a desperate love it has solicited so that it can appropriate the energies invested in that love in order to wage an attack upon the psyche and thereby eventually on life itself.

Given the genius of Catholicism it should come as no surprise that Mel Gibson's *The Passion of the Christ* is the most popular fundamentalist work of our time, hailed and promoted by fundamentalist preachers.[13] What seems odd at first given the fact that Gibson is not strictly speaking a fundamentalist but a reactionary Catholic on the warpath against Vatican II makes perfect sense when seen in terms of the libidinal structure of Gibson's film (sadomasochism) and the psychological need (the creation of rage through sacred snuff-porn) it fuels. The long-standing fundamentalist hatred of Catholicism is misplaced. Equally misplaced is the attempt to confine fundamentalism to preachers in the Bible Belt. Fundamentalism is on the rise today and takes many forms because it speaks to something that has long been active in Christianity, something that the old Church exemplified. Perhaps fundamentalism is the core that cannot be expunged from Judeo-Christianity, its Hegelian Notion, the *telos* and immanent Logos that has today achieved its final and rebarbative incarnation.

# 8

# The Psychodynamics of Terror

In each human heart terror survives
The ravin it has gorged: the loftiest fear
All that they would disdain to think were true:
Hypocrisy and custom make their minds
The fanes of many a worship, now outworn.
They dare not devise good for man's estate,
And yet they know not that they do not dare.
Percy Shelley, *Prometheus Unbound*

## HOME BREWED

Creating a sexuality tied in knots and a heart turned to stone is not sufficient to assure the social order that psyches wedded to Thanatos require. A *practice* is needed which will give such beings the *pleasure*—indeed *jouissance*—suited to their condition. That pleasure is now our subject and following our method we must attempt to comprehend it from within; that is, to trace the malign self-mediation whereby it proceeds to the final state it seeks. The yield of that investigation will be an understanding of the thing that supposedly we are most deeply concerned to fathom today. Terror—and what could motivate and explain human beings who give themselves over to its service.

Understanding the terrorist psyche requires no journey to the Middle East, nor the cribbing of selections from Bernard Lewis on Islam. Terror surrounds us and not primarily as some foreign infection threatening us from outside the body politic. Terror is, rather, one of the things that most of us experienced a steady diet of growing up and something, sadly, many of us have practiced ever since. Terror is perhaps the truth of the American family and as such perhaps the most revealing definition of American society. Every ten seconds in our country someone is the victim of domestic violence. And that statistic, but one of many that could be cited here, refers only to physical violence. Terror strives to penetrate far deeper into the psyche. Its purpose is to produce capitulation in one who has become a victim willing to sacrifice one's dignity and everything one holds dear. All terror has a psychological aim: to destroy another person in their soul or spirit through a systematic assault on the areas of their greatest vulnerability. Terror's goal is to create an inner condition of permanent trauma, so that even when the terrorist is absent, the victim lives under the specter of the blow about to descend. To wage war on terror or protect the homeland against it the first order of business must be an understanding of its psychodynamics. And I would suggest that the best way to such an understanding is to begin with the terror we know best. We will then know why and the ways in which Terror is the underlying domestic policy of the Bush Administration.

A man who hits a woman knows that he's a coward plagued by inner doubts and fears about his masculinity. Projecting them ties the dream of phallic identity to a fundamental resentment of women and the threat they represent. There's something about them—their cunning, their sexuality, their resemblance to the mother—that has the power to unman unless one assumes an absolute control over it. The domestic space is that theater. The details differ—"The meal must be ready when I arrive home; I'll decide the color of the carpet; I don't do that because I find the smell of your genitals distasteful"—but the project is always the same. To work on the woman's psyche in order to extinguish anxieties within oneself that will otherwise prove unmanageable. Bringing the woman's psyche into line is what is necessary to achieve the peace and safety that can come only through power and dominance. Physical violence is the sign that one is losing this battle. The beauty of the opening round in domestic relations is that both parties are often in pursuit of psychological conquest; so that each action activates a greater reaction until mutual frustration reaches a peak. It is then that some persons make a fatal decision: the use of physical force to win a battle one knows one is losing. The goal of such action, however, remains transformation rather than simple domination; the reduction of the other to an abject psyche ruled by an omnipresent fear. But with physical violence the stakes are raised. No less than total capitulation will now suffice. Accordingly, the fear one inspires must become so pervasive that it produces in the victim the search to seek out and extinguish anything in themselves that the master finds unacceptable, since taking such action before the fact is the only way to tailor one's behavior to a *demand* that has become irrational. *A terrorized subject is one who has internalized the other's brutality as their self-reference.* One lives so dominated by the threat of violence that nothing else, properly speaking, exists. One lives constantly on the lookout for the slightest sign of a displeasure that must be immediately allayed. The master's psyche has become the prime agent of one's perceptions. Bringing the victim to such a point is the project of terror. The goal is to assure total control over the other's consciousness by installing a fear that floods the psyche at various times throughout the day. *Terror is the permanent inner state of a subject who will do anything to escape a fear that never recedes.* Any thought of one's liberation from this state has become a thought that fills one with anxiety. That is the proof that the internalization is complete. One lives under the *gaze* of the terrorist. And one does not dare look back at that look. In philosophic terms, terror is the negation of the Hegelian dialectic of recognition. In Hegel the slave has the liberated consciousness because he or she sustains an inwardness in which the meaning drawn from dehumanizing experiences of domination fructifies in future revolutions. The inwardness of the slave defeats thus the efforts of the master to reduce human *recognition* to the conditions of power. In this regard terror is an effort to *cancel* the most important chapter in modern thought.[1] Terror is the revenge that the fascism of the heart takes on all threats to the hegemony it demands. Through terror those who believe in power—and only in power—establish the conditions that mock all other forms of recognition. As we'll see, they thereby also establish a libidinal pleasure of a unique order.

But in order to understand such things we must tunnel to the heart of this darkness. The above gives us the image that can guide us throughout our search—the image of a husband and father his upraised fist about to descend on the faces of those he supposedly loves. Thus far we only have a foretaste, however, of what those who resort to terror are trying to effect in their own psyche as well as in those of their victims. Before proceeding I hasten to add an important point. Though I generally employ the male pronoun, many domestic terrorists are women who have devised innumerable ways to enact on a psychological level what is denied them on a physical one. Thereby they underscore the primary point: physical violence is but one way to achieve a psychological goal. Indeed, the true masterpieces of psychological terror are often crafted by those who never raise their voice, let alone their hand, but know how to deliver blows that open traumatic wounds. The same consideration applies to political terror. The threat of the boot is but one of the measures Big Brother employs to invade and colonize the consciousness of his subjects.

### EVACUATION THROUGH PROJECTIVE IDENTIFICATION

What follows is an attempt, by tunneling to the core of the terrorist psyche, to comprehend the domestic policies of the Bush Administration in terms of its deepest psychological sources.[2] This story begins with two things: the terrible *wound* one finds at the heart of every terrorist and the equally terrible *choice* made in response to that condition. The former may activate our sympathy since it reveals the common condition that perhaps defines us, but the latter demands a judgment shorn of pity. Because psyche is that which emerges when we are wounded in a way that puts our being at issue, giving oneself over to terror is one of the possibilities that defines us. All the more reason to know it from the inside.

Terror's *origin* is a feeling of inner powerlessness. Its purpose is to reverse that condition by reducing others to it. At the center of the terrorist's psyche one invariably finds an overpowering presence: that of a malevolent, destructive other who has a command over the psyche more complete than that of the most extreme superego. In terms of an image, think of Norman Bates' mother in Hitchcock's *Psycho*. The terrorist's inner world is one of ceaseless persecution and unbridled cruelty. The malevolent other has reduced the psyche to a condition of abjection; i.e., the utter loss of any possible identity in a horror within that cannot be overcome. Humiliations have eradicated the ability to sustain any positive feelings toward oneself. One's inner world is defined by a single reality: cruelty. That cruelty has produced the only possible result: self-hatred. The malevolent other has shattered every other possibility of psychic cohesion and identity, rendering the inner world one permanently tottering on the brink of self-fragmentation and psychotic self-dissolution. Only one route to an identity remains. Empowerment through hate, externalizing the hate one has been made to feel toward oneself by projecting it onto others. Power is the only reality and its abiding purpose is the prosecution of cruelty. Everything else is a sign of weakness. That's the lesson one learned from one's victimage: one must take the blow, welcome it even, with a frozen and steely grin, accepting punishment as an opportunity to toughen oneself. Self-brutalization provides the only safety from the malevolent force that presides over one's psyche. There's only one solution to one's condition. *Wounds must be turned into weapons.*

Caught in that project, a bitter necessity has seized one's being: to evacuate one's inner condition by finding those objects fitted to receive its projections. Cumulatively, such a project constitutes a systematic inversion of the golden rule. For one principle promises the inner transformation that the terrorist psyche seeks: do unto others what was done onto you. For this project to effect the inner transformation that is sought, those one targets must fulfill two conditions that appear contradictory. They must embody both one's weakness *and* the malevolent other. Terror attempts to reverse an inner condition by reversing an external one that mirrors it the moment one is able to strike through the mask of the other's apparent power, finding the underlying weakness on which one can act in order to reduce the other to the abject condition that one thereby no longer occupies. Through terror one thus attains a double triumph. Cruelty proves that one is no longer a weak victim but in fact one of the truly strong who've triumphed over the force that once had power over them. Such is the dirty little secret, for example, of those men who attack women for precisely those qualities—sensitivity, access to one's emotions, responsiveness to tenderness—that once made those men vulnerable. By making those qualities the vulnerabilities on which one's terror feeds, one purges oneself of them while solidifying one's identification with the original aggressor. Terror is thus the repetition and ritual memorializing of the scene of the psyche's original wound but with the roles reversed. That reversal, however, produces a new contradiction that can only lead to an increased violence. A transformation that may be irreversible has taken place. The victim has become a victimizer.[3] The power and pleasure of Thanatos have thus seized the terrorist in a grip that threatens to reduce everything to the self-reifying progression of a simple and deadly logic. The first issue of this logic is the cycle of escalating violence examined with such great insight by Rene Girard.[4] Violence begets violence with no way to arrest the begetting of further violence. This is so for two reasons. (1) Terror has expanded the range of the objects upon which it must be projected, since one now hates anything that makes one feel weak as well as anything that reminds one of the malevolent other. (2) More destructive still is the inner transformation because the psyche has now eradicated those things in itself that could halt the projection. They can only be signs of a weakness that must be denied. That's why there's no way to stop. No reason to stop. No objects sufficient to sate a need that is already implicitly global in its reach; and that has refined itself and now knows what terror must strike at and what its method must be. The object changes—colonizer to colonized, white man to black man, man and woman, Bush and bin Laden—but the method and the goal are always the same.

## THE PERFECT MURDER: SOUL MURDER

That is so because all terror has its genesis in the contradictions of the following situation. A person or nation can't stand something about themselves that makes them feel weak. They seek out someone weaker who represents it. Through violence toward that other one attacks something within oneself. The problem is the project doesn't work. The inner doubts and fears return. Brutality and violence offer no solution. An act of a special kind is required. Psychological cruelty is born. It seeks the conditions for a finalizing drama capable of destroying the other's psyche. Verbal abuse is self-defeating. Physical violence is trapped in a Sartrean dilemma: the eyes of the other may resemble those of a terrified animal, but they also harbor the possibility of a consciousness that is free, the way the Hegelian slave is, aware of one's humanity, one's moral superiority and one's duty to reverse one's condition. Those who attack only the body of the other are always unsure of conquering their psyche. What terror requires is what Hegel called a *standing negation*. The other must render their psyche into the terrorist's hands, proving thereby that every source of inner resistance has been conquered. Bringing about such a result requires creating a drama with the following structure. The area of the other's maximum inner vulnerability must be identified then activated in a situation that will force them to stand up in order to preserve their dignity and self-respect. The terrorist then has what he or she seeks—the chance to deliver a blow that will permanently affect the very ability of the other to maintain themselves as a subject. Such is the genius of humiliation and cruelty: to make a person feel contempt for themselves, to experience what is most valuable and personal about them as the thing that opens them to ridicule. One need then no longer fear the Sartrean look. For the eyes of the other are now cast contemptuously upon themselves. One's cruelty has become their self-reference. As a result one reaps the reward that all terror seeks: not the obedience of the battered nor the compliance of the sullen but a true transformation, a subjectivity reduced to the inner condition of those who feel their victimization is what they deserve.

Psychological cruelty is the attempt to bring the other to a condition where they willingly sacrifice the last thread of their self-respect in order to escape the threat of further humiliation. One can now relax because the other, qua psyche, lives in a condition of terror. Terror has become the defining property of their consciousness, an abjection so total that it cries out the words the terrorist longs to hear: "Into thy hands I commend my spirit."

Once one has reduced the other to this condition, the terrorist is ready to reap the long-sought reward: the prospect, through a complete *discharge* of one's *destructiveness*, of attaining the complete reversal of one's inner condition. The founding feeling of inner powerlessness has transformed itself into a feeling of boundless, unrestrained power. Through psychological cruelty one has reversed the roles that defined one's original inner condition. A deadly inner peace descends on the terrorist. All inner conflicts have been successfully externalized. One thing, however, is needed to keep them there: new adventures in cruelty, since psychological torture is the only way to confirm one's identity.

New ways must thus be found to enhance not just one's cruelty but one's contempt for its victims. The danger to the terrorist psyche is regret or remorse. Because then everything turns back inward toward a depression that can only be experienced as regression to the abject condition one was in long ago. Terror has become the way one delays a return of the repressed. The continuous projection of violence becomes the manic side of a manic-depressive syndrome in which the only way to prevent an implosion into the depressive core is through the expansion of one's mania. Destructive mania is the victory dance of an elation that must be sustained to assure oneself that one has triumphed over all inner conflict. Terror solves that problem by liberating the manic triad—triumph, contempt, and dismissal—from any and all restrictions. *Triumph*: torturing one's victim has become a source of ecstasy and elation, thereby unbinding the psyche from the last vestiges of inner conflict. *Contempt*: dehumanizing one's victim exorcises the threat of a return of those weak emotions that could retard the exercise of one's terror. *Dismissal*: rejecting any lingering "humanistic" claims of one's victim confers on one's terror the indifference required to dismiss all consequences as beneath one's consideration. Terror has thereby produced its own form of transcendence. Not change within one's inner world (as in depressive self-mediation) but change by an omnipotent rising above it, one with the mushroom cloud of one's imagination. In terms of terror Hiroshima remains the unexampled masterpiece.

No guilty afterthoughts can enter one's psyche because terror follows a logic antithetical to conscience. (The moment during the debates when a stupefied George W. Bush answered the question about mistakes made during his first administration with the admission that he couldn't think of any was singularly revealing.) The purpose of terror is to effect an absolute unbinding of all inner tensions. Structurally three conditions must be fulfilled for that to happen. (1) The founding condition of inner abjection must be totally *reversed*. (2) All inner *blockage* to one's aggression must be overcome through the abrogation of any human ties that would limit it. (3) That aggression must then be given a fully *unbound* expression, celebrated as an end in itself, uncontaminated by the presence of any other motives. The resulting condition realizes the identity that all terrorists seek. *Narcissistic grandiosity*. There are now no limits to one's power and its arbitrary expression. One submits to only one law: self-aggrandizement. Safety and certitude, inner peace and a lasting identity come through a single operation: the replacement of relations of mutuality and persuasion by ones of force and submission. The fascist ideal realized and with it the achievement of what for lack of a better term we'll call a *phallic identity*, though its pursuit is hardly confined to men. Psychological cruelty is an equal opportunity employer, offering the illusion of an identity to those who find strength in coldness and cruelty.

Because this project depends on unbinding all sources of inner conflict, it proves perforce endless. The threat of depressive inwardness must be constantly allayed by fresh actions taken to prove again that one has the identity one claims, safe from the return of those weak, vacillating feelings that would signify the opposite. Inner conquest remains the ever assured, ever pursued, ever unfulfilled goal of terror, which is why at all times its adherents must be ready to assume again the posture of the playground bully. This was Reagan's genius, his pivotal importance in the development of the Amerikan character. He taught people to hate the poor and feel a righteous pleasure in doing so.

Such pleasure is, however, but a temporary way station on the road to something narcissistically grand. For once a psyche has vanquished all inner restraint it moves within the register of the *sublime*.[5] Global fantasies grip it, longing for the occasion that will legitimize their expression. Such sublimity is the condition of Paul Tibbets in the clouds looking down like an Olympian God on the rubble of Hiroshima, seeing in that spectacle the perfect *image* of the kind of sublimity terror seeks. Once all inner restraint has been vanquished, the dream of terror takes delight in the most horrible imaginings. Horror has become the condition of a pleasure that has become insatiable: the stuff of popular entertainment (disaster movies, Gibson's Sacred snuff porn) and of gaudier imaginings: the twin towers collapsing under bin Laden's astonished gaze, Baghdad littered with depleted uranium, the Arctic Wildlife Refuge opened to pillage, the book of Revelation, its time come round at last, slouching in the terrorist imaginary, toward a fitting expression of cosmic resentment and cosmic rage.

## THANATOS: THE PLEASURE OF TERROR

Having a mind of winter controlled by such fantasies is the innermost necessity of the terrorist psyche because it is ruled by a single desire which remains hot until it has created the conditions required for its pleasure. *Thanatos*. Were one to expose the nuclear core of the terrorist psyche, that's what one would find at the core—the desire to create vast kingdoms where death rules in order to conquer everything that shackles one to life and its demands. Terror is the means to that end. It is the way that *death work* libidinizes itself. The project thus turns on a single necessity. *Thanatos must be eroticized.* All the erotic or libidinal energies that bind one to life must be transformed so that everything vital in the subject concentrates itself in a single project—aggression. Bullying, brutalizing, taunting, contempt for the loser, braying over one's victories (whether in the End Zone or on the decks of the *US Lincoln*)—are so many rituals in service to a single goal: the unbinding of destructiveness from all restraints so that it becomes the only thing that makes one feel truly alive, alive in the certitude that one has cut through all the crap and become a true representative of the bitter truth about human nature. The depressive's fear—that hate will prove stronger than love—was a waste of time, a sentimentalist's failure to grow up. Hate is ever so much stronger than love—and far more satisfying. Thanatos is the only *jouissance* in the sense of an absolute expenditure without reserve. To coincide with Thanatos fully would be true bliss, giving one the ability to practice cruelty with relish on every possible occasion. *Soul murder* would be the informing principle of all relations to the other. Free at last in that supreme pleasure one would be like the cat with the mouse, coming close to the goal then backing up to savor it again until the pressure finally proves irresistible and one delivers the blow one knows will crush the other for good, already sensing the glee that will come later when one relives or crows one's victory to whet one's appetite for the next opportunity. Such is the destructive circle in which the psyches of those wedded to terror turn.

The basic necessity that drives them is the extermination of what Freud saw as death's ancient antagonist. *Eros*.[6] Terror in all its forms is the enemy of Eros because Eros, in its purity, is one thing, the most terrifying and exacting thing: the possibility that opening oneself in love and tenderness is the act that defines our relationship to the other and to ourselves. That possibility contains a terrifying implication: one is only alive when one sustains all the internal conflicts that love activates. Identifying with Thanatos offers the psyche one kind of identity. Eros opens one to another, which is radically different in its direction, defined, as it is, by the necessity of self-overcoming and the recognition that one remains bound to life only if one commits oneself to rooting out all the ways in which one's culture, one's gender, and one's economic position have ensnared one in service to Thanatos. *Eros is the opening of the psyche to the necessity of reversing everything in oneself that aligns one with death.* That's why tenderness is so terrifying. It identifies every way that one is sick within. The project of Eros—which one discovers in the pores in any genuine erotic relationship—is to expand all those connections that wed us to becoming socialists in our "instincts," with instinct lived as that opening to the other which is the basis of any truly radical politics.

Terror is the antithesis of that path. Its effort is to make death the sole term of human relations. Those who have bound their psyches to terror are only satisfied when the attack on every liberating possibility has become the underlying purpose controlling all the institutions that compose the social order. Objectifying terror has become the basis of all domestic policies. Under the banner "pro life" this agenda has under Dubya and Ashcroft–Gonzalez taken giant strides toward realizing a kingdom dedicated to the true work of death, the inner deadening of a collectivity ready to march goose-step to the beat of a common drum. The politics of domestic terror. That's the true purpose of the Patriot Act.

## PATRIOT GAMES

"To be radical is to go to the roots; but the root is man himself."
Karl Marx, "A contribution to the critique of Hegel's Philosophy of Right"

Unfortunately we on the left are quick to dismiss psychoanalytic investigations when the truth of the matter may be that they are essential to our struggle. The value of the concept of terror we've developed here, for example, is that it enables us to measure the velocities of change, to gauge the significance of developments such as the Patriot Act in terms of something deeper than the erosion of civil liberties. The irony of our resistance to psychoanalytic thinking is the belief that we can understand the massive changes in every area of our lives envisioned by Dubya's policies without understanding the cumulative effect of such changes in the psyche.

No socio-political order can last unless it secures in its subjects the conditions of its reproduction. The formation or interpellation of subjects is the essential goal of every institutionalized practice. That's why the psychological model of terror we've constructed offers us a way to chart Dubya's domestic policies in terms of the ideal psychological condition to which they point. The conservative revolution is patient because it rests on a comprehensive game plan that enables its adherents each time they are in power to know what the next step must be. Reagan begets Dubya begets ... ? Marx was wrong. History doesn't repeat itself as farce. That's the delusion that invites us to view Dubya as but a bungling shade of the great communicator. In terms of the logic of the next step he leaves Reagan panting at the post. Yet who knows how many more Dubyas will be needed. Only time will tell. Time—and our resistance. What we can know, however, is the condition that must be reached for the project of the radical right to be fulfilled. Unlike the confusion defining the patchwork liberal coalitions that share little more than their fear of being radical, the conservative right has a clear and undeviating program. We need one of equal clarity and severity.

Transformations in the collective psyche move slowly and yet produce as their cumulative result changes that may prove irreversible. In the biological order, when a species becomes extinct there's no bringing it back. We love to reassure ourselves that such can never be the case with human qualities. That's why we endlessly recycle an essentialistic view of human nature in order to achieve the comforts of what amounts to a secular religion: the belief in a system of *humanistic guarantees* that we claim are somehow outside history. We can never lose our humanity and the self-identity it confers on us. Renewal is thus assured. No matter how bad things get under Dubya we can always begin again. All we have to do is listen to the voice of our ahistorical humanity. This is the idea that more than any other blinds us to History; and, specifically, to the possibility that Dubya's administration represents a watershed moment ushering in changes that can't be reversed—not just environmentally, geopolitically, or in terms of civil liberties, but at a deeper register of the collective psyche that has been made eager to sacrifice every freedom for the promise of an evangelical security. There is no greater terrorist than YAHWEH. (Yes, or Allah.) As Dostoyevsky's Grand Inquisitor foresaw, "Miracle, Mystery, and Authority" are the true props of ideology because they alone fulfill the need on which enslavement depends: to find in mass worship deliverance from the terror of freedom. For Dostoyevsky Christ represents that terror, his essential message being the responsibility of the individual to decide for him or herself "with a free heart, what is good and what is evil."[7] Christianity, in contrast, is a history defined by the desire "to complete the happiness of man" by giving the weak "someone to bow down to" so that politics will fulfill "the need for universal union" by "uniting everyone at last into a common, concordant, and incontestable anthill."[8] In Dubya's Amerika that bliss will be attained when the enjoyment of one's infantilization has become condition general. All other forms of inwardness will have been eradicated. Thinking for oneself or feeling in a way different from the generalized other and its unending hosannah will have become the Kafkaesque condition of a terror that has now been planted in the center of each subject's consciousness. A society of surveillance of the kind that Ashcroft (as Foucault's idiot child) envisions is but the externalization of what happens within as subjects living under such a regime install as the deepest voice of their own conscience absolute obedience to beliefs that they live in terror of ever violating. Within the innermost privacy of the self—that's where Big Brother is always watching and where the religious right campaigns from conception far beyond natural death. Everything must be colonized by the force of beliefs that cannot be questioned because they've become the collective and political unconscious of subjects who are incapable of any self-reference other than fealty to what the Grand Inquisitors of their faith command them to believe—and do. Theocratic politics is the endless iteration of the thought-denying commonplaces that mass subjects have been taught to proclaim not because they love God or He them but because their fear of His Judgment is so great that they're willing to sacrifice everything—indeed, the whole world—to prove their literal allegiance to all the articles of their faith, every last one: unbridled capitalism, devastation of the environment, pre-emptive unilateralism, religious fanaticism. All this coalesces in Dubya, finding in him the realization of a role that Reagan in retrospect played in a half-hearted way.

To put the issue in philosophic terms, we won't begin to understand history, let alone take the necessary actions in it, until we see that we are given over to it *ontologically*. Nothing protects or delivers us from history. Our identity as subjects is a function of our effort to know and combat our historical situation or be blown along like leaves in autumn, not toward the rebirth Shelley envisioned in the great wind he celebrated, but toward the terrified trembling of subjects so habituated to living in death's dream kingdom that they can only see their lives as something already past; or, whenever loss visits them, it can be nothing but the call to embrace what has happened to them in the only way they can: "I love Big Brother." Once the State has established to its citizens the relationship of the familial terrorist to his victims the year 1984 will have arrived. Dubya gives us a Pisgah vision of that prospect.

One argument made often by pundits in the early months after 9-11 was singularly revealing of the change that was then in progress. The argument, made both for the necessity of the Patriot Act and for more general changes in the evolution of a surveillance society, went something like this. The government gave us many freedoms and now it's taking some of them back. The falseness of that view is an index of its profound historical significance. American democracy rests on the recognition of inalienable freedoms. The government doesn't give them to me; nor can I ever permit it to take them away from me. Amerika rests on the opposite assumption, which is why terror is essential to its working. One form of that terror consists in the idea that we should be thankful to the government for whatever freedoms it gives us and thus unperturbed when it withdraws them. Once the populace has internalized this assumption we will live in a nation of terrorized subjects grateful for whatever the master lets them have and afraid to complain about whatever he takes away.

Moving in that direction has been the primary goal of ideological instruction since 9-11. No message has been clearer than this one: apply the term terror only to the other while endorsing global and domestic war against anything that our leaders include under that umbrella. Such is the primary way that state terror operates today; the frequent ratcheting up of the terror watch index by the Department of Homeland Security has become, as it were, the central nervous system of a populace interpellated to live at all times ready to move to red alert. It's everywhere, you know, the terror and whatever measures are taken to stamp it out must be given the wholehearted support of all. Whether Dubya is asking or telling us to view the world in this way is *undecidable* because that question depends on a subjectivity able to resist the force of ideology. The possibility of such a subjectivity is precisely what is being currently contested by the Bushian interpellation of the subject: as subject defined by the threat of terror and thus willing to authorize whatever is needed to deliver one from it. To live in death's dream kingdom is to find oneself in the condition of Faulkner's Rosa Coldfield trapped in "that dream-state in which you run without moving from a terror in which you cannot believe, toward a safety in which you have no faith."[9]

# 9
# Evil: As Psychological Process and as Philosophic Concept

### The psychogenesis of evil

"Hitler gave the world a new categorical imperative. So act that Auschwitz will never again be possible." This statement by Theodor Adorno is generally thought to refer primarily to history and politics. I will argue that its most telling application is to the many little choices we make that result in what is called our *character*; i.e., our ability to feel in certain ways and as a result to open ourselves to the ethical demands of experience. It is here that Adorno's imperative will show its power to deliver us over to the burden of our humanity.

My subject now is the process whereby a heart destroys itself; or what amounts to the same thing, the process whereby what we have every right to call *evil* takes root in the psyche. What follows describes that process from its beginning to the final form where there is no longer any hope for such a person because the leukemia of soul has become irreversible. This description will enable us to rethink the central categories of ethics—intention, motive, choice, and freedom—in a way far more concrete than is possible within the rationalist traditions where ethical responsibility remains confined to the orbit of conscious deliberation, bracketing the emotional and psychological factors which we'll show produce the actual ethical determinations in the life of the subject. Reason is a wonderful thing but it's not where the primary action is. As moral beings we are finally what we are able to feel. It is there, I'll show, that we make the *choices* that inform our ethical agency. (To forestall a misinterpretation, I want to indicate that the position I'll develop transcends the opposition between determinism and freedom as that opposition is deployed with respect to ethics. The psychological condition I describe below identifies a way of being that cannot be comprehended within the terms of either behaviorist or rationalist traditions.)

Focusing on the psyche also enables us to address the issue of the banality of evil in a new way, adding to Hannah Arendt's profound meditation on that topic the psychoanalytic dimension she studiously avoided throughout her work.[1] Along with objective responsibility for his deeds, Adolf Eichmann had another responsibility, deeper than any specific intentions he formulated or motives he acted on in performing what he called *duty*: responsibility for having become Adolf Eichmann. It is in terms of the formation of character, moreover, that each of us may discover ways in which we are far closer to him than we realize. One does not become a Nazi only when circumstances call for such beings. The grounds for that choice are prepared long before. One has already become a Nazi in one's heart. And it is there that the disorder sits awaiting the circumstances that provide the objective correlative of what is an inner condition. Understood concretely, Adorno's imperative is perhaps the most radical ever formulated because it puts all of us on trial in the place where we live, though most of us visit it seldom: the psyche. It is there that each of us must be willing to discover the Nazi in us and uproot it in the only way one can, by tracing it to its source.

What follows attempts to describe evil as a *choice* that begins almost imperceptibly then grows through subsequent *choices* until it becomes a settled way of being that has assumed such command over the personality that it is the thing one must do whenever the opportunity presents itself. In conceptual terms the attempt will be to describe the choices that determine our emotional being. This phenomenology of spirit, which Hegel's only dimly approximates, is the process of self-mediation through which the psyche determines itself by choosing to feel one way in order to escape feeling another.

The initial movement is so simple that it's hard not to slide along it like a well-greased sled down packed snow. Love opens us in vulnerability to the other. Then sadly comes the experience of being injured in one's psyche by those one loves. We open ourselves only to discover that for some unfathomable reason others exploit that situation to hurt us in a way that strikes at our ability to go on being.[2] The psyche feels itself shattered within by the trauma of betrayal, humiliation, cruelty. The existential burden of our humanity has descended upon us. We have become what we were not before: a psyche relating to itself in the felt awareness that one's being is at issue.[3] Before we were determined by many principles—neurological, behavioral, cognitive, adaptational. But now an utterly new one has come on the scene, hollowing out a fundamental inwardness. We now *live* a relationship to ourselves that is defined by feelings (anxiety, dread, humiliation, shame) in which we find ourselves utterly at issue.

We *exist* faced with the first (and in a sense the most monumental) *choice*, if we can call it that: to remain *open* in the pain one feels and find in that way of being an incipient ethic of inwardness or to *shut down* by finding a way to feel that will deliver one from vulnerability. The second route is mapped by what is termed *identification with the aggressor*. To protect oneself from psychological pain one begins to fashion oneself in the image of those who have the power to hurt. It is readily acknowledged how cruel children can be and just as strenuously denied that it is from us, and not from instinct,[4] that they derive the motive to undertake what should be seen from its inception as a horrifying and perhaps inexorable process. Usually it starts on the smallest of stages—the child hitting the stuffed animal it loves, destroying the toy village it has just so lovingly and laboriously created. It's a long way from there to the playground bully and later to the single-minded preoccupation of so many teenagers to humiliate other teens; and a long way, we like to think, from there to what a person has become when cruelty is the settled habit of their being. The fundamental transformation has begun, however, and can be seen for what it is if we acknowledge that all these actions have a common denominator: the attempt to humiliate those who remind us of the weakness that once made us an object of humiliation and that still does, we fear, unless we can, through this practice, purge ourselves of it. We identify in the other what we fear others will see in us. Our vulnerability becomes the thing we triumph over by attacking it in the other. *Do unto others what was done unto you.* The inversion of the golden rule has become the relationship one lives to oneself. Projection has become the means of emotional self-mediation. Everything that makes one feel weak has become something one can extinguish by extending the scope of one's identification with the aggressor. One goes forth in search of oneself with a dagger in one's hand. Inserting it in the other's heart has become the act whereby one solidifies an identity bound to the power to hurt. The exercise of such power is the practice that keeps *closed* all those things in oneself that could *open* one to hurt. Closing down was initially perhaps a necessity for survival. It has now become the basis for a self-brutalizing relationship to oneself. Perfecting that relationship is the *use* to which one puts the other.[5]

To underscore what has happened let us pause and consider another kind of child. For some children sustain the other way of being. They keep themselves open in their pain and thereby gain entry into the suffering *in* others, especially those who injure them. Brooding on the causes of cruelty, such children are born psychologists who live the *why* in its immediacy. There is only one way to sustain that question however. By keeping oneself open to suffering. Psychological suffering has become both the way to preserve oneself and the route to the heart of the other; not the other's power, but something deeper: their psyche—the wounds behind their rage and cruelty. Living the question why hollows out within oneself an inwardness in which one broods on love's bitter mysteries: on how radically love opens us up, how easily love is violated, and at what great cost. Such children are born into an impossible project: the effort to fathom the cause that leads human beings to try to hurt one another so deeply. Refusing to identify with the aggressor makes possible another way of being: melancholia or depressive inwardness as the recognition that trying to reverse the cruelty at the heart of human relations is the only project that can give life meaning. For keeping oneself open to being wounded is the only way of appealing to that which may open itself in the other. (Even in the torturer.) How deep must become one's "empathy" for those who cause one's deepest injuries is a question I can't address here, since this is not the place for a full presentation of this way of being. Suffice to say that living the why—and internalizing every experience in which one suffers it—is the source of a psychological and emotional self-mediation antithetical to the one we are tracing. It issues moreover in an inwardness that is the antithesis of *resentment*, an inwardness that grows by grieving over inhumanity and injustice. As such it is the origin of Hannah Arendt's starting point in her great meditation on the evil of the Holocaust: "This should not have happened."[6] But it did. Many times, in many ways and many places: in Hiroshima, in the Gulag, in the middle passage, in the Trail of Tears, and today in Iraq. That's why the only way to understand it is by suffering it from within in an effort to track down its roots in the darkest registers of the human psyche. There is only one preparation for such a task. It began the first time one took a suffering fully into oneself and was remade by it. For one then became a *psyche* defined by the burden of a tragic inwardness which is the only thing that can save us from our own cruelty by enabling us to recognize it for what it is and either nip it in the bud or bear a guilt that can only be purged when one roots it out. The effort to do so is among the most fortunate experiences, since it can show us how far we've advanced in a process of inner deadening that can only be reversed by reopening ourselves to the path or Tao of a suffering which has, without our knowing it, become the only *hope* for us.

In contrast the pivotal emotional *transformation* in the hardening of the heart comes when the prospect of hurting others becomes a pleasure that is sought and savored. The love of power over others has then become the wedding of one's being to *psychological cruelty*. And there is only one way that project can advance its logic. To show concern for one's victims is to confess one's inner vulnerability. To overcome that threat the attack on the other must become more brutal and strike deeper inward, seeking out what is most vulnerable in order to inflict the deepest hurts, the kind from which there can be no recovery. Cruelty now has its object—the ability of the other to go on being—and its method, a cold indifference, for to feel any other way about one's action signifies weakness and vulnerability. The project implicit in identification with the aggressor is here attained: inner deadening through *soul murder*, a project pursued in a desire that has become insatiable—to destroy others in their souls.

Such projects remain conveniently unconscious. There is, however, one infallible sign that one has completed the process of inner deadening. The banality of evil. Psychological cruelty is something one no longer needs to think about; and the pleasure one took earlier in its practice is no longer part of the equation. One does this thing now without thinking about it or deriving any particular pleasure from it, except for the indifference that has now become an iron necessity. It signifies another kind of pleasure, one that cannot celebrate itself lest that act beget a self-knowledge that must remain suppressed. Inner deadening gives out the proof of itself in another way. One rejects all *appeals* from the other. It has become impossible to hear them, except as an occasion to bray one's triumph. The inability to see others except from one's own point of view, which Arendt lists as a primary characteristic of the banality of evil, is grounded psychologically in the inability to see the other's suffering except as an opportunity to celebrate one's power.

Consider, as one instance, the performance our President couldn't resist when, as Governor of Texas, he had the pleasure of denying clemency to Karla Faye Tucker, while exploiting the situation in the media as the profound inner drama of a "compassionate conservative" faced with the claims of Duty. Recounting the event privately to Tucker Carlson, Dubya couldn't resist the chance to mimic the voice of Karla Faye Tucker in the last minute plea for her life that had been broadcast on national television. "'Please,' Bush whispered, his lips pursed in mock desperation, 'please don't kill me.'"[7] I know, conversion to Jesus is the ploy all prisoners use to fool us sentimentalists, but despite his widely trumpeted born-again status, in Dubya Christian charity couldn't detain a psyche seized by a deeper imperative. The true necessity was hot upon Dubya. The brutalizing pleasure of the playground bully who's never outgrown the need to make fun of his victims, to crow the proof of his heart against sympathy, through mimicry, like the adolescent he remains, to assure himself that unlike those he torments, he isn't weak.

"I'm a loving guy," Dubya loves to boast. As are they all. But when it came to Karla Faye Tucker, psyche, intention, and expression were in sync for once. Caught in an inner necessity, Dubya couldn't resist letting his pleasure cackle a brief appearance on the stage. It's the same pleasure that comes when one speeds up to hit another crazed squirrel scurrying across the road; the pleasure one gets from the look one sees in the wife one slowly backs into a corner under an upraised fist; and at a subtler and more destructive register, it's the pleasure that comes to those who see sadness and disappointment at work in a child and say, "it's good for him; it'll toughen him up." And finally, such is the justice of this thing, it's what happens when in *self-pity* striking one's heart one only hurts one's hand. One has then completed a process that begins in those earliest, barely perceptible choices one makes when one is young that give birth to a dialectic of self-mediation that completes itself in the wedding of a person's being to what must be termed evil. What follows attempts to outline the basic structure of that process.

(1) Identifying with the aggressor banishes the *shame* of humiliation. In attacking the sources of vulnerability in others one acts simultaneously on two fronts, killing within oneself what one persecutes outside. This emotional self-mediation has fatal results. The psyche has made a basic *choice*: to shut down that which opens it up and to feel empowered in the extent to which one does so. Shame and humiliation are thereby transformed into what should be called by its right name. *Self-hatred.* This is the emotion that now regulates the subject's self-reference, issuing in what can for the first time be termed an identity, that of an ego committed to the process of building defenses in order to erect a mighty fortress to protect oneself from all inner and outer threats. But how? Since the process of the psyche's determination is an emotional one, what feelings are needed to advance the process?

(2) Self-hatred must find a way to assure its triumph over every inner source of vulnerability. Only one emotion is adequate to that task. *Envy*. Unlike jealousy, vanity, and narcissism, envy is no small emotion and seeks no little victories. As Melanie Klein shows, it is defined by a titanic desire: *envy desires the destruction of that which is good precisely because it is good*.[8] Jealousy is but a way station on the road to envy: whereas jealousy seeks to possess what it does not have and admires, envy is satisfied only with destruction. The things one sees in others that one lacks are not qualities one could pursue because that would involve reopening oneself to vulnerability. What one lacks, however, eats on the psyche and bleeds within whenever one finds oneself like Iago in the presence of those who have "a daily beauty in their life" that makes one "ugly." Because the cost of killing things in oneself is to live haunted by them, this is the comparison that constantly imposes itself on one's consciousness. The effort to destroy becomes accordingly both peremptory and the only pleasure. Envy is that leukemia of soul that bleeds anew each time one's heart is rubbed raw by the *memory* of all that one sacrificed and must sacrifice in order to complete the process of inner deadening by rooting out everything that remains alive within oneself. In envy self-hatred finds the emotion that becomes for it the prime agent of all perception, the very way of one's being-in-the-world.

(3) To advance its project, however, envy must transform itself into an even darker force. *Cruelty*. For in a sense envy remains a passive emotion, at the mercy of everything that rubs it raw. Cruelty makes it active in a way perfectly suited to the process of inner deadening. Those one envies must be destroyed. But the only way to assure success is to find a way to destroy them from within. Thereby one gets the proof one needs—that we're all alike, equally corruptible, with goodness merely the illusion of those who haven't tasted the bitter apple of experience. Giving them a good bite is the task of cruelty. Cruelty is defined by the effort to operate on the core of another's vulnerability in a way that will make humiliation take hold where before there was something open and vital and spontaneous. Its goal is to act on the area of another's maximum vulnerability, on that thing in their psyche more important than their life because it is what enables them to live. The project of cruelty is to produce a humiliation so complete that the other begins to die within. One thus gets to witness in another the poison that has long been working in oneself. The emotional self-mediation one sought is completed when indifference to the injury one causes proves that one can now do this

thing for no reason other than to do it again. It's the first time one puts a person on a train to Auschwitz that's hard; after that it becomes relatively easy to send millions. Indifference is the triumph of cruelty, the proof one has killed off everything in oneself that could produce a crack in the ice that encases one's heart. No ice axe can trouble one's sleep. Guilt, remorse, concern—these are no longer threats one must battle within. They're so many shards one tosses on the pile of all that one willingly consigns to the ashes. One is ripe for the final emotional self-mediation. All that's needed is time.

(4) For one has completed a process and now experiences its result. *Despair*. But not the kind we talk about when we picture a soul like Lear's writhing in the discipline of tragic self-knowledge. There is another despair—the kind that befits soul murder. It's the feeling that comes whenever a moment of nostalgia or a crying jag seizes one and one knows in the midst of it that there's nothing one can do about this despair, not even acknowledge it as such. All one can do is live it through in a *resentment* that ultimately has only oneself as its object. It too passes in the fleeting consciousness that in extinguishing everything within that makes one vulnerable one has lost everything that makes life worth living. Despair is the self-consciousness that comes only intermittently to give a cold kiss to a psyche that feeling it plunges back into the surface of its life, seeking deliverance from the inner void. The banality of evil is characterized, as Hannah Arendt argues, by the absence of depth. But this is so only as long as the psyche remains actively tied to the surface, seeking perforce new ways to extend its cruelty, like the capitalist desperately reinvesting surplus profits lest the whole thing grind to a halt. Like Eichmann one embraces the banality of the surface because it offers a way to render self-knowledge Unconscious. There's only one problem with this solution. It reveals the truth of the Unconscious. What one feels toward oneself is of necessity how one acts. What we don't know about ourselves is what we do—to the other. What Sartre terms concrete relations with others have their basis in our emotional self-reference. Whenever such relationships activate inner conflicts and disorders, the actions we take derive not from deliberative reason or conscious intentions but from emotional necessities. Choice, motive, and ethical responsibility must accordingly be located there.

But before rethinking those concepts in psychological and emotional terms I want to suggest that the process described above constitutes, metapsychologically, the way that Thanatos works within the psyche to produce the total unbinding that it requires. Unbinding is what the psyche we've described seeks: the complete *discharge* of tension through the abolition of everything that opens one up to inner pain. Unbinding is the action performed on and in oneself repeatedly. Soul murder is the process whereby the psyche severs all the bonds of sufferance that must be sustained in order to keep one's heart open to experience. In cultures dedicated to "happy talk" this is the tension that has proven too great to bear. All painful, "negative" emotions must accordingly be shunned and everything must be done to pump up those happy, tranquilizing emotions that produce a false elation. Underneath it a desperate deadening necessarily rules. Anything that causes inner pain creates panic anxiety. The inability to experience depression becomes sign of a mock progress. Through it Thanatos proceeds toward the unbinding of everything vital within the collective psyche. Once "negative" emotions have been rendered impossible the work of Thanatos is complete. The result, for all its apparent affirmative bliss, is psyches wedded to evil because the absolute discharge of tension has become the goal that is collectively pursued in policies dedicated to creating for global America a world ruled by that principle. *Evil is something a soul does to itself and as a result something it can't resist doing to others.* Death work is first and foremost a practice one lives in one's relationship to oneself. It thereby becomes perforce the relationship one projects in all one's relations with others. The cold fantasm of death's dream kingdom then becomes a prospect that no longer troubles the psyche: a world ruled by Thanatos, an order that, as we'll see, is a lot closer to attainment than we imagine.

## Choice as an existential and psychological process

A rethinking of the central concepts of ethics is implicit in the foregoing discussion. That rethinking begins moreover with what is perhaps its most provocative conclusion. Evil is what happens as a result of abrogating a psychological self-knowledge that one is able to keep repressed only through a strenuous effort. Of course one also takes care to render the whole thing unconscious. Such is the deleterious function defenses play in the maintenance of the ego. The resulting banishment of self-knowledge and the restriction of one's conscious "intentions" to those that enhance one's self-image are sustained through two subsequent operations: (1) refusal to see the harm one's actions do to others, and (2) refusal to change whenever one has a fleeting consciousness of that fact since doing so would require confronting the inner disorder of one's psyche. Flight from that prospect is the process whereby evil becomes the settled state of both one's personality and one's moral *character*. For once the defense ego has solidified its reign, all the things that Kant established as the conditions of radical and demonic evil have been fulfilled, even though that fact is barred from rising to the level of conscious awareness and intentions. One now has a *will* that is corrupted in its essence, a will so dedicated to preserving the ego, that relating to oneself in any other way than defensively has become impossible. One has attained what Arendt saw as the primary characteristic of evil—the incapacity for thought. The primary thing one can't think about, however, is oneself, for one is no longer able to access within oneself that opening of the psyche to experience from which such thought derives.

This recognition implies a primary question. What is the nature and extent of the ethical responsibility human beings have for such a condition? To what extent can evil and the actions that flow from it be said to be *chosen* in the exercise of a *freedom* for which one bears ethical responsibility? Traditionally ethical responsibility only applies to *actions* that are taken after *deliberation* and with full knowledge of the consequences: actions where choice is a function of our ability to reason; where the moral law is known; and where one chooses to violate it for *motives* that can be specified as functions of a *self-interest* that overrides all other motives and considerations. Mitigate any of these factors and one mitigates ethical responsibility. Ethical responsibility is compromised or eliminated, for example, if one's action is determined by forces outside one's control: if one acts without premeditation, under duress, in blind obedience to customs or authorities, as the result of a pathology, because of some limitation in the ability to think or to understand the consequences of one's action, or because one acted without any conscious intention to do wrong. However deplorable their deeds the mad, for example, are not evil. Evil requires consciousness, choice, freedom. If evil is to be a human possibility on a par with the possibility of goodness it must be something that is determined within the order of freedom.

The trouble with the traditional understanding of these conditions, however, is the effort to confine them within the limits of rationalism and a purely cognitive model of the mind. Rationality is noble but single-minded devotion to it leaves the true life of the psyche undetected. Focusing on it prematurely shifts discussion to a rarefied mode of mentation that is then cut off from the rest of the personality. To sustain and deny that split reason is then given disproportionate weight in determining what we are and do. But the dream of reason is precisely that. A dream: a desire—to bring one's being into correspondence with reason and thereby eliminate everything else, especially in determining the questions of ethics. No one brought this dream to bear on moral experience more rigorously than Immanuel Kant. That effort is the sublime beauty of his thought. But experiencing oneself in terms of *a priori* rationality comes at a terrible cost. Life becomes a process in which we sleepwalk our way through most of what we do because we've cut ourselves off from the actual bases of our actions. Our psyche becomes a stranger to us. We fixate on giving rational accounts of ourselves and in the process alienate ourselves from everything else. Emotions become irrationalities, breaks with reason, things we must overcome; or, worse, things we can only acknowledge when they are good, proper, and in tune with reason. The rest of our being becomes brute inclinations, frailties of our nature, desires that disrupt an otherwise rational identity. As a result, in terms of ethics, whether we know it or not, under the guise of reason we've made an offer that most human beings cannot refuse. Claiming not to consciously intend what one does has become the grand excuse. Traditional definitions of the three cardinal categories of ethics are a monument to that motive. Restricting *intention*, *motive*, and *choice* to the canons of rationality fashions them to the designs of human mendacity. For if by *intention* we mean a deliberate rational choice with full knowledge of the consequences, evil, as I've described it, is not chosen. If along the same lines we restrict *motive* to purposes for which we bear responsibility because they issue not from frailties of our nature or the force of circumstances but from an explicit knowledge of what one is doing and why, evil, as thus far described, does not exist within the order of human motivation. One can identify self-interest, careerism, and happiness as motives, but to say that many agents act in order to advance Thanatos is hard to fathom. Unless, that is, we expand the category of motive to include purposes that derive from the psyche in all its inherent conflictedness. But once posit such a possibility, *choice* becomes a concept that must be rethought in a radically new way.

My goal is to show that our primary ethical responsibility is not just for what we consciously intend but for who we are. That is, for our *character* as the end result of a process of psychological self-determination. The previous discussion described choice as a concrete process of emotional self-mediation. Choice so understood is not restricted to rational deliberation or conscious intentions but reaches down into the very quick of what makes us subjects. Such a view of choice is the most radical reach of my argument because it situates ethical responsibility at a deeper register of our being than one finds in other ethical theories. The choice that matters—that determines all others—is the choice one makes in determining one's emotional and psychological self-reference; i.e., the *decision* to feel one way rather than another when faced with those conflicts that activate an *anxiety* in which the psyche feels its very being at risk. All choices derive from the choice one makes in and about that situation and constitute dialectical moments in its progression. As emotional self-mediation, choice is a process that develops through crisis experiences that are only lived through by finding a way to feel which thereby becomes a *determination* of one's being. *How* one feels becomes *who* one is—until the next crisis produces the need for the next self-mediation. Such is the emotional life of the psyche. The operations one performs on oneself in the crucible of conflict constitute the drama that makes us human. Each time the conflicts central to our being weigh on us we either take the next step in a deadening process or undertake the struggle to reverse the whole thing. Genuine change requires no less. This is the justice of living. We choose how we'll feel and the outcome is *character* as that way of feeling toward oneself that informs the way one acts toward others. Our emotional self-reference is what we'd know about ourselves if we ever got around to experiencing self-knowledge in a way that burns.

In terms of choice, the cardinal concept of ethics, my effort is to uncover and sustain that register of experience where the most concrete choices are made, those whereby the heart gives itself determination. An adequate concept of choice requires comprehending *how* the psyche chooses and the *continuum* of the process of self-mediation through which it determines itself. The descriptions provided earlier describe such a dialectic in terms of the purest structural sequence. Phenomenologically, however, choices—and especially the most horrifying choices—almost always find the human being *in media res*. Consider, for example, a man who has become far crueler in his being than he realizes but who because he wants it is still able to fall in love. And so one day he finds that he loves someone. But then soon he experiences in anxiety the conflicts that love reactivates in him and all he would have to change within in order to let this new motive bloom. The burden proves too great. He abridges the process that had begun to open within him. It is a common tale. It is also an example of how the imperceptible history of its *choices* first becomes evident to a human being. We do things to and within ourselves without knowing the consequences. And then we find ourselves in a situation that presents the bill. The determination we've given our heart assaults us. We find ourselves in a situation that requires a reversal within. In fact, we desire it. If we could it is what we would *choose*. But then the effort proves too great because it runs up against all that we'd have to *change* in ourselves in order to bring it about. And so we *choose* to remain who we are.

This choice *retroactively* reveals an entire series of prior *choices* that seldom, if ever, entered our conscious minds or submitted themselves to rational deliberation. In the anguish of losing again what one lost without realizing it, however, one experiences concretely the knowledge that the person one is derives from the history of *choices* that pass fleetly in review, raised for the first time to the level of a self-consciousness. One sees, for example, that all the early *choices* one made to protect oneself from inner pain and the subsequent acts one took to empower those choices have resulted in the need to kill off anything that opens one's heart. One's entire life passes as in a dumb show before saddened eyes awakened finally to the Nietzschean recognition that "memory is what hurts." In the pain of it one's entire life is briefly present in its unity. And one sees it in the right way—feelingly, with the ways one has determined oneself to feel recoiling in rage against the new way of feeling that would shatter one's "identity." The heart is in conflict with itself again, however briefly, experiencing in pain the choices that have brought it to this situation and then, by shrinking within itself again, choosing them for the first time in a sense, retroactively becoming who one is by choosing to persist in a process that thereby creeps on toward a final solution. For the man who turns away from love, for example, is not the same man he was before. Refusing one kind of change advances another. Through *repetition*, all that one was without knowing it, one becomes in a new way. Deadlier. Each time we find ourselves in a situation that puts us in conflict with ourselves we enact of necessity a complete emotional self-mediation. Such is what happens deep in the psyche of the man who refused the possibility that called to him. He has begun to live a despair, and that emotion now starts to move him to another kind of *choice*. It comes when nothing can any longer open in his heart and he feels in that absence the presence of something else. A cold indifference. The inability to care, aided and abetted by the cruelty he must now project not only toward others but *toward himself.* What he may have suffered when another kind of choice (and with it hope for him) was possible is no longer. He has completed the *choice* that weds him to an antithetical way of being. Inner deadening is now his occupation. And because that is so the only *choice* now possible for him is to spread the contagion. He has become one with Adolf Eichmann and enjoys full membership in that brotherhood. Those who claim they did not choose such an inner condition avail themselves of the last measure of their bad faith. All miserable people say it: "I didn't choose to be this way." That is their greatest lie. (The italicized words in the last two paragraphs indicate the range of meanings *choice* has in the framework we are constructing.)

Choice as an act of the psyche is the process of repeating a way of feeling until it becomes a habit of being. To get from the one to the other involves a number of distinct ways of choosing. We've emphasized three here: *the initial choice* that doesn't seem like a choice until one discovers the full force of its determinations when in the *second kind of choice* one refuses the burden of its reversal thereby moving toward that *third kind of choice* in which one completes the process that has been at work in one's psyche from the beginning. These three pivotal moments in choosing involve a number of other choices one makes along the way, all entailing different levels of self-consciousness. But on a deeper level all modes of choice are deliberate acts: the acts through which a *psyche* burdened with itself *chooses* to sustain that burden or to perform upon itself the action that delivers one from it. This decision is the one whereby we *freely determine* ourselves in depth because its issue is the emotional self-mediation that forms our self-reference; i.e., the submission of all choices to that choice that can't be escaped.

To underscore the most important point. People often mitigate or deny responsibility for their actions by claiming they were just following beliefs and practices they were indoctrinated to perform. This is the plea for excuses, for example, of a woman who, following custom, has a clitoridectomy performed on her daughter in order to safeguard the family honor from the shame of possible promiscuity; or the claim of the good German or American who heeds the call of the nation as superego because he's been so indoctrinated in jingoistic flag-waving that "my country right or wrong" is in him an imperative that washes away all other considerations. An understanding of the psyche deprives such positions of their supports because it places us squarely before the origin of the choice that defines us. Those who remain open to suffering preserve in themselves that principle that will always question the given and when necessary rebel. Those who close down to escape inner pain will always go the other way, kidding themselves they're just following what they were taught to believe, while studiously disavowing the pleasures they derive from doing what comes naturally. Rebellion and conformity are choices prepared by the earliest movements of the psyche toward or away from its inmost possibility. Anton Schmidt, a German soldier who sacrificed his life trying to save Jews from the death camps is an exception, but that fact does not absolve any of us of the ethical responsibility to act as he did.[9]

That order of responsibility points to a concept of evil fitted to the reality of the psyche and indeed appropriate as the only adequate term to designate the actions through which some subjects systematically eradicate their humanity. *Evil* as a psychological process is the perfecting of an emotional self-mediation. Hannah Arendt argues that evil in its banality has no psychological depth, no monstrous or demonic cause, which is why, she argues, Shakespeare could not write a drama representing it because "his instinctive aesthetic sense would lead to falsification of it."[10] But contra Arendt, whose thought here is limited by her life-long resistance to psychoanalysis, this does not mean that evil lacks a psyche nor that an in-depth account of the inner processes whereby it comes to be cannot be given. Such an account is needed, moreover, lest we think with Dubya and the Christian right that evil is something we can put outside ourselves as if the very effort to do so were not one of the primary signs of its working within.

Thus far I have of course only accounted for the most ordinary forms of human cruelty: the household terrorist, the professor who gets his kicks out of wounding students, the playground bully who knows he's a coward. Another account is needed if we are to attain a philosophic understanding of that evil which is a matter of reasoning and conscious intentions. Such an account must begin where Kant left off in his great mediation on evil, which has been the basis of all subsequent philosophic efforts to fix that concept. When, shortly, I renew Kant's effort to establish *the rational conditions of evil* I will try to provide what Kant could not for the same reason that limits Arendt, the need to ignore or distance himself from the psyche. As we'll see, it is in the psyche that we will also discover the source of that evil that preoccupied Kant, an evil which is radical or demonic whereas the one we've discussed thusfar is merely human all too human.

But first an example that is betwixt and between the two and which, as we'll learn, thereby reveals the thing that unites them, consider this. (The following is an imaginative reconstruction of a moment in Primo Levi's *Survival in Auschwitz*.)

*Snow is falling gently on the living and the dead. In Auschwitz. It is the kind of night when it is rich to watch a wood fill up with snow or, a child again, to reach out one's cupped hand to catch snow one raises to one's lips like the tip of a vanilla ice cream cone. Icicles form at the windows, catching in a dancing pageant of colors the life within each building. Primo Levi opens a window, breaks off an icicle and raises it to his lips. Before he can complete that act a guard snatches it away. "That is forbidden." "Why?" asks Levi, a question that preserves the innocence of the child in the mind of the man. The men's eyes meet, two alone in a moment charged with recognition. The guard holds the pause so that the full force of what he says will sink in. "There is no why here."[11] Formulating that principle is the fulfillment of his duty. The absence of why is the new why. It is what the camps must produce, in a thousand incidentals, in order to realize the project of dehumanization. Something is more important than mass murder. Something that must precede it. Every thread of meaning that bound the inmates to life must be destroyed. They must be reduced within their souls to the condition of death-in-life. That is the rationale that informs every action taken in Auschwitz, a logic that must be worked out in all its ramifications, however minute. Only then can the victim be disposed of, thrown on the pile of refuse. When the project is soul murder extinction must always be after the fact.*

What's most striking in this scene is the guard's *intuitive* awareness of this logic, his ability to give it metaphysical articulation. We can presume him an ordinary fellow, a minor functionary and thus probably not a man who reflects deeply on his choices or intentions. Here, however, he performs an act of intelligence deeper than the one Styron posits as the act of "genius" that delivered Sophie over to an impossible choice. "There is no *why* here," an absence lived intuitively by the guard as an imperative that must be applied comprehensively, down to the most childlike gestures and desires. Unlike Eichmann the guard is not banal in his evil. He lives it in an awareness that is immediate. He knows the horror his statement will bring once it begins to work in Levi's consciousness as another support of his humanity collapses. That's the reason for the statement. Its why. To force the other to experience the canceling of the human *why?* by the inhuman *why not?* Unlike Eichmann, Tibbets and those who create the legal precedents for places like Abu Ghraib and Guantanamo Bay so that others will realize their intentions, this guard makes no effort to hide the overarching intention. He revels in it. And as a result he receives the full measure of a pleasure that bureaucrats can only see dimly reflected back to them from the spotless glass surfaces of their desks or only express gleefully like Dubya in an unguarded moment. It's the pleasure of going beyond any conceivable limits to the exercise of one's cruelty by turning that cruelty into a morbid joke, a witty phrase, the arbitrary announcing itself in the smug certainty of its power to dehumanize. It's the pleasure of Thanatos proclaiming that it has broken free of everything save the *unbinding* of all that connects one to the human. The guard in Auschwitz has not thought through any of this. He doesn't have to. He knows it intuitively, knows all that a vast chain of philosophic reasoning would be required to articulate. And knowing it he chooses it in an expression metaphysically *adequate* to that choice. "There is no why here"—an idea as adequate as anything one finds in Spinoza. In that articulation the guard reveals how little we understand of the operations of *intentionality* when we confine it to deliberative reason and conscious choices. The psyche lives choice in a far more concrete way. It knows and chooses in ways that make mind in its rationality but a pale afterthought that seldom catches up with desire, which is where the action is and the essential choices made, often in the profoundest intuitive self-consciousness of all that those choices involve. "There is no why here."

### The ethics of psychoanalysis

Two texts are central to contemporary philosophic discussions of evil: Kant's *Religion Within the Limits of Reason Alone* and Arendt's *Eichmann in Jerusalem*. My attempt here is to provide the psychoanalytic complement to these works, both of which are studious in their avoidance of the psyche. Kant and Arendt together illustrate the limits of what we can know about evil as long as ethics remains within the paradigm of rationality and intentionality. What their perspective blinds them to, ironically, is the extent to which their work is already psychoanalytic without knowing it and requires the addition of the psychoanalytic dimension to sustain and extend it. Crucial to this stage of the inquiry will be the work of three creative writers—Shakespeare, Dostoyevsky, and Nabokov—who in studying evil reveal the independent cognitive power of Literature to offer us an original mode of access to experience that comprehends places in the mind that Philosophy rarely reaches. Even more important to the inquiry is the still unrecognized revolution that Sigmund Freud offers ethics, especially with respect to the problem of evil. The common view of psychoanalysis is of a determinism which eliminates (or severely limits) moral responsibility. Actually, the opposite is the case: psychoanalysis redefines and maximizes ethical responsibility by revealing that place in the subject from which all our choices derive. Freud thereby offers the possibility of transforming not only our ethical self-knowledge but, more importantly, the relationship we live to ourselves as ethical beings. What else would one expect of one who dared to say that we are *responsible* for our dreams? What Freud meant by that striking proposition is that we are responsible for what our dreams *reveal* as well as for the totally new understanding that *The Interpretation of Dreams* reveals of what it means to be a subject. Freud is (arguably) the most radical figure in the history of thought because he transforms our understanding of thought itself by grounding reason, consciousness, and intentionality in a more primary reality: psyche as conflict and desire relating to itself in *agons* charged with the ineradicable force of tragic emotions. In inaugurating that "Copernican" revolution in our self-understanding Freud did not, I hasten to add, fully develop the ethical implications of his discoveries. Especially with respect to the problem of evil. That is one of the many tasks he bequeathed to us.

Freud discovered more than the Unconscious. He discovered our responsibility for it; for becoming aware of how what we repress rules our life and therefore our *duty* to gain knowledge of our unconscious as the precondition for becoming an ethically responsible agent. In terms of ethics there's a quick way to summarize the significance of the Unconscious. *What we don't know about ourselves is what we do—to the other.* In calling us to such a reflection on ourselves Freud also taught us a new way to reflect, one that forces us to move beyond the rational world of conscious deliberations and intentions. Once make the psychoanalytic turn and the sources of self-knowledge increase exponentially. Every time one understands a dream, a paraphraxis, an aesthetic experience, a fantasy, one suffers in principle a revolution in one's life. For such experiences put one in touch with the deep conflicts that define the psyche. A dream, for example, does not tell us about something outside the realm of our conscious grasp, though this view of repression typifies how a convenient misunderstanding blunts the force of psychoanalysis. A good dream reveals the desires and conflicts structuring our life. It thereby opens our quotidian life to an in-depth exploration. Listen to a dream rightly and one finds that one must confront something one has been avoiding—or doing. Such is what it would mean to assume responsibility for one's dreams. One would start to live *from* an awareness of one's psyche rather than *in* a continued attempt to escape that awareness.

Freud doesn't abolish *intention*, he expands it by showing how often consciousness is defense mechanism and rationality the cover that conceals the actual motives on which we act; and how often accordingly insistence on conscious intentions is the lie we cling to in order to deny our responsibility. The seductive or prohibitive way of relating that a parent adopts toward a child, for example, may carry as its primary repressed intention the desire to wound that child in their sexuality. This is why it's so necessary at a later point in time for such parents to deny that they ever harbored let alone acted on such an intention. And yet our actions do indeed speak louder than words in conveying our actual intentions. Action is concrete intentionality because it is through it that we live out our feelings, desires, and conflicts. And they are what the other invariably receives, as a message that is often sharply different from what we say, especially when through the exercise of *intentionality* we reassure ourselves about what good, loving human beings we are. The psyche is a lonely hunter, avid in the pursuit of purposes it carefully conceals from itself. The ethical greatness of Sigmund Freud is the crisis he introduced into that practice. Rather than getting us off the hook, psychoanalysis sticks it far deeper in us than any previous ethic. Intentionality is convenient because it absolves us of the greatest responsibility—responsibility for *who* we are. Everything stays in the safely guarded space of deliberative, discursive, quasi-judicial rationality as if this were the primary way we relate to ourselves or, to turn the screw a peg further, as if when we aren't relating to ourselves this way we aren't fully moral agents fully responsible for our actions. But once let responsibility expand into the inner life of the psyche and we take on a new ethical burden: to know oneself in depth and not recoil in horror from what one learns or persist in virtuous denial of the hidden motives one must confront in order to become responsible for one's psyche. Indeed, deliberation is itself transformed by the psychoanalytic turn. Freud shows that to deliberate correctly one must focus the inquiry on those motives that one tries to conceal from oneself, since they are where the truth of one's conduct may lie.

In terms of the problem of evil this line of thought has an obvious implication. Our primary responsibility, which we continually shirk, is to find the evil in ourselves. Theoretically and emotionally the same thing prevents that discovery: the desire to uphold the idea that human nature is inherently or basically good, with evil an aberration, a fall, a break with the natural order of things, an exception to the rule of human decency. Psychoanalysis, like history, renders such sentiments questionable at best. And irrelevant to where inquiry must begin—with psychological conflict, the primary fact that defines us. To be human is to live defined by wounds and disorders that are prior to the mediations (themselves rare) that result in a moral character that can be termed good. Goodness is not something essentialistically guaranteed in a nature; it's an achievement that comes through the overcoming of ways of being that have a foothold in us long before some human beings take up the effort to reverse them.

Psychoanalysis from this point of view is neither pessimistic nor relativistic. It is humanistic in the deepest way, seeing the human as an achievement and valuing it by demonstrating what that achievement requires. Psychoanalysis doesn't point to ethical relativism. It points instead to an *order of rank* among human beings based on the degree to which a knowledge of one's psyche has become the basis of one's actions. Ethically, to know one's psyche is of necessity to engage in an effort to transform it, since inner change is the only way to halt the projection of what otherwise does harm to others. Psychological change is the primary task; ethics the result.

When speaking of evil the honest course is always to begin at home. Or to see how invoking evil for purposes of othering, as Dubya does on every possible occasion, is one of the defining gestures of ideology. Evil thereby becomes the catch-all for all that Dubya wants us to hate while demanding that analysis go no further than the mystical force of that term. As such the term evil functions as a floating signifier that circulates to designate by implication, coyly, and without naming them directly, Islam, Islamic fundamentalism and any other enemy, foreign or domestic, that Dubya targets as evil for failing to support the vision that he and his cohorts would impose upon the world. The term evil renders the other perfidious and unintelligible—as in Dubya's all-purpose explanation for 9-11 and everything since: "they hate us for our freedom." Invoking the term thus enables one to wrap one's cause, and whatever horrors are perpetrated in its name, in the mantle of goodness. Dubya and his henchmen are not alone in this. It's an old and common tale. Evil in its general use is, as Alain Badiou argues, an ideological ploy commonly used to prohibit the close, historical analysis of a situation.[12] But if for that reason we follow the convenient conclusion of Frederic Jameson and reduce ethics to ideology, we sacrifice what may turn out to be the most important category for defining our historical situation; a category we need to recoup not only so that Dubya, Falwell, and others can't continue to use it to prevent the understanding of things Americans know far too little about (Islam, the history of the Middle East, the difference between Sunni and Shia Muslims) but so that we can unlock its power to lay bare a condition at the heart of the heartland.

## RADICAL EVIL

### What Kant didn't know

Is there an evil that is self-conscious, reasoned, chosen, deriving from an act of will that is equivalent in its realm to the position that Kant accords to the good will in the order of the ethical? This is the question Kant takes up in *Religion Within the Limits of Reason Alone*. In the course of that discussion he distinguishes four types and levels of evil: (1) one does bad because of a frailty of human nature, as when pathological forces take over; (2) one does bad due to an impurity of the will, as when one does the right thing for the wrong reason; (3) radical evil: one chooses to do wrong out of self-love; (4) diabolical evil: one chooses to do wrong against one's own self-love and self-interest. (For purposes that will emerge I combine the last two forms and use the term radical evil throughout to avoid the misleading, theological connotations of the term demonic. The important thing is what numbers 3 and 4 share—the calculated desire to violate the moral law.)

My effort is to rethink Kant's concepts from a psychodynamic perspective. This effort will, I hope, deepen Kant's seminal discussion by locating ethical responsibility precisely where it lies. Radical evil is that evil for which one would claim a total responsibility as cause, with that causality the result of a fully self-conscious process. One thereby chooses what no less a philosopher than Aquinas argued was impossible: one chooses evil not out of a mistaken understanding of what is good for one nor as the function of base inclinations and instincts, but for the sake of evil, to make evil the principle of one's conduct and follow that principle through to the end of the line. "Evil be thou my good," as Milton's Satan puts it in *Paradise Lost*. To attain radical evil this choice must become a necessity that exercises the brain to attain a systematic understanding of evil's *a priori* requirements—and a plan for how to fulfill them. Evil must become a self-consciousness raised to the level of a principle of reasoning. Only thereby can one attain a *will* that is corrupt at its roots, a will that is in its realm equivalent to what for Kant the positively good will is in the ethical order.

A methodological caveat. One could question the usefulness of such a discussion since, presumptively, evil of this order, if possible, only exists in the rarest of cases. Let me suggest, however, another way to consider what follows. Perhaps the evil conceptualized here is not fundamentally different from the evil described in the first section of this chapter, but different only in degree. Perhaps radical evil is the need that itches in the psyche of all evil agents, as it did intuitively in a guard in Auschwitz and in so many of us had we the will to know it. But then we'd know that the petty devils and the great are finally the same, the only difference being that the latter raise the shared project to the level of an explicit self-consciousness. That is, they allow themselves to know what the others claim not to know. Those who are radically evil allow themselves no hiding places, make no attempt to deny what they are or to dissimulate by claiming they don't intend what they do. Unlike those wedded to ordinary evil, they have put themselves beyond bad faith. In this there is a terrible honesty about the heart of their darkness. It is almost as if they were the *conscience* of all the lesser devils and expose the excuses and arguments that such use to mitigate responsibility for oneself and one's actions. What follows will thus reveal the first section of this chapter in a new and darker light. For within the order of evil the only difference is, finally, that between a consciousness refusing knowledge of the principles upon which it acts and one that brings those principles into the light of day—all the better to act upon them.

Three literary examples offer us the possibility of experiencing radical evil in its horrible purity. Such is one function of Literature, to represent possibilities that exceed the limits of philosophic conceptualization.

Iago already knows everything the moralists will say about him. Cassio "hath a daily beauty in his life/That makes me ugly." That quality in Cassio, the decency of Desdemona, the nobility of Othello is all Iago needs to activate his will. He knows far better than we that envy is his motive, and that living in fealty to it requires doing evil for the sake of evil. He also knows that satisfying the demands of evil requires exploiting the goodness of others to create a *plot* in which that very goodness is the thing that brings about general destruction. Thereby envy proves itself the author of a perfect action. "So will I turn her virtue into pitch/ And out of her own goodness make the net/ That shall enmesh them all." Goodness, that's what activates one's venom. "The Moor is of a free and open nature/That thinks men honest that but seem to be so." Othello's good qualities must therefore be what brings about his undoing. And only one method is adequate to that project. One must insinuate oneself into what is trusting in the other's psyche and plant there the seeds that will bring about their undoing. Thereby Iago proves himself the master psychologist who knows the true motives and passions that drive people: jealousy, lust, rage, and that vindictive cruelty that so unmans Othello that he becomes nothing but Iago's double. For what Iago relishes in torturing Othello, Othello repeats with Desdemona before making a grandiose effort to lie to himself about his motives. Iago knows better. His intense pleasure at the end of the play is the knowledge that he's gotten inside all of them, destroyed their beliefs, and set them on the rack not only of trying to comprehend his evil but what it's revealed about all of them. He thus attains an incomparable pleasure: the self-consciousness that one has taken envy, the emotion that defines one's being, and realized it fully in a project equal to its demands. Envy here is no longer petty, eaten up by itself and the countless little cruelties it daily requires. It is pure, refined, reified in the confidence that it knows the truth that everyone else tries to deny.

"The motive-hunting of motiveless malignity." Thus Coleridge on Iago's soliloquies as self-revelation. It is the closest criticism has come to understanding Iago and yet the truth of the matter is the exact opposite. Iago knows precisely why he does what he does. The soliloquies stage that knowledge as a game Iago plays to gull the audience and thereby do to them the same thing he does to the characters in the play. Through extended asides addressed to the audience Iago spins the web to enmesh his interpreters so that he will get the last laugh at their stupidity. He invents causes and motives not in order to come finally to a knowledge of himself—he knows full well what he is—but to play with the audience like those serial killers who need to prove themselves smarter than all the stupid detectives who think they can understand them. Iago loves to put the audience on the track of his psyche then mock the ease with which they've clutched at a false lead. Maybe he's acting out of revenge because he was overlooked for a deserved promotion. Maybe there are grounds for his apparent (and preposterous) belief that Othello slept with his wife. Maybe, like Roderigo, he is another of Desdemona's jealous and disappointed suitors, a lover driven by love's madness to desperate acts. Or maybe we can conjure up something more exotic that he's failed to mention. Perhaps Othello is his homoerotic love object; making Othello think he's a cuckold is the only way Iago can possess him sexually. Etc. Or maybe sensing the inadequacy of any and all explanations we all throw up our hands and return to Coleridge, though now as a way to avoid an issue that has begun to eat on us. Whatever we do, Iago wins because he's exposed the limits of our understanding and left us haunted by the specter of something terribly awry in the human psyche that we desperately need to understand but cannot because we fear to confront the place in the psyche from which it derives. Iago knows we'll always seek some secondary, peripheral explanation in order to displace the understanding that would open us to the heart of our own darkness. For envy as overweening motive is far too close to us. And thus, in his silence at the end, one suspects Iago's pleasure is intense. Everyone demands an explanation, some way to accommodate his act to a more comforting view of human nature and thereby achieve some kind of catharsis. Iago's pleasure is his knowledge that it won't work; that he'll continue to be a nightmare pressure on our brains. At the beginning of *The Silence of the Lambs* Jack Crawford in sending Clarice Starling to interview Hannibal Lector leaves her with a warning. "Don't let Hannibal Lector inside your head." Iago issues the same warning then through his soliloquies turns it into an offer we can't refuse: the chance to get inside an evil consciousness and pin down its motives. Our confidence in our interpretive frameworks and the beliefs about human nature that inform them is the object that Iago delightfully deconstructs throughout the play. It is in our failure, especially when we think we understand, that Iago laughs loudest in the knowledge that his project has followed a Cartesian logic of clear and distinct ideas.

Thus: an envious person hates the other because of the qualities that the other possesses. One's inner condition, however, is something one can't or won't change. One is therefore prevented from desiring what the other has or is. One must, instead, raise desire to a new form. The desire to destroy. Psychological cruelty then emerges as the only method adequate to the project. Simple destruction is external negation. The thing one destroys retains the qualities that define it. Psychological cruelty, however, undermines it from within. That is the requirement that must be fulfilled. One must get at the very source of the other's spontaneity, the vital source of their moral character (Desdemona's ability to love, Othello's honor, Cassio's trust) and plant the poison there. For only then does one truly destroy the quality one envies by destroying its spring in the other's psyche. Such is the methodological purity to which Iago raises envy; and such, in effect, is the soliloquy he'd share with us were he to let us in on the secret of his motives. In Iago envy rises to the level of a self-consciousness that attains radical evil.

Nikolai Stavrogin pursues the self-consciousness of an even darker motive, which he plays out in what is finally a vicious parody of "confession" and the beliefs about human nature on which confession depends. In the suppressed chapter of Dostoyevsky's *The Possessed* titled "At Tikhon's: Stavrogin's Confession" Stavrogin offers perhaps the most explicit account of evil in Literature. With scrupulous accuracy he tells the priest Tikhon exactly what he did and why. Unlike Iago his crime began not in some deep seated emotional ulcer but in the *boredom* of a man leading a life dedicated to dissolute pleasure. Only one day, and ironically out of that boredom, he notices the signs of psychological complexity in a young girl, Matroysa, the 13-year-old daughter in the family where he boards. When punished, unjustly, for suspicion of stealing Stavrogin's penknife Matroysa looks in her innocence directly into the faces first of her parents and then of Stavrogin. All are aware she is innocent. And she knows they know. This knowledge eats on Stavrogin. When he finds the penknife he makes no effort to exonerate her. Studying her character provides the irresistible opportunity to savor the damage that injustice effects in a soul. And so after a time, though only to study its effect, Stavrogin makes a half-hearted effort to comfort her. That effort tears open the depth of her need, her pain, and the unmistakable sexuality of its expression. Stavrogin exploits the situation to seduce her, not for pleasure but for something else: to study the results of this new action in her soul. Her self-torment fascinates him, especially since he knows that what drives it is the fact that she knows he is watching. She once possessed the power of the look. He has it now and looks on fascinated as her personality unravels and he anticipates the act that she will be driven to. Intervening to stop it is impossible. He has to see it, to watch from the next room as she goes to her suicide by hanging. For what he's waited for, the object of his deepest fascination, is the look she gives him right before she does it. There's where the source of real evil lies and he knows it. Stavrogin's desire is to see the power he has had to destroy another person's soul as it is written on her face right before the end. His story thus reveals a series of choices, each more terrifying than the one before, and each made in full awareness.

The confession of the crime, however, is even more terrifying. For Stavrogin tells this tale not out of remorse, to expiate through punishment, or in the desire for forgiveness. These are but lures to catch the conscience of the confessor—and the reader, who Dostoyevsky places in a position analogous to that of Iago's audience. Stavrogin confesses the most horrible act—destroying another person in their soul simply to prove to oneself that one can do so—but only in order to attain an even greater horror. That horror comes from the recognition that Stavrogin's act had no motive but meaninglessness; so that looking back on it all Stavrogin can say is "what for?" No deep motive drove him to this act nor did its aftermath initiate some complex (and thus potentially redemptive) struggle to plumb the depths of his disorder. Evil for Stavrogin is simply irresistible. And thus unfathomable. To the question "what for?" he gives the answer "why not?" Psychological cruelty for him cancels all explanations of evil in the purest nihilism. There is no reason to do anything. And no reason not to. Action can be no more that a calculus of ways to relieve one's boredom in order to give oneself the momentary feeling that one exists and the only way to do so is by devising new cruelties that go beyond previous cruelties until one achieves the worst. Stavrogin is a "sensualist" of his own depravity, always seeking a new, heightened experience of a fixed inner condition. Inevitably other emotions, many of a broadly humanistic character, will arise during and after one's actions: pity, empathy, regret, even love. That's the challenge of evil: to coldly pass them by as nostalgias exposed by their failure to strike any genuine chord within. Stavrogin has a single need, in which he triumphs: to prove to himself that all claims from the other are dead in him. "Confession" for him is thus the last step needed to complete that process; an empty ritual subjects play to conjure up feelings of remorse and the need for forgiveness in order to delay and deny their despair. In parodying that act Stavrogin's target is thus the belief that the deepest need of a despairing soul is for a compassionate understanding of its torment. The real kick thus comes from Tikhon's response, which is perhaps a model of ours. Christian charity in its worst form. Motivism. The assumption that there must be a deep and authentic suffering behind evil actions and that those who do evil thus remain human in their need for forgiveness and redemption.

Tikhon is not without profound insights into Stavrogin's condition. He knows, for example, that Stavrogin is already contemplating a new crime, one that will be even worse. But Tikhon's predictable invocation of traditional Christian redemptive "platitudes" makes him the final object of Stavrogin's scorn. Religion here proves itself inadequate to the phenomenon of evil. For Stavrogin, like Iago, is driven by a necessity far deeper than any desire for redemption. To know one's evil in the full bitterness of it; to know it for what it is, without remorse; to love it coldly for what it is; to know it and to love it and then to put it away as indifferently as the piece of lint one flicks off one's coat. In Stavrogin evil has, as in Iago, moved to a pure self-consciousness and the correspondence of one's being with that knowledge. This is no mean despair with all its noisy self-pity. This is the real thing—pure, refined, articulate, and certain of itself in a logic it has taken to the end of the line.

A similar purity informs the inwardness of a final example. Another confession, but one that aestheticizes what in Stavrogin's hands remains within the orbit of the morality it would mock; and one that through confession gulls an even larger audience than the ones Iago and Stavrogin worked on. *Lolita* is a masterful exercise in the lengths to which an evil psyche will go to lie to itself in full consciousness that it's doing so; and the delight it will take in implicating us in the process. For all his skill in trying to convince the reader to the contrary, the corruption of innocence is precisely what fires Humbert Humbert's heart. He speaks as if Lolita's sexual precocity is exculpatory and goes to great lengths trying to convince us that it was she who seduced him. Yet he knows (as we do?) that the sexuality of the child is a given and, as such, not a justification of adult desire but the circumstance that holds it in check. Or inflames it—in those who see the child's trust as the opportunity, by inflicting a traumatic wound, to gain lasting power over a tormented psyche. That is the true crime of those who sexually abuse the young. When Humbert tells us that he heard Lolita sobbing every night the moment he "feigned sleep" he gives us the key to his despair—and his game. For he is unable to hear that cry except as another chance to savor his perversity. He listens and remains powerless to stop himself. Two years back and forth across the country on a journey dedicated not to his lust but to what is, finally, an experiment in despair: its *aestheticization* through devising new ways to corrupt her so that he can decant his deed through a feast of language in an attempt to confer transcendence on what he knows is a sordid process. Turning everything into an aesthetic phenomenon—that is perhaps the innermost project of evil. For then the refinement of one's sensibility in its solipsism becomes the only reality. Experience is stripped of all qualities save those that enable the aesthetic sensibility to express itself as an end in itself. To aestheticize the most recalcitrant subject becomes the irresistible challenge. What better subject than the sexual abuse of a child?

The greatest delight of such a sensibility, however, is to draw us into the net so that we experience a pleasure we must perforce then disavow. Perhaps that's the inherent and resolutely anti-Platonic pleasure of reading: to let all other considerations recede before the power of language to seduce us, mocking the moralism from which we will later rail in reaction against it. The pleasure of the text, of reading *Lolita*, is the simultaneous experience of the inadequacy of both moralism and aestheticism to the immanent process of Humbert's confession. For this confession enacts a condemnation more extreme than that of the most severe moralist through the pursuit of an aestheticism that knows its superiority to all other frameworks of explanation. That superiority lies, however, not in the pleasure that aestheticization gives, but in the awareness that despair informs that pleasure. Such is Humbert's success in playing a game with us that he alone perhaps comprehends two things: that the saddest thing is not just the absence of her voice among the children he hears at play toward the end of the book, but that he is not taken in by the incomparable beauty of the words he uses to evoke that scene, knowing that evocation changes nothing. It is but another performance, another exercise in the aestheticization of experience. That is "the consolation of articulate art." Humbert knows that his book is nothing but a catalogue of the language games that can be devised to disguise and displace, to dignify and decant despair not in order to be delivered from it but in order to be delivered into it. Such a language delights and annihilates itself in one and the same act. It seduces the reader while laughing at the reader for being seduced; outrages the moralist while showing contempt for the moralist's flight from experience. Above all, it is a language that has contempt for itself and finds in that contempt a way to "deconstruct" its own irony. *Lolita* is the end of irony, its most eloquent self-deconstruction; the knowledge that one is in a trap without wanting or being able to extricate oneself from that trap. The trap, as Wittgenstein would be quick to point out, is the belief in a "private language," one equal in its beauty to Santayana's solipsism of the moment. *Lolita* is not only a monument to that belief; it also demonstrates how readily the most private language can be shared by others seduced by the lotus of Nabokov's language to forget everything and lose the desire to ever stop reading. "My victory is verbal." A favorite statement of one who always went beyond it—Jean-Paul Sartre. Championship in that contest goes to Humbert whose language is so enchanting it half convinces him that he loved Lolita and loves her still in a love that endures, as in a kingdom by the sea, wholly cut off from the deeds that would give it the lie.

Yet no sooner does he say it than he knows and embraces the truth. That everything is a ploy—aestheticization *and* repentance; writing, a ploy to lure the audience into participating in the game without knowing that they are being played by it, played by an author who remains supremely indifferent, "pairing his fingernails," laughing a transcendent laugh at the limited sensibilities of those who toil in the net in which it has enmeshed them, a net far wider in its reach than the ones crafted by Iago and Stavrogin. To aestheticize evil—that is perhaps the furthest reach of the intelligence of evil. For what is radical evil, after all, but the exercise of a superior intelligence working out the implications of that superiority? Or, what amounts to the same thing, despair savoring the one pleasure that remains, the taste of Thanatos when it is free of all restraints.

Our three examples point to one end which they've made it possible for us to conceptualize: a full and fully rational self-consciousness of evil. This is the difference between these examples and the banal practicing of evil. Banality is the refusal to know oneself. Radical evil is the refusal to compromise that knowledge; to equivocate about it, repress it, or seek rationales to mitigate it. There is, it turns out, an order of rank among the servants of soul murder: at the pinnacle stand those who, in a strict Kantian meaning of the term, are *sublime* in evil because they know in depth the motives for their actions and in that knowledge pass judgment on themselves; below them flock all those who are banal because they play the cheap game of bad faith, introducing gaps and blank spots in their consciousness so that they can simultaneously do evil and repress that awareness.

### Evil in and for itself

With the above examples as basis, my effort now will be to construct an analytic that presents in purely conceptual terms the *a priori* conditions that must be met for radical evil to be attained. That is, for the evil will to realize conditions analogous to those that Kant establishes for the positively good will. Arranged in an order of increasing complexity, this analytic of concepts forms a structure that will move to a definition that, I'll argue, captures the essence of radical evil.

### Evil as choice

Iago, Stavrogin and Humbert point to the same defining characteristic. Radical evil is the rejection of all behaviorisms and determinisms, all reductions of human conduct to social conditions and social programming. The pursuit of radical evil must be the product of a free choice, freely chosen in full knowledge of *all* its consequences. Freedom, as we'll learn, is of the essence here. To attain radical evil one must purify oneself of all lesser motives, such as self-interest and the search for happiness. Moreover, one must overcome all factors that could mitigate one's responsibility. A deliberative reasoning of unexampled severity is therefore required. One must know that what one does is wrong and do it anyway. The wrongness of the action is in fact the reason *why* one does it.

Evil is thus the fashioning of a will. Kant argues that for the good will, the moral law is incentive enough. Its violation must have the same status for a will that would make itself evil. The will's self-corruption can't proceed from frailty, inclination, or the natural desires that define our sensuous nature. It must be that free act of will through which the will gives itself determination. To attain that end one must seek out actions that will raise evil to the level of a categorical imperative and then make oneself capable of such actions by purifying one's psyche of everything but those motives that befit that purpose.

### Evil as motive

Those whose choice of evil is motivated by pleasure or self-interest compromise the act. To be radical evil can't be a reaction or the indulgence of a pathology. It must incarnate a radically different order of *desire*, one that puts one beyond all ordinary creaturely concerns. We will never understand evil as long as we keep thinking about human beings within the optimistic, humanistic assumptions set down by Aristotle: the belief that all humans desire happiness and follow that principle in all their actions so that though one can be mistaken about what will make one happy, the desire for happiness remains superordinate. Radical evil introduces us to an entirely different order of human motivation: one where the basis of one's actions has nothing to do with self-interest; where, in fact, one performs certain deeds in contempt of negative consequences. An evil will must refuse to be restricted by such mundane concerns as happiness and well-being. In rejecting self-interest as the subject's relationship to itself, one raises *desire* to another level. Radical evil can be seen, in fact, as an attempt to purify desire by engaging in a unique form of self-overcoming. One only becomes capable of radical evil by cleansing one's psyche of all ordinary and pathological motives. Those who pursue radical evil are thus ironically engaged in a process that has much in common with an authentic psychoanalysis. Essential to radical evil is the effort to explore one's psyche in depth—to know its deepest, darkest caverns, so that one can act from there by purging one's will of everything else; of all the petty *excuses* people give for their actions and the banal motives they cling to in order to conceal or repress the abiding perversities of the heart. That darkness is the truth about the human that the evil will must know, know so that it can refine it into something pure, even crystalline.

The desire for self-knowledge has here become something to which one will readily sacrifice all forms of human happiness and yet this desire no longer serves the comforting psychoanalytic belief that self-knowledge is a source of creative change and growth. An evil will pursues something deeper, darker—a knowledge of that which cannot be overcome, of that which is foul about the human. One must know it so that one can freely choose it and will it, thereby transforming everything that was passive and pathological in one's attraction to evil into something actively chosen. Retroactively one thereby becomes the author of one's being. A satanic pride is realized. All conditioning factors have become properties of one's will.

In pursuing that project one discovers something of inestimable value. There is a force of destruction at the heart of the human being. Base motives are powerful not because they serve our petty interests but because they serve that force. One has finally attained a founding recognition: the desire to destroy is stronger than any other desire. Radical evil is the attempt to activate the logic immanent in all lesser forms of evil and raise it to the status of an absolute, to achieve for evil a condition equivalent to the absolute knowledge Hegel achieves for a far different principle at the end of the *Phenomenology*.

### Evil as act

The only way to do so is by operating on the good. In one sense this is the limit of evil. It is defined by its opposite. (The same cannot be said of goodness. It needs no evil other in order to be; and in that sense it is always in paradise.) Without goodness evil would not be possible nor would it have an object. Radical evil knows what lesser devils only half imagine, that in order to realize its purpose evil must operate on goodness in a very definite way. That recognition is the source of a new inquiry, which must be as disciplined as the prior descent into the heart of darkness. One must know goodness better than it knows itself; everything that constitutes it, every hope on which it depends, every credence of which it is capable. For only then is one in a position to destroy it from within. Knowing the good moreover binds one to a new necessity. One must destroy the good precisely because it is good. And for no other reason. The sight of goodness has become, in fact, the sole thing that activates the *desire* to do evil. It also dictates the method that alone fulfills the demands of the project. Simple destruction is no longer viable; nor are the many forms of abuse that breed terror into a psyche. The look of the victim has the power to defeat every brutalizing project, even to convince one of the superiority of those who suffer. That is the illusion evil must triumph over by destroying goodness in its very roots. It is also the necessity that dictates the terms of the evil act. One must find a way to get goodness to destroy itself. Only thereby does one eliminate the idea that it ever was different; that its difference was ever anything but a naiveté that starts to unravel the moment one injects doubt about itself into a psyche. Thereby radical evil moves toward its feast—the pleasure of watching goodness unravel. And thereby the assurance it seeks: confirmation of the belief that those who think themselves good now stand on the first rung of a ladder that one has climbed all the way to the top, with the prospect of the promised land now in sight. For one's act has confirmed something far more important than the destruction of goodness. It has proven that one could do evil—with malice aforethought and without any stirrings of remorse. In fulfilling that *a priori* condition one has attained the equivalent of a noumenal identity. It lies in the recognition that one has realized a freedom that puts one beyond the claims of the human.

### Evil as freedom

Through radical evil one attains what one sought from the beginning. What couldn't be seen then is now apparent. Radical evil is all about freedom. About the possibility that is implicit in freedom and the act required to realize that possibility. *Inherent in freedom, defining it, is the desire to defy anything that would limit freedom.* Insofar as we are free and value that freedom there will always be in us a motive for radical evil. Or as Kant put it, "the propensity to evil is in the very subjective ground of freedom."[13] To the Thomistic claim that one cannot freely choose evil, freedom replies that one must. A freedom limited by anything but itself is no freedom. Such is the relationship that radical evil creates to its own ground. Which is why the *self-consciousness* it generates can be nothing but the *will to persist in this activity*, to seek out new and better ways to realize evil in order to affirm the power of freedom to go beyond anything that would limit it.

## Evil necessity

Radical evil is bound to its own inner necessity. Opposition to the very principles upon which the moral order depends is the imperative informing the search for those actions one must take in order to establish freedom as that which in violating the moral law puts one beyond it. That effort confers in turn the knowledge one has always sought: that of the nature and the extent of one's evil. In seeking out evil one seeks a self-knowledge that can be attained in no other way. In refusing to compromise that quest or lie to oneself about its personal consequences one remains true to the project. One thus ripens toward the final discovery: an impeccable self-consciousness of all that one has done and, in the teeth of that recognition, a rejection of the possibility of any reversal or "redemption." The entire logic we have traced thereby culminates in the achievement of a will that is corrupt at its root. It proves that fact by severing the last tie to the human order. One is beyond any appeal—from the other or in oneself. One has attained the inner state that defines evil: the severing of human contact, the unbinding of oneself from every claim save that of Thanatos. In radical evil this principle is realized purely as that end in itself richer than all others.

## A definition of evil

We're now in a position to offer a definition of radical evil. *Radical evil is the* project *in which the possibility implicit in freedom—to value freedom beyond anything else—becomes the fully self-consciousness choice to make violation of the moral order the* principle *that will inform one's actions. Action thus becomes the attempt to destroy those who are good precisely because they are good by injecting into their psyches the poison that will lead to their self-destruction. That motive is the* categorical imperative *whereby what once may have been a pathology becomes an innermost necessity. To fulfill its demands evil must be done in complete indifference toward the other and in full self-consciousness of what one does to oneself in putting oneself beyond the possibility of reversing one's inner condition. That's the pleasure and the goal of the project: to know what one is doing to oneself. Only thereby can one forge a will that is corrupt at its root and that, accordingly, finds the only pleasure in the consciousness of one's self-destruction; or what amounts to the same thing, in refining the perversity of one's projects, since the one thing that moves such a psyche is the desire to descend ever deeper into evil, seeking the perfect act.*

What, then, is the difference between radical evil and the other, lesser forms of evil? Nothing finally. Save self-consciousness. Though its achievement may be rare, the value of understanding radical evil is that it enables us to see what's going on—in principle—in all other forms of evil. Radical evil simply raises to the level of a self-consciousness what all evil agents do, thereby making explicit the self-knowledge they could attain were they not so adept at avoiding it. Except in their feelings, that is, where they get the full kick of it all the time. In that sense they are perhaps superior to the apostles of radical evil; and more efficient in finding behavioral forms for the feelings it has resolved into abstraction. Those who practice radical evil receive the cold kiss of the corpse, but the lesser devils get the true joy of this thing. It's what courses through them on countless occasions every day. Evil, the pleasure that comes with cruelty in the assurance that in it one has found the safety and power of a lasting identity.

## SYSTEMIC EVIL—THE PSYCHO-LOGIC OF CAPITALISM

### The objective neurosis

"Only thus shall we gain the living space [Lebensraum] which we need. Who, after all, speaks today of the annihilation of the Armenians?"

Adolf Hitler, *The Obersalzberg Speech*

Can evil in the full psychoanalytic and philosophic understanding we now have of it be applied to political and social orders and, as a result, to those citizens who live lives adapted to the ruling principles of such orders? With respect to totalitarianism this question has already been answered non-psychoanalytically in the affirmative by Hannah Arendt. I want here to suggest another affirmative reply to it, one that strikes closer to home. Against the by now trained reflex that negative categories are only to be applied to the other, I hope to show that the concept of evil I've developed describes capitalism, especially in its global or empire stage. My demonstration will introduce two forms of evil we have not yet discussed; one describing those who have internalized capitalism so thoroughly that it has become the logic that structures their relationship to themselves; the other describing those few who have become, in effect, the self-consciousness of the system and live a pure, disinterested service to its principles. Consideration of this final type of evil will also answer a question that is frequently asked: how could the powers that be have let a religious fanatic like Bush get his finger on the trigger? The answer, as we'll see, involves a historical rethinking of Max Weber: a demonstration that late capitalism requires apocalyptic fundamentalism the way early capitalism required the thrift of Calvinist Puritanism. Or, to put this thesis in more concrete terms, Bush and Cheney form parts of a single psyche, joined at the base of the brain like inseparable twins, with the one the idiot child of ideological passions, the other the refinement of economic necessities into pure mind; the one ego, the other the superego and thus in a position to know what it doesn't deign to let the ego know lest that knowledge impede its readiness to function as its signifying monkey.

We have not yet discussed what may be the worst form of evil—that of those who do massive evil while convinced that they are doing good and who are never likely to know the opposite because they inhabit the privileged position Goebbels spoke of, that of the victors who will write the histories. The goal of ideology is the production of a collective consciousness that leads ordinary citizens to serve the system convinced in their heart of hearts that it is morally good, the ultimate realization in fact of both truth and justice when it comes to both economic and interpersonal relations among "men." Does not such a belief describe the consciousness of most Americans both in their readiness to celebrate all the American platitudes and in their readiness to support the domestic and international policies of their government? Those who fight and die for America and those who don't are united by a body of beliefs that distinguish them from the robber barons of the Bush administration. Which is why most Americans would react with incredulity or rage to the argument that pursuing the American Dream is paid for by the systematic corruption of each individual heart and a systematic Hobbesian injustice of each toward all the extent of which is determined by the place one occupies in the system.

What is the use of psychoanalytic categories to political thought? That large question is so much the same as this smaller one—what does living in capitalism do to the psyche?—that addressing the latter frames an answer to the former. There are many critiques of capitalism. As an economic system, a political ideology, a form of civil society. All these critiques are necessary. So, I hope to show, is the one I'll mount here, using the occasion to outline a new theory of the relationship between the psyche and social structures. This critique of capitalism will focus solely on what capitalism does to the psyche. That story is but a part of the evil that can be attributed to the system. But it is also an essential part because it describes one of the primary conditions that must be assured for capitalism's maintenance. *No ideology is secure until the conditions of its reproduction are the conditions that inform the relationship that the psyche lives to itself. Collectively and individually.* And here too in America capitalism has had its greatest success, producing subjects for whom nothing but the system makes sense because they've so deeply internalized it and identified with its logic that nothing else is real for them. Or can be. For their *inwardness* is a perfect reproduction of the logic of capitalism and their *experience* thus a confirmation of the narrowness of the vicious circle to which capitalism confines them. Here, then, a brief outline of the essential internalizations that define the capitalist subject.

## Competition

Whenever I drive around town I listen to Sports Radio. It's one way of making concrete contact with the folklore of capitalism as it operates in those who will never know the extent to which they're true believers. One of the frequent themes of this chatter is the value of competition. And when these pundits of the *massenmensch* wax eloquent on this theme their talk always turns to the young and the value of getting kids started in sports as early as possible. The constant refrain: "How else are they going to learn to compete?"

There's the foundation in a nutshell. Competition, nature and nurture wedded in the most important activity in the education of the young. Competition isn't simply desirable. It's the overarching necessity. The way one learns and proves one's worth. Also concrete training in what must become one's relationship to the other. Through competition one discovers who one is by discovering whether one has what it takes to succeed in life. That's why winning is everything. Success determines one's worth as a person. Low self-esteem the necessary result of failure. Taunting and gloating are written into the process. For there's always an invidious comparison operating that tells one to win at all costs, including all costs to oneself. Within the child's psyche, as a result, a process of savaging everything in oneself that does not contribute to forming a psyche primed for competition as the only way to prove one's worth has begun. And with it a certain cruelty has already set in. All other human relationships are secondary to the self one discovers and creates through competition. The qualities one discovers there must be cultivated; those that don't serve competitive purposes must be purged. Thereby a deeper transformation comes to pass: an internalization of the belief that the self one is when competing is one's true self. Two self-references result: power through the "thrill of victory" and self-contempt as "the agony of defeat." The end result is two conditions which exist simultaneously in most capitalist subjects: arrogant condescension toward losers and shame whenever one suffers defeat. Both feelings serve the purposes of capitalism. In fact, defeat is often the best outcome, since it reinforces the desire to succeed in the system through an ever stricter adaptation of oneself to its demands.

## Self-interest

Self-interest is the answer capitalism offers to the eternal question of human motivation. There is and can be only one motive. Everything must be organized in terms of it. Every quality that serves it must be cultured; every one that doesn't eliminated. Capitalist self-fashioning is the process of learning to exploit every situation in terms of one's advantage by sacrificing anything that doesn't advance that motive. Iago complained that he never met a man who knew how to value himself. Capitalism offers itself as the corrective. Self-interest is all that matters. Everything in the human person must conform to it. The mind itself is thereby reduced to a severely restricted realization. College becomes a business school where one makes valuable contacts. Only the maladjusted think of it as a chance to explore questions that have nothing to do with that. A single logic informs the relationship that the capitalist subject lives to all human qualities. Capitalism is not niggardly in its appreciation of human talents. On the contrary. The more the better. But with this proviso: all talents and qualities must shape themselves to what they become within capitalism. Natural charm, for example, is valuable because it increases the chances that one will, as Willy Loman put it, "be well liked." A sunny disposition likewise. Likewise, a storehouse of affirmative commonplaces. The ability to turn a phrase, to imagine a new possibility, to make the proper use of one's gumption and sticktoitiveness. The key always is to know how to shape one's gifts in order to maximize one's worth on the marketplace and to sacrifice everything in oneself to that principle while remaining ignorant one is doing so. The transformation is complete when the following principle has become the basis of one's self-reference: one is *proud* whenever one exploits situations for one's self-interest and *ashamed* when one doesn't. Thus, for example, the careerism that controls most of what goes on in the academy, with power, prestige, and privilege accruing to the "operators" who can't see the dishonor they do to thought because thought for them was never anything but the current popular commonplaces one purveys in their simplest form in order to advance careers too fine to be violated by an idea.[14]

### Success

In its third imperative the system synthesizes competition and self-interest. There is only one purpose in life—Success—and only one standard to measure it—money. The circle of capitalist self-fashioning thus closes in one vast tautology. Self-worth equals monetary worth. Sign-exchange value rules. And since one is nothing else, there can never be sufficient signs of one's success. The system thus reduces its subjects to a condition similar to that of the child Paul in Lawrence's great story "The Rocking Horse Winner," frenetically riding his rocking horse in the suicidal knowledge that there will never be enough money. There can't be because money has become both an end in itself and the measure of an evanescent self-worth. One only has value by having more money than those with whom one must incessantly compare oneself. Marx's finely jaundiced insight— "I am 'ugly' but I can buy the most beautiful women for myself, consequently I am not 'ugly' for the effect of ugliness, its power to repel, is annulled by money ... I am a detestable, dishonorable, unscrupulous and stupid man, but money is honored and so is its possessor. Money is the highest good and so its possessor is good"[15]— has a flip side: the consciousness that one remains ugly and the sex one buys lousy because both participants in the exchange have reified themselves. And yet there's no exit from self-commodification because confronting the void at the center of one's life is not in one's self-interest. The same situation holds for the losers. Monetary failure is the superego eating away at the last remnants of their self-esteem. For those who fail to make it in the capitalist order, the interiority of Willy Loman represents condition general.

Producing a void at the center of the subject is the genius of capitalism. Capitalism hollows out a hole in the center of desire and makes that hole the only reality. Those who eat whenever they feel unhappy and who grow as a result to fantastic size realize in their body the *symptom* that defines capitalism. Internalizing capitalism equals constructing a self on two principles that are finally one: self-commodification and consumerism, the doubling of a relationship driven by a flight from the void. This interchangeability is both the lure of the system and the secret that everyone inhabited by it must keep from themselves. That's why narcissism and its double, panic anxiety, define contemporary American society: the empty self polishes its image or spasms in the fear that there's nothing behind it.

None of this can, however, be known for the simplest reason. "You can have it all" is the belief that structures capitalist subjectivity. Such is the purpose of the weekend retreats that corporations offer their young executives in order to bathe them in the mental health jargon needed to assure them that they're happy, productive, forward-looking, optimistic members in a Community of those who benefit the world. Such is the driving purpose of an "affirmative culture" that can't tolerate the slightest hint of negativity and that must therefore appropriate Art to itself by reducing it to entertainment. Such also is the *resentment* that triumphs in the need once one's made it to the top to claim that one possesses all the qualities one sacrificed in order to get there. After all, who's to say one isn't the standard of human worth in all things? One's success in the capitalist order testifies to it. The reductive logic of capitalism with respect to human qualities thus finds its capstone in the capitalist pathos. Love and peace, harmony and understanding, sympathy and trust: none of these can survive in capitalism and yet the innermost necessity of those who have internalized the system is the need to assure themselves they are the embodiment of these and all good things. The same need appropriates more philosophic concepts and values. Freedom, for example, becomes the freedom to enter into economic relations unfettered by any restrictions on self-interest. This is the only freedom that matters, of course, but it's buttressed by the belief that personal freedom realizes itself in the right to indulge oneself in arbitrary opinions the truth of which are determined by no standard other than how good they make one feel. With freedom, as with all other concepts, capitalism reduces a complex idea to its capitalist realization. The same logic applies to the human realm. The cash register is always clicking. Relationships are investments. When they fail the balance sheet of profit and loss reduces experiential knowing to the one standard: the need to wise up and purge whatever made one a blind, romantic, and vulnerable fool; or, at the other end of this operation, the need to stay in an unhappy marriage because one has *invested* far too much time and energy in it to admit an emotional bankruptcy that must remain secondary to more pragmatic considerations.

The predictable objection to the above critique is that such choices are not within the range of a person's control or awareness, since most people think and feel whatever they are socially conditioned to think and feel, so determined by ideology that they could not find their way out of it if they tried and thus can't be held ethically responsible for conditions of which they are the by-product. This chapter has undercut that convenient defense by revealing the psychological reasons why most people find it so easy to go with the flow of social conditioning. The decision not to question the practices into which one is born is a choice one makes in one's feeling from the earliest days of tailoring one's emotional life to the social imperatives that make conformity so attractive and rewarding. Social determinism is a convenient theory conveniently chosen to absolve one of responsibility for oneself.

Ironically, this section has offered a description of capitalist inwardness that is close to the account that those who love the system would give of themselves. In fact, if one substitutes for the negative language the language of Dale Carnegie the above would constitute a burnished mirror reflecting the self-understanding and pride of the capitalist subject. Only one thing would need to be added—the necessity to embrace the system in the greatest complacency so that one is thereby delivered from any consciousness of the darker motives that have sculpted one's passage to this way of being.

### The lower layer: Hannah Arendt applied

"The attitude one manifests toward the other must faithfully reflect the true attitude that one has toward oneself."

Harry Stack Sullivan

Culled from a number of her writings here is a list of what Hannah Arendt identifies as the main characteristics defining the banality of evil.

- The elimination of spontaneity.
- Rendering human beings superfluous or, more strongly, eradicating the human being.

- The inability to have any inwardness or self-awareness.
- The inability to think; or what amounts to the same thing, a mind (and in our expansion of Arendt, a heart and psyche) corrupted at its roots.
- The inability to see from the standpoint of someone else; i.e., inability to relate to the other as a subject and not an object.
- The inability to know or feel that one is doing wrong. This characteristic signals the emergence of what Arendt calls a new kind of criminal.

And on a slightly different level the following:

- The commission of a wrong that is beyond comprehension.
- And, accordingly, a guilt beyond the ability of the legal system to comprehend or redress.

I'll try to show in what follows that all these characteristics apply to capitalism in two ways that are necessarily connected: (1) as what one does to oneself in internalizing the logic of capitalism and (2) as what consequently one does to the other. The first constitutes the subjective neurosis; the second the objective neurosis.[16] Or, as a more concrete version of the aphorism that what one does not know about oneself is what one does—to the other: *in capitalism the evil one does to oneself becomes the evil one necessarily does to the other.* What follows will always precede from the former act to the latter. Thereby we'll discover the chilling application of Sullivan's statement quoted above to the ethic of human relations. One can, of course, displace ethical responsibility, thereby reading what follows not as a desire but as an objective function of the adherence of subjects to the rules of the system.

### To eliminate spontaneity

Eliminating spontaneity is the primary thing one does to oneself in internalizing capitalism; so successfully, in fact, that one doesn't realize that one has sacrificed the quality that most deeply attaches and attunes us to life. Spontaneity is the ability to act from an independent, creatively open register of one's being and to welcome being at issue in that adventure. Spontaneity embraces the exploration of life in all its forms. It's also what surprises one about oneself. A spontaneous person is able to respond in unprogrammed and unprecedented ways because for such a person feeling is what opens one to experience rather than what one must close down to protect oneself from it. The same spirit holds with respect to thought. Spontaneity is the source of that curiosity which questions everything, maintaining a child's love affair with the world. Spontaneity is the deepest spring of freedom, that living in its immediacy of a liberation from social rigidities and conventions of behavior. The spontaneous person lives a self-reference defined by an expansiveness of spirit that welcomes conflict and change. Spontaneity is the heart of that Romanticism that refuses to subordinate the imagination to the restrictions of the analytic intelligence. It is the primordial why lived through broad leaps of thought in an expanding awareness that puts passion at the center of perception.

All of this is subjected to systematic assault, of course, by the school system as well as by parents eager to instill the logic of competition. Nothing is more out of keeping with the spirit of capitalism than spontaneity. Capitalism demands that everything become a matter of *calculation* in an unremitting tyranny of the left brain over the right. As one internalizes the imperatives of such a society this becomes the logic that one applies to oneself. Spontaneity one learns is what sets one apart, opening one to ridicule from those better adapted to the system. Moreover, responding spontaneously to experience often floods one with feelings that can only retard one's progress. Those who grieve over injustice, heed the call of passion, suffer the consequences of empathy, thereby reveal their inability to get on with the business of life. Under capitalism spontaneity can only be seen as a sign of trouble: attention deficit disorder or worse, an indication of an asocial or anti-social personality. Everyone must become basically the same. This imperative is the logic of the system as well as the desire that fuels it. Signs of difference identify what must be bent to the rules of conformity. Being like the other is the principle both of success and of happiness. That's why Americans are *individuals by rote*, this the great irony in the constant trumpeting of our freedom, independence, and individualism. Everything that makes the human being a source of surprise and wonder is antithetical to the logic that drives the system. Those who succeed in it necessarily see spontaneity as a barrier to their advancement; and in those who fail a barrier to their productivity and their exploitation. One might have thought that the elimination of spontaneity would be incidental to the system. It is actually an evil that the system renders systemic. Capitalism not only requires one kind of human being; it is actively engaged in the elimination of another.

## Rendering human beings superfluous

Those who internalize capitalism render superfluous everything in themselves that doesn't conform to its libidinal economy. Bergson defines the comic as the presence of the mechanical where one would expect the flexibility of the human. Under capitalism this great formula becomes condition general. Capitalism's secret history is the self-brutalization that each person does to themselves in fashioning an interiority impeccably fitted to the only principle that makes sense: the profit motive. To become a smoothly functioning member of the system any relationship to oneself or to others that exceeds this logic becomes superfluous. Despite an excessively affirmative hyperconsciousness, capitalism thus creates a Hobbesian universe of isolated individuals pitted through the principle of self-interest in a war of each against all. Relating to others in trust, empathy or solidarity is but a temporary move in the game. The appeal of the TV show *The Apprentice* (the true *Survivor*) is the nakedness with which it foregrounds this logic, which also applies to intimate relationships. Under capitalism any relationship is ultimately an investment with a calculus of profit and loss constantly keeping score in each consciousness. The relationship reaches its incipient crisis whenever events force this logic to the surface. For the question "what's in it for me?" can have only one answer: the incessant repetition of that question as it eats away at every other principle of human relatedness. The ideal capitalist couple: two narcissists each feeding the other's narcissism because it enhances their own. For the payoff then is constant in a perfect marriage sure to last because it's based on mutual commodification. Everything else has been rendered superfluous.

## Banality

Banality is that relationship to oneself that one must dissimulate. Under capitalism this need takes the form of the incessant happy talk of affirmative culture, the inability to experience one's world except in the mode of celebration. Inwardness becomes a haven of optimistic commonplaces running like a tape that loops back into itself in endless iteration: self-hypnosis dedicated to forever forestalling the prospect of anxiety. Once self-interest has become supreme, the impossibility of any critical or dialectical relationship to oneself and one's experience is assured. Everything that transpires in the head must reinforce one's identification with a system that must be wholly positive and beyond contradiction. Dialectical negativity, the relationship through which inwardness develops, finds in capitalist interiority its annulling antithesis. Everything is ruled by the need to sustain a smooth and productive functioning within the system. That's the rationale, for example, behind the weekend *retreats* that corporations arrange for their employees. The purpose is not just to program happy employees, but to create happiness itself as the one inner voice. The same goal informs the mental health professions under capitalism: social engineering in the production of the emotional self-references that adaptation requires. Everyone must be made happy and once that interiority exists nothing can be permitted to disrupt it. To complete what Dostoyevsky's Grand Inquisitor called "the happiness of man," dissatisfaction must be eliminated and with it the possibility of that reflective consciousness which constitutes itself by calling life into question. Insofar as that act is the achievement that makes us human, capitalism is defined by the attempt to extinguish the human, to replace what Heidegger termed the call of conscience with the prattle of self-congratulation.

### The inability to think

The inability to think is the end result of affirmative culture. One who has internalized capitalism is unable to conceive or comprehend any idea that challenges the system. Freedom, for example, can only be arbitrary indulgence in one's opinions and tastes, with "it's a free country" serving as the justification for reducing one's mind to a condition of self-indulgent mush. The notion that freedom may be the most exacting relationship of responsibility that one could live to oneself has been rendered impossible. Thought can be nothing but the reproduction of ideological affirmations in the pseudo-space of private deliberation. The same condition controls more academic exercises of thought. Thought's role is to justify acquiescence in what is: positivism, common language philosophy, Chicago School Economics, and the new Darwinism of Dennett and Pinker are among the more conspicuous realization of this imperative. The highest act of mind within capitalism is a sort of degraded Kantianism: the proclamation of thought's reifying limitations so that one can acquiesce in what has long since become the only way one can be.

### The inability to see things from the point of view of the other

The inability to think produces as its necessary consequence the inability to see anything from the perspective of the other. Others can only be mirrors of oneself. Those who are different or who fail to conform to the dominant model must be labeled "weird." Failure to become a capitalist is the sign of a fundamental character disorder. Deviance from the norm of conformity signifies a failure to adapt. Adaptation, moreover, has been raised to the apex of psychological values. That's what ego, self, identity, attachment and relationality are all about. How could it be otherwise? Subjectivity in capitalism is reduced to consensual validations and reflected appraisals. The same imperative that puts a stop to thought arrests the possibility of genuine otherness. This, too, is vanquished by necessity. The System is the highest realization of the human. Failure to correspond to its ruling principles can only signal a failure to realize one's humanity. Pre-emptive unilateralism is not just Bush's gift to international relations; it's the attitude the capitalist subject takes toward every form of otherness.

## The new criminal

Capitalism goes Hannah Arendt one better. The flaw inherent to it isn't that one does wrong without being able to know it, but that one does it without being able to know it as anything but good. The beauty of the system lies in this: those who internalize it never experience that internalization as a violation of themselves nor the way they relate to the other as a reduction of humanity to the conditions of exchange value. Successful internalization of capitalism systematically alienates the human being from everything in oneself save what reproduces the conditions of the system. Thus the rigidity of body, the obsessional concern with petty details, the excessive legalism or contractualism in human relationships, the alienation from every form of pleasure except those that discharge tension or stimulate aggression, and, above all, the need at all times to feel good about oneself. Such practices produce the desired reification. One blesses all one's actions, unable to experience anything one does except as good and necessary.

All of this remains, of course, on the periphery of consciousness, either as that which one never quite knows about oneself or as what one knows only in the mode of a celebratory hyperconsciousness. That does not mean, however, that deeper psychological forces aren't at work here. On the contrary, capitalist internalization succeeds because it's perfectly fitted to the emotional self-mediations required to solidify one's attachment to the system: envy, cruelty, resentment, and greed. *Envy*: the relationship one lives in prideful contempt for everything one is not. *Cruelty*: the relationship one lives to the other whenever faced either with a threat to one's self-esteem or with a chance to enjoy the right and power that befits one's situation. *Resentment*: the relationship one has to anything that presumes to question the supreme value one places on the kind of human being one has become. *Greed*: the emptiness of that void within that can never have enough. All this naturally is something one doesn't let oneself think about or consciously intend. It works ever so much better when it has become habitual, unthought, that which goes without saying. There is, however, one place where the whole arrangement crows. When the worker is the other who is submitted to the logic of capitalism, the psychological forces objectified in it make a full and naked appearance on the stage.

## Wal-Mart: The way of the future

This too has a history with the latest chapter exemplified by Wal-Mart whose treatment of its workers represents the model for the relationship of global capitalism to the third world, a world which as we know exists in Flint and Detroit as well as in the outsourced colonies of Bombay, Jakarta, and the Philippines.

That model is one of terrorism. "Think of the future as a huge boot being brought down on the human face forever."[17] The genius of Wal-Mart is to have realized the requirements of that process in minute particulars that constitute a systematic attempt to destroy any solidarity among workers not just through a spy system meant to quash any union activity, but through systematic techniques of harassment used to isolate, demean, and terrorize each worker. Workers are under constant panoptic surveillance, especially for signs of "time theft," and subjected to periodic Kafkaesque reprimands where they are forced to justify their continued employment; i.e., Orwell's "five minutes hate." The result is workers stripped of any pride they could find in their work and any chance to experience Labor as either realization of or alienation from one's species being.[18] Everything is done to make workers feel their disposability and exchangeability. And in all this an overtly sexist dimension also operates. Wal-Mart employs far more women than men, pays them less, and systematically bars them from promotion, often through the fabrication on the spot of *ad hoc*, belittling requirements. Thus does Wal-Mart announce the glad tidings: global capitalism turns back the social clock as well as the economic one.

Wal-Mart also represents the vanguard of the future in understanding the role of the State. Since only 41–46 percent of its employees can afford the health insurance it "offers," and because the majority of its employees remain below the poverty line, U.S. taxpayers annually pay over $2,000 dollars for every person Wal-Mart employs. It's the perfect arrangement: the government is used to finance workers who are kept in minimum conditions so that the profiteers can extract the utmost in the surplus value of their labor. Wal-Mart suffers an over 50 percent yearly turnover of employees who would rather accept unemployment than continued association with Wal-Mart. But this fact serves only to confirm the meaninglessness of their freedom, since what the turnover establishes is the disposability of each worker with replacements readily available within the community or in the global village. The vampiristic logic of capitalism finds here one of its most grotesque realizations. Wal-Mart is not the store of choice among the rich, but is of necessity among the poor where the bulk of Wal-Mart stores are located, each one resulting in the collapse of small competitors and with that a significant loss of employment and revenue within the community. Wal-Mart has effectively set the poor in opposition to one another, with the same person occupying both positions in the food chain (employee and clientele) in a vicious circle of workers replaced by others eager to accept any conditions in order to escape that great army of the unemployed which the disgruntled worker has just fallen back into. The new employee, always more docile, has already bowed to kiss the Orwellian boot that will shortly descend.

The cheaper the better, such is the logic Wal-Mart follows in all things in fealty to an old law that Wal-Mart restores to the level of a self-conscious corporate imperative. *Extracting surplus value is the purpose of capitalism. Reducing labor costs is the primary way one does so.* All the rest is window dressing, temporary palliatives, misguided liberal ventures. Capitalism has no place for sentiment. As Wal-Mart testifies, everything human must be stripped away so that its logic can shine as clear as the white, glistening tiles of the floors that sweep one's passage through Wal-Mart, as through the dream kingdom of everyman the consumer: everything you desire is visible to you here, all under one roof, at the tip of your fingers, the great consumerist circus in which one gets to feel like a child again visiting Santa; or those not blinded by the *jouissance* of it all, get to see what Rilke saw at the back of the carnival, "money's genitals, nothing concealed, the whole action"[19] visible and then again invisible because one's consciousness is arrested again by the brightly colored prospect of the next object of desire. A tour of Wal-Mart is a surreal passage through the collective fantasm. As such, however, it is but an overture to a descent into the belly of the beast.

## Cheney, or The Grand Inquisitor

"Most of you know what it means when 100 corpses lie there, or when 500 corpses lie there, or when 1,000 corpses lie there. To have gone through this and—apart from a few exceptions caused by human weakness—to have remained decent, that has made us great."

Heinrich Himmler

"It's not personal, Sonny, it's strictly business."

Michael Corleone, in *The Godfather*

Nixon had his Agnew. Sure that the latter would plow the low road, tricky Dick could assume the high one. Ideological platitudes dripped like honey from his pursed lips while his idiot child prattled on about "the nagging nabobs of negativism." Cheney and Bush represent a far deadlier form of ideological incest. Their union, like that of inseparable twins joined at the head, reveals the relationship of ego and superego required for the global reach of capitalism. It is as if the two had gotten together to rewrite Max Weber, to historicize his argument about the Protestant ethic and the spirit of capitalism by revealing the final twist of that logic. "Thrift, thrift Horatio" may have been sufficient to get the engine going, but a psychotic split is needed to bring it to its final form: an apocalyptic religious fanaticism equal to the global expanse of capital and an aloof indifference regarding the negative results of that process. The answer to the oft repeated question—Why would the stony lords of high finance let a fanatic like Bush assume a position of such power?—is very simple. Bush is precisely what's needed because he can organize the masses into a crusading consciousness that will embrace, with religious fervor, political ventures that are necessary for far more calculating purposes. Fundamentalist Christianity is the ego required for global capitalism: an apocalyptic faith based on a stark and omnipotent opposition of good and evil that justifies the absence of all restraint in a manic and destructive relationship toward the other. An equally ardent faith, tuned to the conditions of Empire, inhabits Cheney as the superego who commands the ego the way Hamlet's father tried to command his son. "If thou hast manhood in thee," this the refrain that with respect to all policy decisions leaves a salivating Dubya the adolescent cowboy eager to strut forth on the global stage dressed in religious garb. Bush, the ego full of all its passions and stupidities, seeking an identity through action; Cheney the superego, aloof and serene in a dispassionate proclamation of economic laws that through his ministry will attain the character of transhistorical truths. Cheney is Fukuyama realized because Cheney knows that History has progressed beyond all ideological needs, even Dubya's gushing theocratic ideology of the saved. There is only the truth of global capital. The rest is silence, though the noise from Iraq remains deafening to those who fail to hear in it the music of necessity.

Christian fundamentalism and global capitalism, Bush and Cheney, are Dostoyevskian doubles; the former the infantile incarnation of destructiveness; the latter its abstraction into pure law. But in that relationship there should be no mistaking which agent is in command. The son does not understand the father's purposes, nor does he question them. Dubya is the antithesis of Hamlet. He obeys in the frenzy of his passion to prove himself Laertes. It is doubtful Dubya could hold his own in discussions of economic policy. He doesn't have to. He has the faith, an unquestioning belief in capitalism as firm as his allegiance to Jesus. Moreover, for him the two are one. Capitalism, freedom, moral values, one and indivisible. That's the unity signified when he tells us "*they* hate us for our freedom." This statement also exemplifies Dubya's psychological economy: you either have *it* or you envy *it*. The inability to think or feel outside this circle makes him the perfect mouthpiece of a capitalism that has always needed to find ways to offer itself to its subjects as a popular religion.

But while Dubya is necessary he is also, as Hegel would say, the Absolute Idea still clothed *in a sensuous form* and thus not yet realized in the required condition of pure rationality. In Cheney, however, the Absolute Idea attains the form necessary to it. To understand capitalism in its global phase we must understand the inner workings of Cheney's consciousness, which unlike Dubya's, is of necessity a *self-consciousness* that intends and acts *impersonally* in service to impersonal trans-historical laws.

What follows does not fully describe Dick Cheney the man, though the affectlessness of his personal demeanor is uncannily in keeping with the logic of the pure position represented here. That impersonal affectlessness represents what Dick Cheney would be were he able to strip away all human coordinates and coincide purely with the Idea he serves. Dubya needs religion to pull off his role. Cheney has overcome such needs. Religion is of no importance to him because he is the pure apostle of a greater necessity, which he serves in the one way that is adequate to it—impersonally. If radical evil requires that one act independent of and even against self-interest, Cheney is the capitalist realization of that necessity. It isn't that he doesn't have self-interests—in the interim between bouts of "public service" he knew how to fill his coffers with the riches of a Midas—but that in him self-interest so coincides with the interests of the system that the monetary service he does himself is but a grace note to the larger service he renders to it. In the purity of that service Cheney offers the most chilling realization of the characteristics of evil that Arendt identifies. Cheney can do massive wrong while, unlike Dubya, knowing both that it is wrong *and* that the wrong serves the greater good. He needs no religious blinders to obscure his vision of what must be done in Iraq and elsewhere. He knows that countless human beings must die for the capitalist order to secure global hegemony. He cannot, however, know that such action is wrong because he knows that whatever the system requires is for the greater good. Of all—even the dead. So what if we have to destroy most of the Middle East, sacrificing our boys and girls with an indifference beyond the reach of Henry Kissinger's comment that "Military men are just dumb animals to be used as pawns in foreign policy."[20] It's all part of the transformation. Eventually the entire world, incorporated into the new world order, will reap untold benefits. In Cheney the "inability to think" is cloaked in an iron necessity that accords itself a position beyond good and evil. Whatever is required to realize the new world order is justified because capitalism, not the proletariat, is Marx and Lukács' identical subject–object of history. Any means necessary are justified by History's one end.

Cheney knows, with a cold clarity that has no need for Dubya's apocalyptic imaginings, that this end requires the abolition of otherness in all its forms. A memorable instance of this truth was witnessed when his dam, Lynne, was head of the National Endowment for the Humanities. Dubya can hate intellectuals for their uppity airs and artists for their libidinal pretensions. The Cheneys, however, know the truth of the matter, that art and the life of the mind form the basis of an oppositional culture that must be conquered from within by withdrawing support from all projects that don't pass the litmus test of neocon political correctness; though Cheney himself, possessed of the Transcendent Truth, is beyond the lingering ideological needs of his neocon colleagues. Even an ideology of the victors is dross. One who serves the Absolute Idea of Capitalism correctly is thoroughly demystified. Thus the affectless detachment of the man's personal style. Cheney simply announces truths impersonally as if he were the pure medium through which they present themselves. Such demystification is beyond the systematic reach of Paul deMan's concern to perfect an aesthetic of irony. Even neocon ideologues find no resonance within the iron necessity of Cheney's mind. Contra Samuel Huntington, Cheney knows we're not in Iraq as part of some grand *cultural* struggle of civilizations nor, following Wolfowitz's perversion of Leo Straus, to bring freedom to the people of the Middle East. Cheney alone, one suspects, was not taken in by the fantasy that there'd be a groundswell of popular Iraqi support for our troops. He knows we're in Iraq for one reason and one reason only. "It's the *oil*, stupid." In knowing that Cheney knows the good in a way that liberates him from the neocon imaginary. Capitalism is the absolute good because it has proven itself in the only *philosophic* forum that matters—the economic battleground where self-interest, as Adam Smith taught, finds realization in pure, impersonal laws. Any action taken to advance capitalism is therefore good. Anything that retards its movement is bad. Stalin was wrong: it is neither the first death warrant nor the millionth that matters because the death order is never signed. It is given *a priori* by the impersonal laws of Capital. Cheney thus has no trouble taking responsibility for the many who must die for the sake of global capitalism. Because he's a sentimentalist at heart, Dubya needs the troops (and their families) to feel that they're dying for their country. Cheney only needs to know, in the capitalist perversion of Krishna's message to Arjuna, that both friend and foe perish of necessity. But while their service to the Idea is blind, Cheney's is pure because he has identified with the principle that directs History and purged everything else from his being. Cheney has attained what Wallace Stevens could only imagine: a mind of winter. He sits, accordingly, in the position of pure service, beyond any reward or the need for reward. If Dubya has a weak spot, it's his desire for the love and admiration of the masses. Cheney labors under no such need and, accordingly, refuses to let the position of true power he occupies sully itself with the populist posturings of Dubya.

Cheney is beyond all mundane human concerns; beyond all the hot appeals to fear, hate, and manic religiosity of the new McCarthyism; beyond the late, degraded exercises of neocon political theorizing. Cheney doesn't need any of this to summon in himself the full measure of his devotion. He is one with the abstraction *Kapital* in its pure abstractness. Nothing else matters because nothing else is; which is why everything else must be washed away, without a moment's pause or the blink of an eye, and without the slightest stirring of regret or remorse. The inability to see otherness except from one's own point of view achieves in Cheney its capitalist apotheosis. Bush scares us because he's so irrational; Cheney should terrify us because with him everything is a matter of the purest reason.

### On becoming a socialist in one's instincts

Early in Doris Lessing's *The Golden Notebook* the narrator makes brief mention of a former lover as the only man she ever knew who was "a socialist in his instincts."[21] It is, I would argue, the condition we must all attain. Instinct here, of course, refers not to a biological given but to a human process. Of transformation—that becomes historically more exacting with each new reach of the capitalist hegemony. To become a socialist in one's instincts is to reverse the instincts that living under capitalism breeds in us so deeply that we regard them as universal, ahistorical truths of human nature. If we are to sustain the idea of overturning capitalism, this is the place where the struggle must begin. Socialism is a way of being before it's an economic system. And until we attain the former we cannot hope to secure possibilities for the latter because they'll rest on the sand of a bad faith always willing to make compromises when self-interest is at stake. Socialism depends on the internalization of a single principle. *One cannot own anything.* Owning must become a way of being foreign to one's nature, a way one can't feel toward anything, especially the things one has. Sharing must become natural. Giving oneself freely must become an inner necessity. And not giving what one has to the other must become a source of shame. Relationships can't be investments. Which means there can be no resentment when they end. The pettiness that feeds capitalism is its niggardliness of the heart. In opposition to the constricted arteries of capitalist circulation, where the blood pounds away at the chambers until something bursts under the pressure, the heart of a socialist must become a fire that opens the self in love and responsibility to all incarnate nature. Such an expansiveness of being is the primary source of the recognition that one is not, in one's self-interest, the center of the universe, but rather the humble servant of all the environments one shares with everything else that lives in a mutuality that unites one's being with all creatures great and small; with the grandeur of trees, the meanest flower that blows, the fecundity of natural life in all its aching beauty, and our human life in the struggles that define it. "Perhaps we are *here* in order to say: house, bridge, fountain, gate, pitcher, fruit-tree, window—at most: column, tower ... But to *say* them, you must understand, oh to say them *more* intensely than the Things themselves ever dreamed of existing."[22] To become a socialist in one's instincts is to recover the *spontaneity* of the child, to shed the wrinkled skin of capitalism and live again in the erotic expansiveness of a body cleansed of it, a mind quick in the perception of the connections that bind us in single-minded commitment to the least of things and to all that we see for the first time, as it were, once we move into what Rilke calls *The Open*,[23] aware of the Thing not as object but as duty, the Other not as other but as the opening of oneself to the possibility and discipline of love.

All of the above, which I must leave in the briefest of formulations here, goes by another name. Romanticism. Perhaps that once and future revolution remains the way of being we must recover in order to become socialists in our instincts and thereby to live a relationship to ourselves that is antithetical to the one enforced by capitalism. Everything capitalism sacrifices we must recover and then constitute as ways of being that bind us to others. Only then will the possibility of socialism be secured as a libidinal ordering of desire. And only then will evil no longer have a way to work in us. Our being will stir to the demands of another ethic. It forms the subject of our final chapter.

# 10
# Men of Good Will:
# Toward an Ethic of the Tragic

"It is impossible to conceive anything at all in the world, or even out of it, which can be taken as good without qualification, except a *good will*."

Immanuel Kant, *Foundation of the Metaphysics of Morals*

"Individuals have international duties which transcend the national obligations of obedience. Therefore, individual citizens have the duty to violate domestic laws to prevent crimes against peace and humanity from occurring."

The Nuremburg Tribunal (1945–64)

### THE ETHICAL SIGNIFICANCE OF PAT TILLMAN

Two examples will take us to the center of the ethical problem I want to develop here.

On September 12, 2001 Pat Tillman, an NFL football player with the Arizona Cardinals decided to forsake an 8.5 million dollar contract and enlist in an army special forces unit in order to join the fight against terrorism. In keeping with the ethical character of that choice, Tillman refused all media efforts to publicize his action. Tillman's unit was deployed in Iraq and later in Afghanistan where Tillman was killed in action in April of 2004. Pat Tillman is regarded by many as an ethical hero. His action also fulfills, as we'll see, the criteria Immanuel Kant established in the theory that remains central to contemporary ethical philosophy.[1]

My second example is taken from a play by Shakespeare. Hamlet, faced with a situation analogous to Tillman's, makes very different choices. Called by his father to avenge his murder, Hamlet gives the moment of decision over to the delays and detours of reflection. In the process he discovers complications that overturn all the assumptions on which his father's command—or what Lacan calls the Symbolic Order—is based. Hamlet discovers not just the impossibility of any direct or simple action but the need to reject the central beliefs of his age. Out of that revolution of thought, which is also an *existentializing* process that completely transforms his relationship to himself, Hamlet comes to a new ethic, one shorn of all guarantees, given over to the contingencies of existence.

Both examples, as I'll show, address the questions and criteria that Kant brought to the center of ethics. Kant's basic effort, briefly, is to ground ethics in the autonomy of the individual ethical agent by establishing the rational criteria that must be satisfied to attain a positively good will. All other foundations for ethics—religious belief, social norms, ideological allegiances, pragmatic exigencies—are invalid because they compromise the principle on which ethics must depend: that one's values, choices, and actions be a function of one's freedom. To possess ethical quality one's act must proceed from a motive that is purely ethical. To preserve the purity of that criterion Kant insists on purging the will of all other motives or, at the very least, relegating them to a strictly secondary status. One must do what is good because it is good irrespective of one's self-interest, inclinations, and desires and irrespective of the cost. Pure Duty is the sole motive that can guarantee a good will. To do the good thing because it will make you feel good or win you esteem in the eyes of others compromises the ethical character of one's act. Though he probably was not a reader of Kant, Pat Tillman provides a compelling recent attempt to fulfill the criteria of the Kantian ethic.

In satisfying the Kantian paradigm Tillman reveals both its power and its limitations. Hamlet, in violating it before the fact, points toward a different ethic—one that is inherently tragic. Such an ethic I hope to show is the one required by our historical situation. Hitler, Adorno argued, gave us a new imperative: so act that Auschwitz will never again be possible. Freud gave us another, one directed at the heart of our inwardness: know thyself, become responsible for one's psyche, by becoming aware of all the "unconscious" motives, conflicts, desires, and disorders that inform one's actions: one must assume responsibility not just for one's conscious intentions and rational deliberations but for the deep and inherent conflictedness of one's psyche. The two imperatives, as we'll see, are necessarily connected and equally extreme in the responsibilities they place on us. Dialectically the synthesis of those extremities is perhaps the true measure of our historical situation.

## PSYCHOANALYSIS AND ETHICS

"The role of the intellectual is to make emotional comparisons that will shock people into understanding."

José Saramago, Ha'aretz

The implications of psychoanalysis for ethics derive from what we may formulate as Freud's deepest discovery. *There is something in us that demands our destruction. And there is in us something that radically opposes itself to that force.* The human psyche is the *conflict* between these two principles, a conflict that is unavoidable though it takes an infinite variety of forms. In studying that conflict Freud offers a new self-understanding tied to a new appreciation of the centrality of the tragic to the life of the psyche. Contra Aristotle and the traditional views of the tragic that derive from him, Freud shows that the tragic is not an avoidable event that befalls some subjects as the result of either a flaw or bad luck, and thus something we can regard as a departure from an otherwise rational, healthy, normal human nature. *The tragic is the situation that all subjects face insofar as they are subjects.* The reorientation implicit in this idea has major consequences both for ethics and for the practice of analysis. For it suggests that all ways of being other than the tragic may constitute so many flights from and defenses against it, whether through quiet desperation or noisy affirmation.

Freud's thought constitutes, in fact, a fundamental challenge to the very project of ethics. Contra Kant, what Freud reveals is that ethics is not opposed to desire; it is, rather, one of the primary and most intransigent forms of desire. The superego is a harsh and unremitting force that demands compliance and that tortures, even unto death, the subject who tries to resist it. Though it clothes itself in the mantle of goodness, duty, and virtue it is often little more than the most twisted and life denying form of desire. To move directly to the most radical implication of this line of thought: *ethics must begin with a critique of the superego that contains as its innermost possibility exposing ethics itself as a pathological condition.* Since Freud a major effort within psychoanalysis has been to limit the attack on the superego in order to sustain it as a viable ethical principle; as in the efforts of Erikson, Schafer, and others to establish a loving and beloved superego that can be separated from the harsh, punitive superego. The benign superego, we are told, is aligned with permanent cultural values: it only wants what is ultimately good for us. Once again normalizing values have found a way to reassert themselves in the teeth of Freud's discoveries. The alternative view, which I'll develop here, sustains the Freudian critique of the superego by extending it to all the ways the superego preserves its power. As we'll see, the primary target of this critique will be the ego itself and the subsequent concepts of self and identity that have been developed by a psychoanalysis eager to sustain the illusion that the "developmental process" issues in a permanent and socially adapted identity that cannot be lost. My effort, in opposition to this view, is to sustain the radical wounding that is Freud's basic gift to those who seek self-knowledge as the condition for their freedom and who are therefore willing to suffer the discovery of everything they don't want to know about themselves and those they love. Psychoanalysis offers us a new categorical imperative: not just to know but to become responsible for one's Unconscious, for everything that is buried in one's psyche. The activity through which one pursues that goal is, I'll show, the process through which ethical agency is attained. To put it in the simplest terms: ethics must begin with the effort to discover all the ways in which one is not free followed by the effort to attain freedom by reversing that condition.

As Kant demonstrated, the fundamental issue of ethics (as opposed to morals) is that of autonomy; i.e., whether it is possible for the individual human agent to attain a freedom that will issue in actions that will testify to universal values. Freud does not render the quest for autonomy impossible; he concretizes it by revealing the essential struggle required to attain the required end. The following question posed by Alenka Zupančič in her Lacanian study of Kantian ethics provides a useful formulation of the problem: "Is it possible to conceive of an ethics that is not subject to the logic of the superego in all its resonances; free, on the one hand, from the often-stressed 'irrationality' of its demands and, on the other, from its socializing function as the 'internal' representative of 'external' authorities, values, and norms?" One answer to this question is the Lacanian one Zupančič provides: the famous "refusal to give way as to one's desire."[2] My effort is to provide another: *an ethic based on an internalization of the Tragic so radical that sustaining tragic awareness becomes the principle regulating one's relationship to oneself and consequently to everything one experiences.* The internal regulator one thereby establishes replaces the superego with a principle that coincides with the self-reference that defines the subject. To Kant's categorical imperative—so act that your every action could be made a universal law—it substitutes an existentially *and* psychoanalytically exacting principle: *so be (and act) that your every action opens you to a tragic discovery of everything you don't want to know about your psyche as the burden you must assume.* Discovering all the ways one isn't free is the first moment of the tragic process; overcoming that condition the second. Dialectically these two moments define the being of the tragic subject.

## THE APOSTLE OF DUTY AND THE SUBJECT OF EXISTENCE

"The Court wants nothing from you. It receives you when you come and it dismisses you when you go."

Franz Kafka, *The Trial*

I want now to outline the main principles that inform that ethic and develop them through a systematic contrast with the Kant; i.e., a contast between an ethic that heeds the call of Duty or the Symbolic Order and one that sustains the claims of self-analysis and existence. Most people are content to base their choices and values on a principle outside themselves: religion, custom, legal norms, social constraints, etc. But for those rare individuals such bases compromise the ethical quality of an act. For them one's ethic must be a function of one's freedom. The primary ethical task accordingly is to establish one's autonomy as an ethical agent and derive all ethical values from the conditions of that autonomy. Pat Tillman and Hamlet exemplify the two basic ways a human being can take up this task.

A crucial caveat at the very beginning. For good reason Pat Tillman has been lionized as a model of ethical heroism. In trying to show the limits and the contradictions of the position he exemplifies I intend no disrespect to his memory. Nor is it my intention to engage in unfounded speculation about Tillman's psyche. My concern is solely with the ideal ethical status that certain actions appear to confer upon a subject. Indeed, a primary function of the logic of Duty is to render psychoanalytic considerations irrelevant. Through the Kantian purity of his choice Pat Tillman, in effect, attained a psyche identified with the rational criteria that must be satisfied to attain *a positively good will*. In following Duty all other motives are burnt and purged away. My effort will be to reveal the *impossibility* of that *project* in order to show what it really effects in the inner structure of any psyche bound to it. The focus of such an analysis, then, is not with all the things Pat Tillman may have thought and the psychological considerations that may have entered into his act, but with what takes place in the order of psychic structure whenever a human being makes the kind of choice Pat Tillman made.[3]

Though in radically different ways, for Tillman and for Hamlet ethics begins with the recognition of the superego and its power. Tillman serves the superego. Hamlet rejects it. For Tillman the way to attain a good will and through it an essentialistic identity is to hear and heed the call of Duty. Hamlet, in contrast, finds in the superego a host of values that one has not chosen. He then suffers the consequences of that recognition: *the assault upon oneself within oneself* that begins the moment one tries to say No to the superego. Persisting in that effort he learns the true nature of the identity he thought he had. It resides in obedience to a voice that resists any change or modification, that is initially more powerful in us than anything else, and that persists in dogmatic refusal to acknowledge the complexities of experience. Hamlet's famous "to be or not to be" articulates the complexities that come to define the inner condition of one who rejects that voice in favor of the hard path of reflection.[4] Reflection, Hamlet reveals, is that radical force in the human subject that lays bare all the contradictions and ruptures between thought, feeling, will, desire, and action. The tidy picture that Hamlet's father draws of duty and the swift, uncomplicated, manly course of action is torn to shreds.

The apostle of duty, of course, knows little or nothing of this. The kind of thinking that enters into Hamlet's soliloquy is not merely beyond the possibilities of that position. The position renders such thought irrelevant—and morally suspect. Two radically different modes of self-reference inform the two projects. The ethic Tillman exemplifies grounds ethics in the thing outside oneself that commands *Reverence* and that one serves by overcoming all motives other than duty. One thereby attains an inner condition that delivers one from all doubts and fears over who one is and what one should do. Hamlet, in contrast, grounds ethics in the self-torture that one must embrace in order to bring about a comprehensive change in the very structure of one's psyche. Such an act is impossible in Tillman's world because there *identification* constitutes one's relationship to the Symbolic Order. The two men accordingly take up completely different attitudes toward self-knowledge. From the first soliloquy on, forcing oneself to change is for Hamlet the entire rationale of trying to know one's psyche. Tillman follows a different rationale: by serving the Symbolic one overcomes the threat of change. Reflection for Hamlet is the discovery of contradictions, conflicts, and the necessity of self-overcoming. For the apostle of duty it is the process of finding within oneself—quickly and without any deep effort—those few true and simple principles that one believes with all one's heart and for which one is willing, if necessary, to sacrifice one's life.

The two positions thus entail opposed attitudes toward a shared *starting point*. Both begin with a situation in which the call of the superego is heard in an overpowering way. The apostle of duty answers the call. The subject of existence exposes it. As anyone who studies it knows, the superego is protean. When our compliance is immediate and heartfelt it is quite willing to present itself as a loving inner voice, one that seems in fact to to be our own voice speaking to us in a language that is apparently our own. It is only when we resist or disobey that the superego reveals itself as a force that attacks us with extreme prejudice and that will do anything to compel our submission. "If thou hast nature in thee ...." If ever thou didst thy dear father love ..."—such, Hamlet learns, is the true voice of the superego, tying the psyche in knots by activating the threat that holds the whole structure in place: the loss of the superego's love or, in a subtler form, the loss of the chance to one day prove worthy of and thereby win its love. In all its forms (and the above description is far from exhaustive) one thing is clear: the superego is a terrorist who uses every psychological device to eradicate that within the subject that resists submission.

For Tillman as for Kant there is a fundamental opposition between Duty and Happiness, between the claims of the ethical and the life of self-interested inclination and desire. But in that conflict there is only one correct response. Doing the good often requires that one act against one's self-interest. The happiness one gives up at the beginning, however, one gets back in spades at the end. There is no greater happiness than serving the Good. It confers on one a noumenal identity and symbolic immortality. For Hamlet, in contrast, the true opposition is between Self-consciousness and Inauthenticity. One lacks moral agency as long as one lives in bondage to the superego, in unquestioning fealty to the values, beliefs, and ideology of one's culture. When faced with a conflict between the duties one owes to oneself to sustain the burden of self-consciousness and the duties one has to the Symbolic Order, one must always choose the former. Because self-consciousness remains for Hamlet a supreme value, despite the suffering it brings, Happiness and the desire for it become supremely irrelevant.

For both Tillman and Hamlet ethics begins with a traumatic situation, with the recognition that "something is rotten in the state of Denmark." Tillman feels called by the suffering of his country to do whatever is required to resolve its trauma. For him the lesson of history is clear: all ethical subjects are called on to sacrifice happiness and self-interest to the service required to restore the health of the whole. What Hamlet learns, in contrast, is that it is impossible to locate, simplify, or contain the rottenness nor is there any action one can take that would "set it right." The rottenness is condition general. One finds within oneself that one is fully implicated in it. No heroic or annealing action is possible. In fact, rather than resolving the trauma one must do everything in one's power to sustain and constitute it by destroying all illusions, exposing all hiding places, and eradicating all guarantees so that everyone will see the situation for what it is. That action is the primary action of a play that some claim delays action. Through it Hamlet liberates an ontology of existence or being-in-the-world that overturns all received beliefs. Tillman in acting knows that he acts for all good men, doing what one must to assure the kingdom of universal, trans-historical ends. Hamlet knows that everything he does is an exception, a pure possibility dependent on the rarest and loneliest of actions, the sustaining of a tragic inwardness willing to suffer the loss of everything.

One of the great charms of the Kantian ethic is the satisfaction it offers to a Will that wants to be assured of its goodness. Kant argues that the good will cannot be in conflict with itself. Nor can there be a conflict within the order of the good. The world of value forms a harmonious totality. A conflict between two ethical values that must both be honored or of a situation where in serving one value one necessarily violates the other is impossible. The Kantian ethic offers, in fact, a way of insulating oneself from such experiences. Service to the cause purges one of all doubts about what is Good. For Hamlet the opposite condition maintains. The ethical situation is one in which one is in conflict with oneself fundamentally, in depth, and irretrievably and in which one discovers conflicts in the world that can't be resolved in a way that preserves the harmony of the ethical. Goods are opposed—tragically. Both conditions are for Hamlet primary realities that must enter into the constitution of one's Will. Will must become the radical acceptance of contingency as the source of value.

Through choice the apostle of duty escapes inner contingency. Sustaining that state, however, requires blinding oneself to external contingency. Nothing one sees (in Iraq say) can cause one to question one's choice. For to question it is to destroy it. The choice must impose itself upon the world. What Hamlet insists we see— and keep ourselves in principle open to seeing—is precisely what must be banished, especially on the field of battle. The apostle of duty is incapable of the kind of soliloquy Hamlet engages in when contemplating the absurdity of mass death on a battlefield that is not large enough to bury those about to be slain (Hamlet, 4.4:22–66). For

Hamlet the reality of war scoffs at all heroic pretensions, makes mock of all heroic resolves. As he sees, an ethic of the Symbolic is tied to a logic of mass slaughter. That is the hidden imperative behind its founding demand: that no appeal from reality can correct the purity of the will; or, to put it in the correct terms, that purity must be sustained through the continual abolishment of contingency. Duty conceals the lesson Nietzsche will formulate: *active forgetting* is what makes pure choices possible and what enables them to be sustained. The world must first be resolved into certain abstractions. Good and Evil, us and them. Choice then becomes possible, easy, necessary. Moreover, once one chooses it's all over; thinking cannot then come to question or complicate one's deed.

The two ethics thus proceed from sharply opposed conceptions of thought and the condition that thinking brings about in a subject. Thinking for Hamlet is the act of radical critique that complicates our situation by discovering its central contradictions. The result is a *melancholia* that deepens with each new development of thought.[5] For the apostle of duty, in contrast, thinking issues in the clarity of a *resolve* that banishes all doubts and confusions. To think is to discover Reason and the certitudes it brings to all deliberations, which is why thought always ends not in melancholy ideas but in the bliss of absolute truths. It is, in fact, the thing that delivers one from the threat of melancholia. The choice of duty puts an end to all inner doubts and discontents, banishing the specter of depression both now and in the future. One achieves through one's resolve a clarity of purpose that one can never lose. Resolve for Hamlet, in contrast, remains what it is for Heidegger: an anticipatory readiness that is open to dread,[6] open, that is, to the discovery that one's choice is untenable, that no project, no action delivers one from the duty to sustain a condition of inner doubt and inner suffering.

The difference turns on the problem of identity. The Kantian ethic offers an *identity* that resides in the total correspondence of one's will to Duty. Through duty one is delivered from the kind of inner condition that haunts the American psyche: that there is no self-identity, only a void given over to panic anxiety and the incessant pursuit of meaningless, insatiable desires. Duty offers one a Self that is free of all that, free of everything that disgusted a man like Tillman with the world of the NFL. Hamlet, in contrast, pursues an inwardness in which the psyche becomes transparent to itself by attaining a knowledge of all that it does not want to know about itself. In coming to that knowledge he learns that there is no self, no ego, no identity able to deliver us from persisting in the act that defines the existential subject: to suffer not just the knowledge of one's inner conflicts but the necessity to engage them in the effort of *active reversal*[7] by seeking out those situations that will bring them to a head. That necessity is for Hamlet where ethics begins.

Action puts the apostle of duty beyond change, while action for Hamlet plunges us into change, putting us at issue and at risk. All Symbolic supports for one's being are thereby overturned. One has attained a deeper necessity: to sustain contempt for the disorders one discovers within oneself. That act is the means whereby the psyche transforms itself from within. The apostle of duty, in contrast, is assured by the Symbolic Order that his action confers on him an Identity that resolves any disorders he may have in himself, not just the discontents he feels at times, but the deep and unconscious disorders that may lurk in his psyche. The subject of existence knows what the apostle of duty through his action assures himself he will never to have to know. *That in order to act one must take up one's disorders, not avoid them.* That process commences when depressive melancholy so overtakes a soul that it becomes the mood through which one experiences the world.[8] Hamlet's first soliloquy—"O that this too too sullied flesh"—transports us into a world of thought that comes to fruition in the recognition of the necessity for actions that violate the primary canon of Kantian ethics. All authentic action is the struggle to discover "what is to be done" by cutting through all the barriers both in oneself and in the symbolic. "By whatever means necessary," said Malcolm X. *Hamlet lays bare the existential conditions that establish the ethical necessity of that position.*

One of the truly beautiful ideas one finds in Kant is that having a good will is not only a condition of our happiness but of "our worthiness to be happy."[9] Honoring that criterion is the deepest and most heroic dimension of Pat Tillman's choice. By all accounts Tillman was a happy man possessed with everything we associate with fulfillment of "the American Dream": a football hero with a beautiful wife and family, millions of dollars, and virtually limitless future prospects. Tillman knows, however, that by the claims of a higher standard this happiness has not yet been earned. He has it, but he doesn't know if he's worthy of it. That worthiness can only be established through answering the call of Duty. That choice, however, commits the psyche to the pursuit of a condition similar to the impossible Sartrean *en-soi-pour-soi*. The apostle of duty wants by serving duty to be assured that he has a substantial identity that can never be lost. Like most Americans Pat Tillman is caught up in the pursuit of "The Self," of that stable, lasting ego-identity that delivers one from the contingencies of existence. His is an exceptional example of this pursuit, one that exposes the narcissism of dominant American quests for identity.

Tillman and Hamlet are both sublime agents for whom the inner worth of an act derives from the fact that it has "few" subjective causes. Both have refined their being into ultimate necessities. The subjective causes of Tillman's action are all functions of the desire to become one with the Symbolic Order. Hamlet's are all functions of the desire to sustain the radical individuation that defines tragic awareness. As Kant proudly notes, "in the kingdom of ethical ends everything has either a price or a dignity." Tillman pays the price by enlisting. Death alone, however, confers the dignity by showing that service to Duty has been "exalted above all price and so admits no equivalent."[10] In a sense, such death is necessary. In another it has already occurred. For one has died to all claims other than Duty. Hamlet discovers a more fundamental relationship to death, one that replaces neurotic guilt, the guilt one feels when one disobeys the superego, with existential guilt. This is the guilt one feels whenever one compromises oneself by capitulating to the superego. Internalizing the recognition that existential guilt cannot be overcome delivers one over to a new duty: to overcome all forms of otherworldliness and all ontological guarantees. One only enters history when one knows and accepts what the apostle of duty must deny: that there is no deliverance from historical contingency and that the only viable values derive from the realization that God—i.e., the order of moral and metaphysical absolutes—is dead. That recognition begets, in turn, a new relationship to one's own death. Death is not a reality that choice can transcend or transform. It's the limit that keeps it in the world. Internalizing one's death brings one back from transcendence to finitude, from solutions grounded in the purity of Reason to ones buried in the murk of contingency. Hamlet's words and actions in Act 5 center on the articulation of this awareness, on what it means to internalize the full ethical and existential consequences of an action *before* one performs it. That is how one ripens existentially in tragic knowledge. Unlike the apostle of duty, Hamlet goes to his death knowing it has no global or metaphysical or political meaning. And yet he must accept, even will it, at the expense, even self-waste, of the inwardness that has made him exceptional because the one thing he has learned above all is that we cannot escape our contingency.

One must do what one's historical situation demands not because it is good but because it is necessary.

The two ethics rest on two totally different conceptions of autonomy. The apostle of duty attains the Kantian autonomy of a good will. Hamlet attains the autonomy of a tragic psyche. The first is a freedom that aligns our individual being with Reason and thereby with the kingdom of transhistorical ends and values. The second is a freedom that aligns us with the suffering of contingencies that cannot be resolved or transcended. Autonomy for Kant is achieved when Reason recognizes Duty and the Will attains the purity required to assure that one's choices are informed by nothing but Reason. Existential autonomy is achieved when one wills to choose only that which will deepen the pain that defines self-consciousness, the unhappiness that accompanies all reflection. Autonomy for Kant is achieved by submitting one's will to Reason. Autonomy for Hamlet is attained by immersing oneself in the disorders of one's psyche and sustaining that process against all the motives and creaturely comforts that would end it.

## THE CHOICE ON WHICH ETHICS TURNS

"The dialectical relationship between desire and the Law causes our desire to flare up only in relation to the Law, through which it becomes the desire for death."

Jacques Lacan, *The Ethics of Psychoanalysis*

The world of Immanuel Kant is of course a far cry from the world of Pat Tillman. It could be argued, in fact, that Duty as Kant conceives it can and must have nothing to do either with military action or the needs of a political community. The ethical community Kant envisions has the universal interests of humanity at its heart. The only service it allows is to that kingdom of ends. That is why, as I'll now show, the real conflict between Kant and Hamlet turns on issues that are only vaguely reflected in the situation Pat Tillman faced. The famous Kantian turn or revolution in philosophy—the attempt to establish the *a priori* principles that the mind brings to experience in order to construct phenomena—can be seen as a last ditch effort to preserve the primacy of Reason and the guarantees that can be derived from it. The existential turn constitutes a revolution of equal scope and far more radical implications. The predictable charge that has persistently been brought against it holds that existentialism grounds everything in psychological and emotional causes in opposition to the rational purity that philosophic thought requires. The irony, as I'll show, is that the apostles of Reason thereby disguise how deeply their position derives from psychological and emotional factors which they are careful to conceal from themselves. My demonstration will take the opposition between a Kantian ethic of Duty and an existential ethic of situated subjectivity to a new level where it can also be engaged in a more concrete way.

A common misreading fostered by Kant holds that an ethic of Duty grounded in Reason is free of psychological factors, especially, he'd add, the kind that psychoanalysts identify. Kant works overtime to purge his ethic of pathological motives and emotional factors. There is one emotion, however, that is "self-produced by a rational concept," and thus free of psychological taint. That emotion, *Reverence*, defines our relationship to Duty and the Law.[11] As an emotion Reverence is constituted by the simultaneous feelings of a *profound fear of* and a *deep attraction to* the Law. Moreover, these feelings are of a special sublime order because "Reverence is properly awareness of a value which demolishes my self-love."[12] What we have then in the simultaneity of these two uniquely powerful feelings is an acknowledgement by Kant of the initial relationship of the psyche to the superego. Self-love is demolished due to the profound libidinal tie that is satisfied by obedience. Profound fear and deep attraction thereby hold in place against any alteration of the psyche's founding condition: *an inner world where "self-love" does not yet exist because its possibility depends on the reversal of a prior condition*. Kant inverts the actual temporality of the relationship he describes. The superego has demolished the possibility of self-love. Individual autonomy can only come into existence through an *agon* in which the subject struggles to surmount the power of the two emotions Reverence fuses to estrange it from itself. As long as these two emotions control the psyche one remains in a condition of abjection, unable to question or modify the Law because of the emotional assault that erupts in the psyche whenever one does. Seldom do philosophers devoted to Reason let us see the psyche behind that allegiance. That's why this passage is so significant. It reveals that displacement into Reason is precisely the method whereby Kant assures that the psychological and emotional conditions that inform his ethic will never come under investigation. They've been transformed into something else. *A psyche has found a way to hide from itself.*

A repeated opposition between inclination and duty reflects the deepest impulse of Kant's ethic: to avoid then overcome psychological and emotional factors. Fear of contamination by them is one with the ultimate principle on which his ethic rests: that of Reverence before the Law. In establishing the necessity of that relationship Kant bows before a force that commands him not to know his psyche nor to change his relationship to the force enjoining that non-knowledge. Kant is at pains throughout his ethic to discover pathological motives so that he can be sure to remove them from his concept of the positively good will. The most pathological motive remains in force throughout, however, carefully concealed in abstract concepts all the better to escape detection. That pathology rests on the following identification: the command of the superego as voice of reason is the supreme principle which must be acknowledged as such by a subject that has purged itself of all other motives and emotions. We are, of course, most familiar with this pathology in its virulent realization: religious fundamentalism. There the thing Lacan detected in Kant's categorical imperative reigns supreme: the sadistic need to sacrifice everything in one's person to a life-denying principle.[13]

Hamlet takes up the opposite stance toward the problem of pathology. For him the essential ethical act is the attempt to discover one's pathological motives so that one can engage them in active reversal. Hamlet knows the truth that most people and most philosophers strive to deny. That we never escape the psyche. We always act from it and not from reason. At its worst reason is the fist the psyche bangs down on everything that threatens it; at its best reason discovers its true dignity and purpose—to be the cutting edge of passion. But it only does so when the heart of our darkness plumbed. In following that imperative Hamlet brings about a reversal of the Kantian imperative. Kant's rests on a Reverence for the Law so total that everything else in the psyche remains in permanent subjection to this emotion. Hamlet's rests on a systematic deracination of everything in the psyche that binds us to that very emotion.

Kant grounds his ethic *emotionally* in the affects that bind the abject subject to the superego. An existential ethic, in contrast, is grounded in melancholia as what Keats in the "Ode to Melancholy" called "the wakeful anguish of the soul." This is the emotional condition that comes to regulate the self-reference of a subject who mediates its condition by saying No to all that the superego commands. One thereby attains the antipode of Reverence, Dread. Dread is the realization that there are no ontological supports for one's being.

There is nothing but an existentializing freedom in its lonely effort to find a way to act in the world without guarantees where nothing delivers the psyche from itself.

The Law for Kant is not only the repository of Reason. It's also the defense of Reason against radical critique. That's what Reverence as motive amounts to: the recognition that the Law has reasons we may never fathom but must obey anyway. In vulgar terms, this is the logic that says "my country right or wrong" and that applauds the belief that our leaders must know what's best because they know things we don't. Hamlet is the perfect contrast because he asserts the necessity for total *personal* accountability. He affirms our duty not just to question the Law, but to demand that it make transparent all its reasons—so that we can assert our right to question them. Kant should not be placed only with deSade, as Lacan so brilliantly does. He must also be placed with Kafka, the great anatomizer of the superego. Kant's position is finally the purest service one can render to The Castle. For true apostles of duty hear the Call even when it isn't placed to them. They are so deeply attuned to the superego as internal regulator that like saints they hear it all the time. It is the foundation of their self-reference, the principle of association controlling the stream of their consciousness, the agency that does all the talking when they talk to themselves. The ought for Kant is that which corrects our imperfections. By serving it we are liberated from the contingencies of the psyche into a sublime identity. That's why service to the ought can have no regard for consequences—including one's life. Their introduction would reintroduce the psyche at precisely the point where it must fade away or, if you will, be transcended.

Since for some audiences everything comes down to a question of Reason, here in terms of that exalted principle is the basic contrast. As Kant shows (and his work remains definitive on this score) Reason as a principle for ethics must produce a condition of ethical purity and a harmony of values in which there can be no contradictions; a condition where certain *a priori* demands must be imposed upon the world. Or, to put it in a more telling way, where we must turn our back on any situation that cannot be mediated through that imposition. An existential subject takes up a radically different relationship to experience. Contradictions and contingencies that cannot be resolved are precisely what one must discover, confront, and sustain. Reason's ethical purposiveness is to produce the imperatives of a good will. *Existential psychoanalysis* finds a countervailing purposiveness in tragic situatedness. Here is one way to describe the ethical dynamic that informs it. To be human is to bear the scars of a deeply wounded psyche that one would love to flee—or indulge. We are faced, however, with responsibilities that establish the primacy of something else: our situatedness. Hamlet's condition is ours: the rottenness in the State of Denmark, the use of depleted uranium in Iraq. The key condition on which ethics turns is this: *it is the situation—and not reason or desire—that establishes the starting point of ethics*. The Kantian ethic is the attempt to absolve us of that fact by setting up the criteria that must be met if we are to retain our moral purity. In this it is but another disguised Platonism, offering us assurance that we will never be touched to the core by existence. An existential ethic, in opposition, makes a demand Kant never makes. For Kant we can never fully know the psychological reasons for our action. And in most cases we don't have to. When we serve Duty we know that they don't matter because they aren't regulative. We've transcended our psyche. An existential ethic rests on a radically different imperative: a total responsibility for one's psyche requiring the constant effort to know and engage one's repressed and disclaimed motives. This too is of course a goal that may never be realized. But that doesn't matter because the effort to attain it remains *the regulative principle* requiring that one sustain the process of depth-analysis rather than finding ways to short-circuit it or render it unnecessary.

Tragic existence is thereby revealed not as a flaw but as the realization of a duty with the status of a categorical imperative comparable to Kant's. This is, however, the most inward of duties because it has no rationale other than the demand that some subjects place on themselves: to sustain a sovereign contempt for everything inauthentic in themselves.[14] This duty, the duty we bear to ourselves as subjects, does not come to us from the essentialized order of what is rational, natural, normal, "healthy," or good. It comes to us out of an inner necessity of another and deeper order: the necessity of taking those actions that will maximize responsibility for one's existence. Like the apostle of duty, the tragic subject wills whatever pain choice brings. The pain, however, is precisely the kind of pain that the apostle of duty escapes. Psychological suffering. In Lacanian terms, the apostle of duty is a hero of the Symbolic whereas Hamlet is a hero of the Real. In being so, however, he concretizes that term in a way Lacan cannot by showing that what trauma really inaugurates is not paralysis before that which absolutely resists signification but the development of an existential self-consciousness that sustains a process of self-overcoming. A just and free society would see as its duty the fostering of such individuals and would do all in its power to create the conditions conducive to the evolution of individuals who would take it as their duty to question the foundations of everything. This fantasy reveals the obvious. All societies depend upon the creation of a Symbolic Order to which subjects are bound by superego ties.

A final contrast. The apostle of duty and the subject of existence incarnate two different relationships of the human being to death.[15] Death for the former is heroic sacrifice to a cause, the privilege of bearing witness to what one regards as an unambiguous historical situation. Thereby one attains the essential identity of the soldier and with it a transcendence of that anxiety that constantly impinges on the consciousness of those who take pride in their normality. Death and the dread of it are the origin of human inwardness. Heroism in war is one attempt to gain deliverance from that condition. Hamlet rejects such a relationship to death. For him the only authentic relationship to death acknowledges it as a force at work in all human relations. Dying within is the worst death. The only way to combat it is to internalize death so deeply that it becomes not that thing that will happen at some distant point in the future nor that intrusive thing we spend most of our lives forcing out of our consciousness, but that finality that must enter into and transform all of our choices in a way that fully delivers us over to our finitude. It is by taking death into ourselves and abiding with it that we become subjects who experience the finality of each of our choices as the further entangling of our being in contingencies for which we bear responsibility. Finitude is the contingency that cannot be overcome. We exist fully alive to its demands only by dying to all other voices.

## TOWARD AN EXISTENTIAL ETHIC

Interviewer: "If you had to choose today between two labels, that of marxist and that of existentialist which would you choose?" Jean-Paul Sartre: "that of existentialist ... absorbed, surpassed, and conserved ... it [existentialism] will cease to be a particular inquiry and will become the foundation of all inquiry."

What follows attempts to distill the ethic of existence into its fundamental principles. I also try here to present those theses in a way that will engage the reader's psyche and emotions at precisely the place within us where each of us makes a basic decision about ourselves. That's the only "self" that matters. The others are self-reifying defenses. The argument thus constitutes both an appeal to the reader's freedom and an attempt to impinge on that freedom, to bring each reader before him or herself by challenging defenses with the power that some ideas have to light a fire in the soul.

(1) We concur with Kant that if a choice is not free it's not moral. The possibility of freedom depends, however, on an in-depth analysis of one's psyche. Such an analysis leads from the destruction of ego identity to the need to bring about a complete *reversal* in one's relationship to oneself by deracinating the voice of the other. *Thinking is ethical* insofar as it engages one thing: the battle of a subject with itself over the meaning of its being.

(2) There is no way to abridge that process nor to provide guarantees that will secure a safe outcome. To sustain the psychoanalytic turn, the psyche must continually throw itself into question and root out the emotions that bind it to a pattern of lies. An ethic of the existential subject depends on maximizing what Keats termed *negative capability*: the ability to be in "uncertainties, Mysteries, doubts without any irritable reaching after fact and reason."[16] Rather than resolving doubts, the purpose of thought and action is to deepen them. *An act is ethical* insofar as it deepens the conflict of the subject with itself.

(3) One acts ethically only when all symbolic and ideological supports have collapsed. Only then can one take on responsibility for oneself because only then is one *at issue* and *at risk*. The ethical act must radically open itself to contingency in a situation where one must create values, yet where those values can derive from nothing but the depth of one's engagement in the situation. By the same token, such values cannot be a final solution but must open themselves to later contingencies. Ethics must always allow itself to be measured by contingency because contingency is precisely what calls up ethical responsibility. The primary ethical situation is not one where there is a clear course of duty, but where a subject trembles before its responsibility to create new values in a situation that reduces received values to rubble.

(4) Ethics begins when there is a genuine crisis of values, even perhaps the need for a re-valuation of all values. For Kant there was not nor could there be such a crisis. The values were known, immutable, and generally agreed upon. The only question was what kind of principle they would be grounded in; which meant for Kant and the *Aufklarung*, how could they be grounded in Reason. For

us, in contrast, the primary fact is a historicity that bites into the very possibility of the ethical. Every ethical value must be willing to historicize itself. That recognition entails the following considerations. The desert grows. Under the guise of fundamentalist crusades, herd moralities dominate. The extent of inhumanity is appalling. So many values that once seemed so solid have been so thoroughly debunked. The possibility of ethics now begins with a systematic exposure of all superego pathologies, all the ethical ideologies that societies use to introduce a fundamental passivity into subjects while convincing those same subjects that they are good in a goodness that depends on willed ignorance. An existential ethic is radically destructive of received beliefs, radically disruptive of the desires of the normal subject. Refusing and exposing all Symbolic supports, it seeks in the struggle of the psyche with its disorders the source of value.

(5) Ethics is a matter of extremity. It begins in the most extreme act—the act of radical individuation in which one opens one's psyche to an interrogation that must be sustained in its extremity. Ethics is about a *choice* in which a subject *risks* the value and meaning of its existence, not about those choices that assure it of that meaning. Moreover, it is only when one does this that one experiences for the first time the terror implicit in the oft-quoted Sartrean statement "existence precedes essence."

(6) Ethics must engage and derive from the dread that defines choice. Let me illustrate this proposition by contrasting Hamlet's choice with the situation in Styron's *Sophie's Choice*. The horrifying choice Sophie faces—to choose which of her children will be sent to the gas chamber—is a forced choice and thus extreme and exceptional in a way that deprives it of the possibility of being normative.[17] Hamlet's choice, in contrast, is a free one that issues from nothing but his freedom and the readiness with which he accepts the self-torture that existence entails. Sophie is tortured from without by the madness of the other; and the inhuman logic that madness requires in order to know itself. (Styron calls the officer who forces the choice on Sophie a "genius" of the Reich.) Hamlet is tortured from within by the logic of self-criticism and self-overcoming that informs the existentializing process. We are fortunate if we never face a situation like Sophie's; nor suffer the death-in-life that is the result of such choices. But insofar as we have a psyche Hamlet's situation is the general one that defines us. Or to put it in properly ethical terms, engaging the kind of situation he faces is the act that activates the inherent possibility that defines us. The choice that founds such an

ethic must therefore be distinguished both from the *a priori* choice made by the apostle of duty and Sophie's forced choice. All three refer to extreme choices and situations. In only one, however, is guilt toward oneself both the origin of the choice and its result. That is, only one of the three choices is the ground of its own possibility and thereby the source of an existentialization that issues in values bound to the tragic contingencies of our situatedness.

## THAT VALUE THAT ADMITS NO EQUIVALENT

"But my intention was certainly not to draw away from the concern for existence itself, for concrete personal commitment, or for the existential pathos that, in a sense, I have never lost ... a philosopher without this ethico-existential pathos does not interest me very much."

Jacques Derrida

In her critique of Kantian ethics Alenka Zupančič often refers to the Lacanian idea that there is a loss deeper than one's life. The loss of one's reason for living. The apostle of duty offers a heroic example of how one escapes the threat of that loss. What I'm suggesting here is that ethics actually begins on the other side of it. With the possibility that first exists when one discovers that one has already lost or violated or fatally compromised one's reason for living because the values one thinks one honors and the actual truth of one's life are thoroughly at odds. The traumatic event that brings one to this recognition is the origin of ethics. This is the ethical task it establishes: to see if one can pay the price for having violated oneself by assuming the full burden of the situation one has thereby created.

The ethical situation, accordingly, confronts the subject with the necessity to choose to be in a radically new way or die inside. Nothing less is demanded than a totally new way of relating to oneself, for the guilt one experiences in such a situation is existentializing. One is guilty toward oneself for having failed to honor the duties that one bears to oneself, for having so thoroughly lied to oneself about one's life. As Hamlet learns, it is through that recognition that one first discovers that one has tragic responsibilities toward oneself that can no longer be evaded because one with this situation is the even deeper discovery that there are failures that can be irreversible. That is the possibility defining the situation one is now in. What one does will reveal the truth of who one is. Guilt toward oneself has overtaken all possibilities of displacement and denial. Fail now and one dies within. Most people will, of course, do just about anything to avoid guilt or to get cleansed of it as quickly as possible. That is why so many fail the test when it comes to them, shrinking inside rather than expanding to the demands of our innermost possibility, the one defining our humanity.

An ethics of existence begins with the traumatic experience in which everything we've tried to escape about ourselves catches up with us. One then knows that one's prior life has been a flight. And all one's brave ideas and bright ethical claims airy nothing—the indulgence in comforting and self-alienating lies. But now one is finally, like Hamlet, in the situation from which there is no exit. An ethics grounded in the possibility of freedom depends on the actions one performs within oneself when one finds oneself in a *crisis* that can no longer be denied. This is precisely the kind of situation Kant is unable to consider, which is why he constructs in Duty the principle of choice that renders it impossible. In serving Duty one is delivered from the repressed thought that now can never arise: that one's whole life and all its choices, especially the ethical ones, may be no more than a flight from things in oneself that one flees because one fears that if one is ever forced to face oneself one will suffer a destruction worse than death. Destruction within. An existentializing ethic begins on the other side of all the things we do to delay that event. For it is when the thing one fears happens that one first discovers the truth of one's life, the depth of one's inauthenticity. The trauma that will measure one's humanity has arrived. Nothing else now exists but the lonely struggle of the psyche with itself. Suicide (including the primary form of suicide, inner death) is one term of that situation. Ethics is the other. *An ethics of existence is what one does when one finally finds oneself in the traumatic situation that brings one before oneself.*

There is one lesson in this, a lesson that probably can't be learned. Rather than running from the trauma we should plunge toward it, since it is only through it that we can discover both the truth about ourselves and what we are able to do in the face of that truth. To activate that possibility all that's needed perhaps is to drown out the noise and chatter one keeps running in one's head. Perhaps the truth is that the truth about ourselves is not deeply repressed and unknown. It's closer than we think, available to introspection if we but dared. But that's what makes the kind of impassioned reflection Hamlet engages in so terrifying. It exemplifies everything we know and don't want to know about ourselves.[18]

Here is an attempt to offer an image that describes in depth the existential–psychoanalytic condition from which the possibility of ethics derives. In George Orwell's *1984* Winston Smith when tortured with the thing he most fears betrays the thing he loves. To save his life he sacrifices what gives it meaning. He capitulates before an inner torment that reduces the psyche to a condition of catastrophic anxiety. (The image of the cage of rats placed over the head they will raven externalizes in a perfect objective correlative the terror that has the power to dissolve the psyche. What is a phobia after all but an inner condition displaced into an external fear?) What I want to suggest here is that Winston Smith's phobia describes the inner condition that defines any subject traumatized by itself. Such a subject lives tortured by the struggle not to betray the thing one loves, the thing that could give one's life meaning. But one saves it only if one is willing to sacrifice everything to the acceptance of the suffering and inner torment that service to it entails. This is the ethical act whereby a subject attains tragic agency. Becoming an existentially autonomous agent is the process of engaging the disorders of one's psyche in the effort of active reversal. The wish to escape that effort, to soften it, or to insist that suffering must always have a happy resolution is the voice of self-betrayal. If one gives in to it one loses, with Winston, the thing one has finally found, the thing one can love more than one's life but only by suffering all that it demands. That thing more precious than life is the tragic struggle that gives life perhaps the only meaning it can have.

## TRAGIC SITUATEDNESS: A MODEST PROPOSAL

In terms of ethics, the stakes of such a struggle are clear. The ethical act can't reflect extant values and ideologies. It must create new values. As one example, in closing let me address again the issue of political action in terms of the gravity of our current historical situation; a situation where older ethical and political ideals are no longer tenable and where we must begin to consider the possibility of dangerous, ethically questionable actions. Consider a contrast. Both the possibility and the political efficacy of Gandhi's ethic of non-violence rests on two conditions: (1) that one's oppressor has a conscience that can be appealed to; and (2) that the conscience of the whole world is watching and has the power to put pressure on the oppressor. These two conditions no longer exist. Bush's pre-emptive unilateralism, the littering of Iraq with depleted uranium, the ravaging of the planet's ecological resources and the contempt for everything except insatiable greed reveal the truth of capitalist Empire. And yet to draw the conclusion—"by whatever means necessary"—remains repugnant to ethical sensibilities devoted to moral absolutes. Perhaps that ideal is the luxury we can no longer indulge. As long as one lives in history, ethics is submitted to history for its validation. The paradise of ethical ideals is available only to those who are afforded a position that frees them from history and the recognition that our responsibility to it is total because there is nothing else. All attempts to transcend the world reek of bad faith.

In hopes of reversing that practice I offer a summary of the orientation that an existential psychoanalysis brings to ethics.

(1) In preserving what is radical in Freud, tragic experience evolves an ethic that both satisfies and concretizes the criteria that Kant established. For it is through the tragic process that *autonomy* becomes existentially concrete.

(2) Exposing the pathological desire that informs Kantian ethical formalism is the essential step that shifts the entire burden of ethics to the psyche and existence. The Kantian demand for a non-pathological basis for ethics reflects a pathology: the pathology called the *Aufklarung*; the demand there be only rational motives. There is only one alternative to this position. A radical appropriation of Freud: the decision to take up the pathological fully by knowing one's psyche in depth and reversing all that one thereby discovers.

(3) The deracination of the superego and all the "values" it enforces is the process that leads to an ethic that is universal *and* existential; that is, an ethic that preserves the individual subject's concrete situatedness as the foundation for an ethics that creates values binding on all subjects.

(4) The route to that ethic is through engagement in the tragic conflicts that define the psyche. That act is the ethical act bound to the only categorical imperative that is existentially and psychoanalytically concrete: so *be* that your being remains at issue in all your choices and actions.

The primary criteria that must be satisfied for such an ethic may be summarized as follows:

(1)  An exposing of the ways that all other ethical theories are grounded in the superego in order thereby to deprive the subject of all symbolic, social supports for action. Destabilized internally, the subject loses all inner supports other than those it itself creates through a process of self-knowledge that is also necessarily one of existential self-overcoming. Ethics depends on a systematic critique of one's motives focused on the possibility that those values and beliefs one most strongly affirms may derive their power from a flight from one's psyche.

(2)  Accepting its situatedness radically opens the subject to the contingencies of existence while abrogating any and all guarantees that would limit contingency. One must assume total responsibility both for one's action and for the situation that it creates. There is no pure act capable of granting the subject a permanent ethical identity. The authentic ethical act embraces contingency in the will to sustain a reflection that continually rubs raw one's existential awareness.

(3)  Ethical action is the risking of oneself in a situation defined by the possibility of discovering things about oneself that may bring about one's destruction. One only acts ethically when one's action opens one to the possibility of subjective destitution, catastrophic anxiety, and the dissolution of the psyche. Or, to put it positively, one only acts ethically when one puts oneself in a situation that has the power to bring about a radical change in one's being. Rather than avoiding such situations, one must seek them out. Action thereby becomes not the witnessing of pre-existent values but the creation of new values that are grounded in nothing other than freedom.

The above theses outline the basic *criteria* whereby the process we've described provides *regulative* principles for conduct.

*Where superego was, existential autonomy must come to be.*[19] Such is one way to highlight the way in which an authentic psychoanalysis is an ethical process. Each step one makes in that process generates an ethic based on two principles: (1) action within oneself is only genuine when it puts one at issue and at risk; (2) the end result of such action is the creation of values grounded in nothing other than freedom. Perhaps that's why each step here is as difficult as it is rare. To confront the superego is to demand radical change in one's relationship to oneself—a reversal of the very structure of the personality. Sustaining that process is the act of a freedom that creates freedom as a value by making it experientially concrete. For one never overcomes a superego demand abstractly; by telling oneself, for example, that one is a rational agent and will be guided only by rational principles. One only overcomes the superego by taking actions that bring one's conflict with it to a head. The struggle for sexual liberation is a good example. It's relatively easy to vow that one will assert one's freedom in this area, but it is only in the act of trying to do so that one discovers the true force of the superego and the long, slow process required to free oneself from all the ways it assaults one in body and in mind. It is from that process that a new value emerges however. For one discovers through it the power of the erotic and thereby ways of relating to others that reveal the kind of complexities that superego morality abhors. The ethical here, in short, is what emerges when one descends from the purity of abstract ethical thought to conflicts, choices, and values that can only be known by being lived. The ethical is what one discovers when one engages one's conflicts directly in experience and not just in thought.

To take up the tragic dimension of Freud's discoveries goes against the grain of all the motives subjects invoke to limit their responsibility for themselves. There can, in opposition, be only one motive for pursuing the tragic. An ethical one. The desire to assume true responsibility for oneself by suffering all that one must in order to become honest and clean in one's relationship to oneself. Such a will goes much further than the Kantian demand that the good will be free of motives deriving from inclination and self-interest. For in willing to suffer of oneself one goes beyond both the pleasure and reality principles; i.e., beyond the metapsychological framework in which Freud tried to contain his insights. One has uncovered a third principle of mental functioning: *the ability of the human being to regulate its self-reference by that which maximizes its existence.* Unlike the other two principles, this principle is strictly speaking unmotivated by anything in the natural order since it is grounded in nothing but the possibility of freedom.[20] That is, it arises through the free act in which an individual calls itself to account. Whenever one does so one transcends the idea of a reward, which Kant correctly saw as a fatal barrier to the ethical act. To open one's psyche to the discovery of all one has buried, denied, and lied to oneself about is to risk a process in which there can be no guarantee of a reward or a successful outcome. The psyche opens itself instead to the possibility of its own dissolution. That possibility, moreover, remains the one constant that must be willed and experienced, the primary condition for progress in this dialectic being that each new discovery have the power to overthrow everything one believes about oneself. Psychoanalysis violates itself whenever it plays the mental health game of guaranteeing good results; especially when that need comes from analysts and their unacknowledged allegiance to adaptational ideologies. The ethical value of psychoanalysis is its power to expose all systems of value that abridge the only process through which we can become free, autonomous agents, knowing that agency is nothing but the effort to create values.

In summary the position I've developed here can be formulated thus: an ethic of tragic autonomy is grounded in the effort to assume total responsibility for one's psyche on the basis of a systematic psychoanalytic self-knowledge that exposes the superego, thereby engaging the subject in the effort to overcome it as the necessary process through which one becomes capable of the ethical act; i.e., of those acts that create what Nietzsche called a "value for the earth" by maximizing our situatedness and the imperatives it imposes on us. In following that course one learns that existing without guarantees, without any metaphysical supports for our being, does not remove the claims of the universal. It increases them while establishing the only context in which they can be actualized. *This is the task of Orpheus: to sing us back from death into a new way of being that blossoms in those who can suffer the contradictions of their time as the untranscendable horizon of thought, action, and passion.*

### SINGING IN THE HARD RAIN

What's in a title? As, hopefully, it plays in your head as you read. That moment of sublime romantic hopefulness celebrated by Gene Kelly, its transformation by Alec in Kubrick's *A Clockwork Orange* (with Dubya cast in that part in the remake) as *both* renditions play off Bob Dylan's great, prophetic ballad about the ecological future. Who knows? All we can say, with the Eliot of the "Four Quartets," is that "you are the music while the music lasts." The same register of your inwardness is where words sometimes try to take root.

The critique of humanistic and essentialistic *guarantees* is an attempt to get us into history by depriving us of the *a priori* ethical absolutes we've traditionally interposed between ourselves—i.e., our essential human nature—and History in order to protect ourselves from it and assure ourselves that in our essential humanity we are not touched to the quick by History and can always recover from its traumas and renew ourselves at the eternal spring of the *guarantees*. (Even Marx, and I think of my thought as a continuation of his staggering work, needed to impose a system of guarantees on history that assured the collapse of capitalism and the eventual triumph of the proletariat. *Das Kapital* is a great book but it is also yet another Hegelian translation of Logic into temporal, and in Marx's case, economic terms.) Ontologically, we never could afford to have such views, but in the present circumstances they are positively destructive. The choice we face is a simple one. Be in history or find a way out, but don't sustain the bad faith of the contradiction. Once *time* permitted the endless abstract debating of what relationship universal, substantialist principles of human nature have to historical change. But *time* is now defined by the crisis of the environment, the prospect that we are killing the planet on which we depend for our very life. The debacle of Iraq is finally a provincial backwater in the tsunami crest of that crisis. *Time* today is defined by the urgency of radical intervention. It may even breed the necessity for a new form of terror. But ethically terror can never be justified as an isolated individual action. Narcissistic ahistorical nostalgia feeds on that grandiose pathos. Historical responsibility, in contrast, is always a matter of organized political action. But that condition is also our dilemma. The virtual absence of any discourse about the environmental crisis was one of the most conspicuous features of the 2002 US election. This absence speaks of more than the bankruptcy and cowardice of the Democratic Party and its standard appeal once again to its loyal left: "let us temporize until we get elected and then you'll see how radical we are." The facts confirm the opposite. The Democratic Party is not part of the solution; it's part of the problem. But that recognition transforms the very terms of the problem! For there simply is not *time* within our political system to build a party that will have a realistic chance of being elected to power. By the time we did we'd all be choking on the perception that it's too late. But then, to return to the question that Lenin and Tolstoy shared: "what is to be done?" Is the knowledge of history finally that "highway of despair" that Hegel invented modern thought and consciousness in order to exorcise? Or, more concretely, there are certain *actions* that one can take ethically only if those actions have a legitimate chance of seizing power and are thus bound to a political group who are prepared to govern. This, of course, was the sage advice Colin Powell whispered to Dubya: take out Saddam—and apologies to Pat

Robertson he didn't mean for dinner—and you inherit a country. What's good for the goose is also good for us. *Action* is the translation of the full depth and complexity of one's thought, one's inwardness into the terms of *responsibility*. Lucidity is terror. Nietzsche calls for a "pessimism of strength" (i.e., to have the courage to face a negative reality and to grow stronger as a result of doing so) and I suppose that for most readers this book constitutes a similar call. Which doesn't mean it can't be answered affirmatively, since all you have to do is overcome the belief that any argument that doesn't end up restoring the guarantees and thereby making us feel happy and secure again is a counsel to despair. Due to the forces of global capitalism that find their current signifying monkey in Dubya, history once again weighs like a nightmare on the brains of the living.

# Notes

## PREFACE

1. But for a delightful example of old-style psychohistory applied to George W. Bush, see Justin A. Frank, *Bush on the Couch* (New York: Regan Books, 2004). The moral/political extension of psychoanalysis that I practice here is something quite different. It stands in a long line of thought that was first charted by Freud in a series of examinations of European society and culture during and after the period of the First World War. Walter Benjamin and the members of the Frankfurt School (specifically Adorno, Horkheimer, and Marcuse) extended this tradition into a full-scale critique of capitalist ideologies. Psychoanalytic thinking thereby became one with Marxism in a synthesis that took as one of the objects of critique psychoanalysis itself; and specifically what happened to it in America once its mandate became to preach adaptation and the defense of the ego. The history of psychoanalysis in America remains under the control of that mandate which is why it is often no more than the mental health wing of capitalist ideology. For an incisive critique of earlier chapters in that history, see Russell Jacoby, *Social Amnesia* (Boston: Beacon Press, 1975). Today the old wine is circulated under a number of new names: self psychology, intersubjectivity, attachment theory, and relationality.
2. I've developed this critique at length in *Deracination: Historicity, Hiroshima and the Tragic Imperative* (Albany: SUNY Press, 2001). The present book is an application of that theory to contemporary events. At key points in the argument I offer the reader references to those pages in *Deracination* that ground the discussion, but reading them is not necessary to understanding the present book.

## CHAPTER 1

1. My source for this is a scene in Richard Attenborough's *Gandhi*.
2. The major texts on psychosis that underlie the concept of it that I will develop are: W.R. Bion, *Transformations* (New York: Jason Aronson, 1965), *Second Thoughts* (New York: Jason Aronson, 1983), *Cogitations* (London: Karnac Books, 1992); Michael Eigen, *The Psychotic Core* (New York: Jason Aronson, 1986); Melanie Klein, *Envy and Gratitude* (New York: Delta, 1967); D.W. Winnicott, *Collected Papers: Through Paedatrics to Psycho-Analysis* (New York: Basic Books, 1958) and "Fear Of Breakdown," *International Review of Psycho-Analysis* 1, 1974, pp. 103–07.
3. See Davis, *Deracination*, pp. 193–232.
4. For the development of such a hermeneutic and the ways in which it contrasts with the hermeneutic theories developed by Heidegger, Gadamer, and Riceour, see Walter A. Davis, *Inwardness and Existence:*

*Subjectivity In/And Hegel, Heidegger, Marx, and Freud* (Madison: University of Wisconsin Press, 1989). Engagement renders hermeneutics existential, political, and psychoanalytic.

5.  The article was written by McGeorge Bundy but published under Secretary of War Henry Stimson's name: "The Decision to Use the Atomic Bomb," *Harper's*, February 1947. Bundy, architect of the myth, admitted the truth in *Danger and Survival: Choices About the Bomb in the First Fifty Years* (New York: Knopf, 1992).

6.  In establishing these as the four reasons for the bombing of Hiroshima, pride of place among historians goes to the seminal work by Gar Alperovitz, *The Decision To Use the Atomic Bomb and the Architecture of an American Myth* (New York: Knopf, 1995). See also, Robert J. Lifton and Greg Mitchell, *Hiroshima in America: A Half Century of Denial* (New York: Putnam, 1995).

7.  Leslie Groves cited in Richard Rhodes, *The Making of the Atomic Bomb* (New York: Simon and Schuster, 1986), p. 627.

8.  See Davis, *Deracination*, pp. 47–97.

9.  Klein, *Envy and Gratitude*.

10. See Melanie Klein, "A Contribution to the Psychogenesis of Manic-Depressive States," and "Mourning and its Relation to Manic-Depressive States," in *Love, Guilt and Reparation* (New York: Delta, 1975).

11. Wilfred R. Bian, *Second Thoughts* (London: Pitman, 1967).

12. Paul Boyer, *When Time Shall Be No More* (Cambridge, MA: Harvard University Press, 1992).

13. Guy Debord, *The Society of the Spectacle* (Detroit: Black and Red, 1983).

14. For a critique of this position, see below, Chapter 5.

15. For a development of this theory of trauma and its contrast with the way trauma is conceived in American psychology, see Walter A. Davis, *An Evening with JonBenét Ramsey: A Play and Two Essays* (Nebraska: iUniverse, 2004). For the theory of trauma within mainline American psychoanalytic psychology and the guarantees that underlie this theory, see Charles B. Strozier and Michael Flynn (eds) *Trauma and Self* (Maryland: Rowman and Littlefield, 1996).

## CHAPTER 2

1.  Though we both focus the study of ideology on fantasy, the concept of fantasy I develop and its connection to psychotic anxieties is very different from the Lacanian theory of the fantasmatic developed by Slavoj Žižek. For extended contrast, see below, Chapter 6.

2.  See *Boston Herald*, August 4, 2003, Technology section; *Wired News*, July 30, 2003, Business section.

3.  See *Democracy Now*, August 5, 2003, <http://www.democracynow.org/article.pl?sid=03/08/05/1455235>.

4.  Raymond Williams deserves great credit for trying to introduce this concept to Marxist theorizing. Unfortunately, Williams operates with a very traditional concept of emotion. See, *Marxism and Literature* (Oxford: Oxford University Press, 2000).

5.  See Davis, *Deracination*, pp. 183–91.
6.  *New York Times*, August 3, 2003, "Week in Review."
7.  Studs Terkel, *Guardian*. August 5, 2002. For this and related links on Guardian Unlimited go to <http://www.guardian.co.uk>.
8.  Robert Lowell, "Waking Early Sunday Morning," *Near the Ocean* (London: Faber, 1967).

## CHAPTER 3

1.  The conceptual pun here is deliberate. Primary process ideation operates whenever the psyche cognizes through image or is affected by image. As such, primary process ideation is present in all areas of quotidian life, both in the way ideology plants structures in the psyche and in the rupture that occurs whenever a radical image enters the psyche. We don't live in two worlds, but in one; one where, qua psyche, we are always simultaneously in the real and in the dream; or, better, in a process in which knowledge is the mediation of experience through all the processes whereby the psyche responds to phenomena. See Davis, *Deracination*, pp. 151–3 and 193–222.
2.  On the concept of the Event, see ibid., pp. 35–9, 106–7, 153–62, and 235–6.
3.  Rene Girard, *Violence and the Sacred* (Baltimore: Johns Hopkins University Press, 1977).
4.  Laura Mulvey, "Visual Pleasure and Narrative Cinema," in *Visual and Other Pleasures* (London: Macmillan, 1989).
5.  Garry Wills has a fine essay on the connection between Gibson's film and reactionary movements within Catholicism. See "God in the Hands of Angry Sinners," *New York Review of Books* 51 (6), April 8, 2004, pp. 68–74.
6.  The book that was a favored reading among the neocons is Raphael Patai's *The Arab Mind* (London: Macmillan, 1973). Needless to say there is no evidence of their making the acquaintance of Edward Said's *Orientalism* (New York: Vintage, 2000). Samuel Huntington, *The Clash of Civilizations and the Making of New World Order* (New York: Simon and Schuster, 1996) is, of course, the primary architect of the ideology behind a quasi-Hegelian application of an ahistorical cultural essentialism to world politics. On Patai and the neocon fascination with "Arab sexuality," see Seymour M. Hersh, "The Gray Zone," *New Yorker*, May 24, 2004, p. 42.
7.  For a quick and insightful study of this concept, which is central to Žižek and to Lacan's late thought, see Todd McGowan, *The End of Dissatisfaction* (Albany: SUNY Press, 2004).
8.  See Robert J. Lifton, "Conditions of Atrocity," *Nation* (May 31, 2004), pp. 4–5.
9.  See Shankar Vedantam, "The Psychology of Torture," *Washington Post*, May 20, 2004. See also Dr. Michael A. Weinstein "Abu Ghraib Means Impunity" in PINR (Power and Interest News Report) Dispatch of May 24, 2004.

10. On historicizing the dialectic of Eros and Thanatos and a critique of Freud's ahistorical formulation of this dialectic, see Davis, *Deracination*, pp. 133–50.

11. For Bion's psychoanalytic development of this concept, see Bion, *Cogitations*, pp. 1–98 . See also Michael Eigen *The Sensitive Self* (Middletown, CT: Wesleyan University Press, 2004).

12. Artaud of course never developed an explicit theory of emotion. His thought on the subject is the explosion that occurs throughout his work. Artaud, *Antonin Artaud: Selected Writings*, edited and with an introduction by Susan Sontag (Berkeley: University of California Press, 1976). I have tried to develop a theory of how tragic drama works on the primary emotions of an audience in *Get the Guests: Psychoanalysis, Modern American Drama, and the Audience* (Madison: University of Wisconsin Press, 1994).

13. Peter Weiss, *The Persecution and Assassination of Jean-Paul Marat as Performed by the Inmates of the Asylum of Charenton under the Direction of the Marquis de Sade* (New York: Athenuem, 1972), p. 163.

## CHAPTER 4

1. Jacques Ellul's *The Technological Society* (New York: Knopf, 1964) remains the finest study of technological rationality and the imperative it imposes on all fields and disciplines to rethink their subjects of inquiry so that they conform to what this way of thinking establishes as the real. Martin Heidegger's *The Question Concerning Technology, and Other Essays* (New York: Garland, 1977) offers a magisterial meditation on the ontological implications of technology. One way to define our world is this: in Wittgensteinian terms, technological rationality has become the "form of life" that renders all other forms unintelligible and archaic.

2. I've relied on numerous sources for the factual bases of this chapter. An extremely useful website is Depleted Uranium Watch: <http//www. stopnato.org.uk/du-watch/index.htm>. See also <http:///www.umrc. net/contact.asp> and <http://www.informationclearinghouse.into/ article5941.htm>. On the nature of depleted uranium see <http://www. umrc.net/whatIsDU.asp>. The entire book from an important conference on DU is now available at <http://www/uraniumweaponsconference.de>. See also the Uranium Medical Research Center in Toronto: <http:www. umrc.net/default.aspx>. Mention should also be made here of a recent and alarming report done by the Institute for Energy and Environmental Research for the Nuclear Regulatory Commission on corporate options for DU disposal and its risks. See <www.ieer.org/reports/du/LESrptfeb05. pdf>.

3. In connection with this paragraph, see <http://www.traprockpeace. org/rokke du 3 ques.html> and <http://traprockpeace.org/chris busby 08may04.html>. Desert Storm was not, however, the first use of DU. DU was used by Israel under U.S. army supervision in 1973.

4. In connection with this paragraph, see <http://www.sfbayview.com/081804/ Depleteduranium081804.shtml>; <http://www.truthout.org/docs;04/

www.americanfreepress.net/html/cancerepidemic.html>; <http://www.truthout.org/docs;04/www.worlduraniumweaponsconference.de/speakers/speakers.htm>; <http://www.rense.com/general56/dep.htm>.

5. Giorgio Agamben, *Homor Sacer: Sovereign Power and Bare Life* (Stanford University Press, 1998).

6. On tactical nuclear weapons currently being planned for development by the U.S. see <www.Haarp.alaska.edu/haarp>; <www.dtic.mil/jointvision/jupub2.htm>; <www.popsci.com> (Defense 2020); and <http://www.fredsadademiet.dk/library/stealth.htm>. Recently 153 million dollars of DU weapons including bunker busters (or to use official language and thus gain insight into the libidinal bases of the new technologies, Robust Nuclear Earth Penetrators) were sold to Israel. The purpose of all these developments is to blur the distinction between conventional and nuclear war. Iraq is the systematic eradication of that distinction, and as such a first sign of things to come.

7. See Ludwig Wittgenstein, *Philosophical Investigations* (London: Macmillan, 1958). For example, number 129: "The aspects of things that are most important for us are hidden because of their simplicity and familiarity ... The real foundations of his inquiry do not strike a person at all.—And this means: we fail to be struck by what, once seen, is most striking and most powerful." One purpose of this chapter is to show that our responsibility is not to acquiesce in this situation but to become aware of it as the ethical duty of historical subjects. Responsibility to history deprives us of the luxury of leaving the social, ideological, and communal bases of our thoughts and practices in the dark, however convenient or natural it is to do so.

8. I ran across this delightful quote in Mark Crispin Miller's *Cruel and Unusual: Bush/Cheney's New World Order* (New York: Norton, 2004), p. 298.

9. See, for example, Harvey Wasserman, *Killing Our Own: The Disaster of America's Experience with Atomic Radiation* (Ohio: Delacorte, 1982).

10. Klein, *Envy and Gratitude*.

11. I intend this proposition quite literally. My effort is to construct a dialectical philosophy of history like Hegel's but one that traces the development of an antithetical principle to his. For Hegel on the Absolute and Absolute Knowledge as the necessary outcome of dialectical reasoning, see the chapter in *The Phenomenology of Mind*, trans J.B. Baillie (London: George Allen and Unwin, 1910) titled "Absolute Knowing" and the chapter in the *Logic* titled "The Absolute Idea."

12. Paul W. Tibbets, Clair Stebbens and Harry Franken, *The Tibbets Story* (New York: Stern and Day, 1978). On Tibbets and Hiroshima, see Walter A. Davis *The Holocaust Memorial: A Play About Hiroshima* (Bloomington: First Books, 2000).

13. The Department of Energy continues to insist that there is no evidence to support the claim that DU is harmful; and of course they've lined up the usual scientists to support the proposition, despite all the medical evidence our soldiers have now brought home in their bodies. Moreover, the claim of non-knowledge by the Department of Energy is also pernicious, since not knowing what the effects of a weapon will be

is a *prima facie* reason *not* to use it. Or, to state the matter in terms of the facts. The U.S. continues to practice what was one of the rationales for bombing Hiroshima: to create a laboratory so that our scientific, medical, and military personnel can study the effects of our weapons. Ethically, to formulate the antithesis: the use of any weapon that has not been fully tested in terms of all its possible consequences should be classified as a war crime. Naturally, the powers that be will always claim that some other cause is to blame. This explanation has already been floated in relation to Iraq, the claim being that the increase in cancers etc. of the Iraqi people stems from Saddam's use of chemical and biological weapons. That is, the cause is not the weapons we used on him but the ones we gave him, a transfer presided over by none other than Donald Rumsfeld (on this see <http://www.newscientist.com/news/news.jsp?id=ns99993627>). All this suggests a concluding fantasy of how the clean-up of Iraq should begin. Each of them—Bush, Cheney, Rumsfeld, Wolfowitz, Rice, Perle, Rove, and all the others—should be given a sack and ordered to fill it with chunks of the radioactive debris that now litters Iraq. They should then be required to take that sack home and use it as their pillow. Pleasant dreams.

## CHAPTER 5

1. Robert J. Lifton, *Superpower Syndrome: America's Apocalyptic Confrontation with the World* (New York: Thunder's Mouth Press, 2003). My treatment of Lifton is comparatively briefer here than my treatment of Žižek/Lacan in the next chapter because I have already in *Deracination* developed a lengthy critique of the essentialistic system of guarantees on which Lifton bases his thought.

2. See especially, Robert J. Lifton, *The Protean Self* (New York: Basic Books, 1993) and *The Life of the Self* (New York: Simon and Schuster, 1976).

3. Robert J. Lifton, *The Broken Connection* (New York: Simon and Schuster, 1979, p. 7. This is Lifton's most philosophic book.

4. For an incisive and detailed critique of Lakoff along lines similar to those adumbrated here, see Richard Lichtman, "The Consolations of George Lakoff," *Counterpunch*, May 28/30, 2005.

## CHAPTER 6

1. A delightful example is Žižek's analysis of the Japanese electronic toy, the tamagochi, in "Is It Possible to Traverse the Fantasy in Cyberspace," in *The Žižek Reader* (Oxford: Blackwell, 1999), pp. 104–24.

2. For Baudrillard's exceedingly glib take on 9-11 see *The Spirit of Terrorism and Requiem for the Twin Towers* (London: Verso, 2002).

3. This is Samuel Huntington's disease, the grand ideological gesture whereby economic and geopolitical conditions are transformed into a "culture war" of moral and religious absolutes. The latest in right Hegelianism.

4. Derrida represents this position in a rethinking of the concept of trauma in the fine dialogue "Autoimmunity: Real and Symbolic Suicides" that he contributes to Giovanna Borradori's *Philosophy in a Time of Terror:*

*Dialogues with Jürgen Habermas and Jacques Derrida* (Chicago: University of Chicago Press, 2003).

5. Herbert Marcuse "Repressive Tolerance" in Robert P. Woolf, Barrington Moore and Herbert Marcuse, *Critique of Pure Tolerance* (Boston: Beacon Press, 1969).

6. In the aforementioned dialogue, Derrida rethinks the concept of democracy with great incisiveness. See Derrida, "Autoimmunity," pp. 118–24.

7. Slavoj Žižek, *Welcome to the Desert of the Real* (London: Verso, 2002), p. 82.

8. For Žižek's best formulation of this concept, see *The Plague of Fantasies* (London: Verso, 1997), Chapter 3.

9. Žižek, *Welcome to the Desert of the Real*, p. 96.

10. Ibid., p. 100.

11. Ibid., p. 112.

12. On these connections, see Michael C. Ruppert, *Crossing the Rubicon* (Canada: New Society Publishers, 2004).

13. Žižek, *Welcome to the Desert of the Real*, p. 128.

14. Ibid., p. 134.

15. Hegel, however, provides only one example of this project. At an opposite extreme one could cite Carnap's *Logical Structure of the World*. And for a position in the middle, the structuralist formalism of binary logic of Levi-Strauss. Other chapters in this story would include all the forms of neo-Kantianism that have dominated modern thought, ranging from Cassirer's Philosophy of Symbolic Forms to Kenneth Burke's pentad.

16. Here too it would be a mistake to think Hegel is the only one who offers such an understanding. The philosophic pluralism of Richard McKeon, for example, provides a synoptic understanding of all discursive possibilities schematized in an overarching pluralistic framework which acknowledges the "truth" of all of them. See his *Thought, Action and Passion* (Chicago: University of Chicago Press, 1954). Moreover, McKeon's position is far more open to the legitimacy of competing positions than Hegel's transcendental monism allows, despite Hegel's claim to honor the inherent truth of every position as a moment in the Hegelian system.

17. Žižek's finest philosophic work, *For They Know Not What They Do* (London: Verso, 1991) is devoted to this reading of Hegel. For a contrasting and more traditional reading of the *Logic*, see Charles Taylor, *Hegel* (Cambridge: Cambridge University Press, 1975).

18. Žižek's work thus stands in the methodological tradition of ideological critique established by Adorno and the Frankfurt School. The difference it that Žižek through the use of Hegel and Lacan takes up the task of wedding Marx and Freud at a far more theoretical level.

19. For what is perhaps the last word from this perspective on the nature of subjectivity, see Derrida's final thoughts on Artaud, "to Unsense the subjectile," in Jacques Derrida and Paule Thévenin, *The Secret Art of Antonin Artaud* (Cambridge, MA: MIT Press, 1998), pp. 61–157.

20. The most extreme example is the claim Žižek makes for the exemplary ethical status of the actions of Bobby Perou in his analysis of David Lynch's *Wild at Heart* in "Fantasy as a Political Category: A Lacanian

Approach," *Journal for the Psychoanalysis of Culture and Society* 1(2), Fall, 1996, pp. 77–85.

21. This is precisely what Heidegger does in *Being and Time* (New York: Harper and Row, 1962) through his distinction of the *existentiell* and *existentiale*, thereby preserving the formalism of the analytic of Dasein from what would happen if he let that analytic be the prelude to a concrete study of existential experience. That is the last thing Heidegger wants. Thus, ironically, his great book leads him away from existence rather than into it.

22. Jacques Lacan, "Of Structure as an Inmixing of Otherness Prerequisite to Any Subject Whatever," in Richard Macksey and Eugenio Donato (eds), *The Structuralist Controversy* (Baltimore: Johns Hopkins Press, 1972), p. 232.

23. This is the issue that Hegel discusses in the famous "Preface" to the *Phenomenology*.

24. Hegel makes precisely this gesture at the end of both the *Logic* and the *Phenomenology*. It is required methodologically to complete the necessary circularity of his thought. It does not, however, deepen the examination of existence and experience.

25. To put it in Hegelian or dialectical terms, what follows is the *Aufhebung* of Lacan, the movement whereby his thought and its important contribution to an understanding of the psyche are cancelled, preserved, and "uplifted."

26. The necessity of imitating one's thought in one's writing style or *ecriture* is frequently used to praise or justify the stylistic excesses of Derrida and Lacan, to my mind two of the worst writers I've read. In Lacan's case a simpler explanation may account for the contortions of his style. For Lacan every utterance must gesture in three directions simultaneously: contempt for other thinkers, self-aggrandizement, and the search for opacity. The alternative to such a style would be a prose dipped in acid and animated by an effort to act on the reader the way the sculpture *Archaic Torso of Apollo* acted on Rilke.

27. The finest philosophic consideration of Lacan's thought in English, Richard Boothby's *Freud as Philosopher* (London: Routledge, 2001) does a masterful job on this crucial issue.

28. See especially Melanie Klein, *The Psychoanalysis of Children* (New York: Dell, 1975).

29. John Keats, "Ode on Melancholy," in *The Selected Poetry of Keats* (New York: NAL, 1966), p. 254.

30. Bergmann, who plays Levy in the movie, is a psychoanalyst and author of the fine book from which Levy's thoughts are derived: *The Anatomy of Loving* (NY: Columbia University Press, 1987).

31. Hegel, *Phenomenology*, p. 231. Hegel's insight into the dynamic that defines love is a pure product of the concept of Reflection from which he deduces it. To be aware of limitations is to be already beyond them: such is the power and principle that define a reflective self-consciousness for Hegel.

32. The section "Concrete Relations With Others" in Sartre's *Being and Nothingness* (New York: Philosophical Library, 1956) pp. 361–430 remains

the most incisive and systematic application of Hegel's *Phenomenology* to intersubjectivity and human relations.

33. In this connection mention should be made of Lacan's considerable and generally unacknowledged debt to Sartre and to Proust for his understanding of how desire generates the perpetual failure of human relations.

34. Jacques Lacan, *Ecrits: A Selection* (New York: Norton, 1977), pp. 292–325.

35. Artaud, *Selected Writings*, p. 258.

36. Jacques Lacan, *Le Seminaire. Livre X. L'Angoisse, 1962–63*. (Paris: Editions du Seuil, 1994). This seminar should put to rest the contention that Lacan has no theory of emotions.

37. The best articulation of Lacan's thought on this central category is in Boothby, *Freud as Philospher*, pp. 242–96.

38. Jacques Lacan, *Encore. The Seminar of Jacques Lacan, Book XX* (New York: W.W. Norton, 1998), pp. 4–6, 144–6.

39. Joan Copjec, "Sex and the Euthenasia of Reason," in *Read My Desire* (Cambridge, MA: MIT Press, 1994), pp. 201–36.

40. Edward Albee, *A Delicate Balance*, in *The Plays. Vol. 2.* (New York: Atheneum, 1981), p. 164.

41. The dialectical theory of Eros and Thanatos I'm developing is radically different from the Utopian and essentialistic theories advanced by Herbert Marcuse in *Eros and Civilization* (New York: Vintage, 1962) and Norman O. Brown in *Life Against Death* (Middleton, CT: Wesleyan University Press, 1959) in the late 1950s, early 1960s. My effort is to make the concepts of Eros and Thanatos historical and utterly immanent in their development. Eros thus here provides no guarantee nor is sexuality conceived in instinctual terms as it is in Marcuse and Brown. Moreover, the submission of Eros to history suggests today that there may be little life left in that principle. The ability of Thanatos to annex and transform those realities considered independent of it, in contrast, grows apace. To put the contrast in more philosophic terms, Marcuse and Brown deploy Eros and Thanatos as comprehensive categories in order to construct an abstract dialectic grounded in a reductive, instinctual understanding of sexuality. As a result history is subsumed under two categories that never enter into any actual dialectical conflict. Instead, we are given the quasi-Utopian charms of those guarantees that can be provided by visionary metaphysics. The way we concretely experience life and death as pressures within us and the way in which this conflict binds us to and alienates us from actual historical processes are thereby sacrificed to abstract dialectics. On the difference between abstract and concrete dialectics, see Davis, *Inwardness and Existence*, pp. 314–63. A final category could be added to the discussion of Lacan. The concept of the death drive that Lacan develops is, however, one of the weakest moments in his thought, a moment where his dependence on linguistics to generate the meaning of his categories forces him into a bizarre rereading of Freud's terms. Thanatos, in contrast, is the through-line of my thought. Contrasting the two positions would thus lead far afield while contributing nothing essential to the critique of Lacan.

42. For the development of this idea the most important text (and one of Lacan's finest) is *The Seminar of Jacques Lacan, Book VII, The Ethics of Psychoanalysis* (New York: Norton, 1992).

43. The allusion, of course, is to Joyce/Stephen Dedalus' definition of the proper stance of the artist as articulated in *A Portrait of the Artist as a Young Man*. Lacan achieves a similar irony toward psychoanalysis through his demystification of the master analyst as "subject supposed to know." He also thereby confirms the necessary contempt of the Master both for his own cult status and also for the inability of his followers to think for themselves.

44. Rainer Maria Rilke, *Letters to a Young Poet* (Boston: Shambhala, 1984), p. 33.

45. Friedrich Nietzsche, *Thus Spake Zarathustra* (New York: Viking, 1966), p. 63.

## CHAPTER 7

1. Charles Strozier, *Apocalypse: On the Psychology of Fundamentalism in America* (Boston: Beacon Press, 1994).

2. See Martin E. Marty and R. Scott Appleby (eds), *The Fundamentalism Project*, 5 vols (Chicago: University of Chicago Press, 1993–95). In terms of the psychological study of religion, two other recent projects should be mentioned here: J. Harold Ellens (ed.), *The Destructive Power of Religion: Violence in Judaism, Christianity and Islam*, 4 vols (London: Praeger, 2004), and J. Harold Ellens and Wayne G. Rollins (eds), *Psychology and the Bible*, 4 vols (London: Praeger, 2004).

3. Sigmund Freud, *The Future of an Illusion*, standard edition, 24 vols (London: Hogarth Press, 1953–74), vol. 21, pp. 57–147.

4. Fundamentalist readings of *Revelation* are an exercise in interpretive ingenuity in service to an ox-like stupidity: every image in the text must be literalized and attached to a specific historical event or person. The great interpretive act would thus match everything in Revelation to every empirical detail of contemporary history. The project ironically calls for constant revision in time. This operation has been performed repeatedly in America since the 1840s when this effort first became fashionable among fundamentalists. For a history of such efforts, see Boyer's *When Time Shall Be No More*. Thus, as the fundamentalist looks at history, the same drama forever approaches, is forever delayed (and mores the pity), with the empirical forever sacrificed to the mechanical iteration of stock figures strutting their allegorical hour upon the stage. All this is both mechanical and mad: the frantic search for those events that will confirm and tie down the bizarre images of Revelation in order to prove—once again—that it provides the secret code to the meaning and direction of history.

5. On the narrative rhetoric of the fundamentalist conversion tale and the "universal" principles of human response and desire that it supposedly satisfies, see Wayne Booth, "The Rhetoric of Fundamentalist Conversion

Narratives," in Marty and Appleby, *The Fundamentalism Project*, Vol. 5, pp. 367–95.

6. Bion, *Transformations*.

7. Bion, *Second Thoughts*.

8. It would be interesting and fun to do a complete reading of Revelation as a psychological text; that is, one where the psyche of the author is projecting the inner drama that defines it. In John's case we have a repetition compulsion in which each attempt to express love gives birth to an eruption of a rage that can never be successfully discharged. As a result, it necessarily expands with each repetition. John can only free himself of it through a cataclysmic projection that realizes the order of destructiveness Bion describes. Only then can love be expressed without a renewal of rage. That love significantly is for a world that can only exist after this one has been destroyed.

9. See Robert Kennedy Jr., *Crimes Against Nature* (New York: HarperCollins, 2004) for discussion of this view in connection with the massive assault of the Bush administration on the environment.

10. For the reliance on physical and psychological abuse in fundamentalist child-rearing, see Philip Greven, *Spare the Child* (New York: Random House, 1992).

11. For a rethinking of Freud's views and an attempt to articulate an existential and historical concept of the dialectic of Thanatos and Eros, see Davis, *Deracination*, pp. 133–50.

12. There's a problem with the above two paragraphs which for reasons of length I must consign to a note. Namely, the formulation offered here is insufficiently dialectical. Eros is pictured in quasi-essentialistic terms, whereas the truth of the matter is that it only comes into being properly speaking when it is activated by Thanatos. When, that is, the conflict issues in what is not a psyche before then. This dialectical connection is the antithesis of binary thinking. It is also the key to what all psychoanalytic concepts must be. Conflict is the reality. Other categories only take on determination out of that process—to which they also remain tied. See Davis, *Inwardness and Existence*, pp. 266–96 and 326–46.

13. As it turns out Hal Lindsey and Tim Le Haye are merely the precursors of Gibson. He alone has developed the art that assures that fundamentalist structures of feeling will take root in the psyche of a mass audience. Perhaps the next logical step is for Gibson to film the Apocalypse. But hush!, we don't want to say this too loudly because one suspects the idea is already rattling around like a loose billiard ball in the empty caverns of his brain.

# CHAPTER 8

1. I refer to Hegel's discussion of master–slave and the struggle for recognition in Hegel's *Phenomenology*, pp. 229–40. This text is central to the genesis of the thought of both Marx and Kierkegaard; and in our own time, through Kojeve's lectures, to the thought of (among others) the following

continental thinkers: Sartre, Lacan, Batallie, Levi-Strauss, Barthes, Derrida, and Queneau.

2. Two observations with respect to the way Bush and the media deploy the term terror and what that usage represses ideologically. It is doubtful the analysis of the terrorist psyche given here applies to Bin Laden whose terror stems not from power but from powerlessness. A further distinction is necessary with respect to the many forms of terror that are legitimate political strategies of the oppressed; as in Algiers, Belfast, and the struggle of the Palestinian people. Getting us to blur such distinctions and lump all "terrorists" under a single image of the demonic is a key example of the use of the theological for ideological purposes. On the saturation of Dubya and his administration with a single-minded and extremist religious ideology, two recent books are of great value: David Domke, *God Willing?* (London: Pluto Press, 2004) and Esther Kaplan, *With God on Their Side* (New York: The New Press, 2004). For a stunning attempt to think the problem of terror outside the terms of humanism, see Maurice Merleau-Ponty, *Humanism and Terror* (Boston: Beacon Press, 1969).

3. I'm indebted for this articulation to a lecture "Trauma, the Invasive Wound" presented by Donna Bentolila at the Annual Conference of the International Federation For Psychoanalytic Education, Chicago, Illinois, November 5–7, 2004.

4. Girard, *Violence and the Sacred*.

5. On the sublime as a psychological desire and its relevance to History, see Davis, *Deracination*, pp. 79–96.

6. For further discussion of the dialectic of Eros and Thanatos, see Davis, *Deracination*, pp. 133–51.

7. Fyodor Dostoyevsky, *The Brothers Karamazov* (London: Quartet Books, 1990), p. 255.

8. Ibid., p. 257.

9. William Faulkner, *Absalom, Absalom!* (New York: Random House, 1964), p. 142.

## CHAPTER 9

1. Two recent books have surveyed the history of philosophic discussions of evil. Susan Nieman's book *Evil in Modern Thought* (Princeton: Princeton University Press, 2002) follows Hannah Arendt in resisting the psychoanalytic claims of the topic. As a result evil gets reduced to something that happens to people otherwise not evil who by "bad luck" find themselves in certain situations. A less popular but far better philosophic survey is in Richard Bernstein's *Radical Evil: A Philosophic Interrogation* (Cambridge: Polity Press, 2002). Evil has become a favorite topic of academic conferences. Two were held recently, one "The Problem of Evil" at Purdue University, April 1–3, 2005, another "Conference on Evil" at the Metreopolitan Center for Mental Health on April 30 and May 1, 2005. For an attempt at a psychoanalytic theory of evil that has some points in common with this chapter, see Christopher Bollas,

"The Structure of Evil," in *Cracking Up* (New York: Hill and Wang, 1995), pp. 180–220.

2. Winnicott sees this ability as the key to the psyche. This is, I think, his greatest contribution to psychoanalysis; for lacking a self-reference defined by sustaining or losing that ability there is no psyche. See D.W. Winnicott, *Human Nature* (New York: Schocken Books, 1988).

3. To state it bluntly, without this experience there is no psyche. See Davis, *Deracination*, pp. 33–35 and 146–7. This is the point where an existential framework provides psychoanalysis with the grounding it needs in order to sustain its insights into the psyche against both scientistic reductionism and abstract humanism.

4. Instinct theory stands in the way of understanding childhood because it posits as a biological given what is determined by the child's response to the m/other's psyche. We develop what are called "instincts" as a result of the pressures placed on us by the psyches of our primary caretakers. For the development of a theory of childhood based on this position, see my essay "Childhood Play as Tragic Drama," in Jon Mills (ed.), *Other Banalities: Exploring the Legacy of Melanie Klein* (London: Routledge forthcoming).

5. In effect, the kind of person described here cannot "use" the other creatively in the way Winnicott describes, but only for purposes of inner deadening. See D.W. Winnicott, "The Use of an Object and Relating Through Identifications," in *Playing and Reality* (London: Penguin, 1980).

6. Hannah Arendt, *Eichmann in Jerusalem* (London: Penguin, 1963), pp. 287–8.

7. Tucker Carlson, "Devil May Care," *Talk*, September 1999.

8. Klein, *Envy and Gratitude*.

9. Arendt, *Eichmann in Jerusalem*, p. 208.

10. Karl Jaspers originally made this point, later adopted by Arendt, in a letter to her. See Hannah Arendt and Karl Jaspers, *Hannah Arendt/Karl Jaspers. Correspondence, 1926–1969* (New York: Harcourt, Brace, Jovanovich, 1992) p. 62. The position I develop in this chapter holds, antithetically, that only poets such as Shakespeare and Dostoyevsky can understand evil both in its quotidian forms and from within.

11. Primo Levi, *Survival in Auschwitz* (New York: Collier, 1961), p. 6.

12. Alain Badiou, *Ethics: An Essay on the Understanding of Evil* (London: Verso, 2001), pp. 2–3.

13. Immanuel Kant, *Religion Within the Limits of Reason Alone* (New York: Harper and Row, 1960), p. 17.

14. The allusion here is to T.S. Eliot's remark that Henry James "had a mind so fine that no idea could violate it" (The Little Review, 1918).

15. Karl Marx, *Early Writings*, trans. Tan Bottomore (Cambridge: Cambridge University Press, 1956), p. 143.

16. On the development of both concepts the seminal work is Sartre's great biography of Flaubert. See *The Family Idiot*, 5 vols (Chicago: University of Chicago Press, 1981–93), especially Vol. 5, Book 1, "Objective Neurosis."

17. George Orwell, *1984* (New York: Signet, 1949).

18. Marx's development of the now nearly forgotten concepts of alientation and labor as the realization of our species-being are in the "Economic and Philosophic Manuscripts of 1844." See Karl Marx, *Early Writings* (New York: McGraw-Hill, 1964).

19. Rainer Maria Rilke, *Duino Elegis*, trans. Stephen Mitchell (Boston: Shambhala, 1992).

20. For this and other uplifting sentiments of Kissinger's, see Monika Jensen-Stevenson, *Kiss the Boys Goodbye* (New York: Dutton, 1990).

21. Doris Lessing, *The Golden Notebook* (New York: Simon and Schuster, 1962), p. 296.

22. Rilke, *Duino Elegies*, 9th Elegy

23. Ibid., 8th Elegy.

## CHAPTER 10

1. My goal here is to establish an ethic of the psyche grounded in what I'll call the existentializing imperative and to outline its basic characteristics through a critique of the Kantian ethic of a categorical imperative grounded in reason. The goal thereby is to awaken the left from what we might call our dogmatic ethical slumber as well as from Jameson's notion that we can simply consign ethics to ideology.

2. Alenka Zupančič, *Ethics of the Real* (London: Verso, 2000), p. 160.

3. To see the world Tillman was coming out of and reacting against one need look no further than the comments of Simeon Rice, a star player in the NFL, who said Tillman's choice was "stupid because making money and having fun is all that matters ... Besides he wasn't a very good player anyway." It is against the background of such remarks that one must measure the magnitude of Tillman's act. As Dave Zirin has revealed in a recent article in the *Nation*, "Pat Tillman, Our Hero" (October 24, 2005), p. 6, Pat Tillman's memory has been ill-served by a White House and media eager to capitalize on Tillman for ideological purposes. As it turns out Mr. Tillman was against the war and an avid reader of leftist thinkers such as Noam Chomsky. Tillman's family is currently attempting to rescue his memory. This chapter joins them in that effort.

4. The reading of Hamlet sketched here is quite different from most readings that are offered both of that character and of the play *Hamlet*. Despite their many disagreements, interpreters of Hamlet are agreed on one thing. The play is the Medusa and some shield must be found to protect us so that we can slay what we fear to look upon. The effort here is to resist that operation—to open up the radicalism of what is perhaps the most radical work of art ever written. For a contrasting effort to fit the play to the Procrustean bed of the conventional views and practices of Shakespeare's time, see Stephen Greenblatt, *Hamlet in Purgatory* (Princeton: Princeton University Press, 2001).

5. On the concept of melancholia as the mood and mode of tragic knowing, see Davis, *Deracination*, pp. 163–75.

6. See Heidegger, *Being and Time*, pp. 349–52.

7. I discuss the concept of active reversal at length in *Inwardness and Existence*. See especially pp. 259–63.

8. The position taken here reverses the position Freud took toward Hamlet in his great essay "Mourning and Melancholia," Standard Ed. (London: Hogarth Press, 1953–74) 14, pp. 243–58. On Mood (*Befindlichkeit*) as a way of knowing, see Heidegger *Being and Time*, pp. 172–84.

9. Immanuel Kant, *Groundwork of the Metaphysic of Morals* (New York: Harper and Row, 1964), p. 61.

10. Ibid., p. 102.

11. Ibid., p. 69.

12. Ibid., p. 69. On sublime emotions and the register of the psyche engaged by them, see Davis, *Deracination*, pp. 57–99. The method I there develop at length for the psychoanalytic interpretation of a philosophic text I can only illustrate in an abbreviated form here. What I offer here is far from a full reading of Kant's ethic, which is one of the greatest and most beautiful works in the history of ethical thought. All I attempt here is to introduce the key psychoanalytic ideas that would inform an extended critique of Kant.

13. Jacques Lacan, "Kant avec Sade," in *Ecrits* (Paris: Editions de Seuil, 1966), pp. 765–90.

14. Terms such as authenticity have supposedly been thoroughly deconstructed, the assumption being that any such term is fatally entangled in the metaphysics of presence. *Eigentlich* refers, however, to the act of making one's existence one's own by appropriating the depth of one's finitude and situatedness. Once that problematic also requires plumbing the hidden conflicts of one's psyche, it has moved outside the orbit of anything that could be readily identified with the metaphysics of presence or self-presence.

15. Or to be more precise of *Dasein* as *Sein-sum-Tode* (Being-toward-Death). On which see Heidegger, *Being and Time*, pp. 279–306.

16. John Keats, "Letter to George and Thomas Keats," December 21, 27(?), 1817, in *The Selected Poetry of Keats*, pp. 328–9.

17. For a Lacanian discussion of the film of *Sophie's Choice* in terms of the forced choice, see Zupančič, *Ethics of the Real*, pp. 213–21. Zupančič there also contrasts that choice with another kind of ethical choice which Lacan discusses at length in *The Seminar of Jacques Lacan, Book VII*.

18. For a discussion of what thinking is for Hamlet and how Shakespeare in *Hamlet* represents a way of thinking that moves outside the limits of the ratio, see Davis, *Deracination*, pp. 175–93. The present chapter constitutes the next step in an ongoing effort to come to terms with that play.

19. Contrast this formulation with Freud's famous statement "where id was, ego shall be" and Lacan's rewriting of it: "There where it was, or there where one was … it is my duty that I should come into being."

20. Though it has no biological basis, this is perhaps the "survival value" of the tragic. Existence is a break with natural processes and yet a necessary way of being if we are to survive. There is, of course, no biological warrant for or guarantee of the persistence of this principle. That is one measure of its value.

# References

Agamben, G. (1998) *Homo Sacer: Sovereign Power and Bare Life*. Stanford: Stanford University Press.

Aikman, D. (2004) *A Man of Faith: The Spiritual Journey of George W. Bush*. Nashville: Thomas Nelson, Inc.

Albee, E. (1981) *The Plays. Vol. 2*. New York: Atheneum.

Ali, T. (2002) *The Clash of Fundamentalisms*. London: Verso.

Almond, G.A. Appleby, R.S. and Sivan E. (2003) *Strong Religion*. Chicago: University of Chicago Press.

Alperovitz, G. (1995) *The Decision to Use the Atomic Bomb and the Architecture of an American Myth*. New York: Knopf.

Altieri, C. (2003) *The Particulars of Rapture*. Ithaca: Cornell University Press.

Arendt, H. (1951) *The Origins of Totalitarianism*. New York: Harcourt, Brace, Jovanovich.

—— (1954) *Between Past and Future*. London: Penguin.

—— (1963) *Eichmann in Jerusalem*. London: Penguin.

—— (2003) *Responsibility and Judgment*. New York: Random House.

Arendt, H. and Jaspers, K. (1992) *Hannah Arendt/Karl Jaspers: Correspondence, 1926–1969*. New York: Harcourt, Brace, Jovanovich.

Armstrong, K. (2000) *The Battle for God*. New York: Knopf.

Artaud, A. (1976) *Antonin Artaud: Selected Writings*. Edited and with an introduction by S. Santag. Berkeley: University of California Press.

Badiou, A. (2001) *Ethics: An Essay on the Understanding of Evil*. London: Verso.

Bateson, G. (1972) *Steps Toward an Ecology of Mind*. New York: Ballantine.

Baudrillard, J. (2002) *The Spirit of Terrorism and Requiem for the Twin Towers*. London: Verso.

Benjamin, J. (1988) *The Bonds of Love*. New York: Pantheon.

Bergmann, M. (1987) *The Anatomy of Loving*. New York: Columbia University Press.

Bernstein, R. (2002) *Radical Evil: A Philosophical Interrogation*. England: Polity Press.

Bion, W.R. (1965) *Transformations*. New York: Jason Aronson.

—— (1967) *Second Thoughts*. London: Pitman.

—— (1992) *Cogitations*. London: Karnac Books.

Blatt, H. (2005) *America's Environmental Report Card: Are We Making the Grade?* Cambridge, MA: MIT Press.

Boal, I., Clark, T.J., Matthews, J. and Watts, M. (2005) *Afflicted Powers*. London: Verso.

Bollas, C. (1995) *Cracking Up*. New York: Hill and Wang.

Boothby, R. (2001) *Freud as Philosopher*. London: Routledge.

Borradori, G. (2003) *Philosophy in a Time of Terror: Dialogues with Jürgen Habermas and Jacques Derrrida*. Chicago: University of Chicago Press.

*Boston Herald*, August 4, 2003, Technology section.

Boyer, P. (1992) *When Time Shall Be No More*. Cambridge, MA: Harvard University Press.

Briody, D. (2003) *The Iron Triangle*. New Jersey: John Wiley and Sons, Inc.

Brown, N.O. (1959) *Life Against Death*. Middletown, CT: Wesleyan University Press.

Bundy, M. (1992) *Danger and Survival: Choices About the Bomb in the First Fifty Years*. New York: Knopf.

Caldicott, H. (2002) *The New Nuclear Danger*. New York: The New Press.

Carlson, T. (1999) "Devil May Care." *Talk*, September.

Chodorow, N. (1999) *The Power of Feelings*. New Haven: Yale University Press.

Chomsky, N. (1999) *Fateful Triangle*. Cambridge, MA: South End Press.

—— (2001) *9-11*. New York: Seven Stories Press.

Copjec, J. (1994) *Read My Desire*. Cambridge, MA: MIT Press.

Davis, W.A (1989) *Inwardness and Existence: Subjectivity In/And Hegel, Heidegger, Marx, and Freud*. Madison: University of Wisconsin Press.

—— (1994) *Get the Guests: Psychoanalysis, Modern American Drama, and the Audience*. Madison: University of Wisconsin Press.

—— (2000) *The Holocaust Memorial: A Play About Hiroshima*. Bloomington: First Books.

—— (2001) *Deracination: Historicity, Hiroshima and the Tragic Imperative*. Albany: SUNY Press.

—— (2004) *An Evening with JonBenét Ramsey: A Play and Two Essays*. Nebraska: iUniverse.

—— (forthcoming) "Childhood Play as Tragic Drama." In J. Mills (ed.) *Other Banalities: Exploring the Legacy of Melanie Klein*. London: Routledge.

Davoine, F. and Gaudilliere, J.-M. (2004) *History Beyond Trauma*. New York: Other Press.

Debord, G. (1983) *The Society of the Spectacle*. Detroit: Black and Red.

*Democracy Now*, August 5, 2003, <http://www.democracynow.org/article.pl?sid=03/08/05/1455235>.

Dempsey, J. and Cole, D. (2004) *Terrorism and the Constitution*. New York: The New Press.

Derrida, J. and Thévenin, P. (1998) *The Secret Art of Antonin Artaud*. Cambridge, MA: MIT Press.

Domke, D. (2004) *God Willing?* London: Pluto Press.

Dostoyevsky, F. (1962) *The Possessed*. Trans. Andrew R. MacAndrew. New York: Signet.

—— (1990) *The Brothers Karamazov*. London: Quartet Books.

Eigen, M. (1986) *The Psychotic Core*. New York: Jason Aronson.

—— (2004) *The Sensitive Self*. Middletown, CT: Wesleyan University Press.

Ellens, J.H. (ed.) (2004) *The Destructive Power of Religion: Violence in Judaism, Christianity and Islam*. 4 vols. London: Praeger.

Ellens, J.H. and Rollins, W.G. (eds) (2004) *Psychology and the Bible*. 4 vols. London: Praeger.

Ellul, J. (1964) *The Technological Society*. New York: Knopf.

Etzioni, A. (2004) *How Patriotic is the Patriot Act*. London: Routledge.

Faulkner, W. (1964) *Absalom, Absalom!* New York: Random House.

—— (1997) *The Sound and the Fury*. New York: Random House.

Frank, J.A. (2004) *Bush on the Couch*. New York: Regan Books.

Frank, T. (2004) *What's the Matter with Kansas?* New York: Henry Holt.

Freud, S. (1912) "The Dynamics of Transference." Standard edition. 24 vols. London: Hogarth Press, 1953–74. Vol. 12, pp. 99–108.

—— (1914) "Remembering, Repeating and Working-Through." Standard edition. 24 vols. London: Hogarth Press, 1953–74. Vol. 12, pp. 147–56.

—— (1917) "Morning and Melancholia." Standard edition. 24 vols. London: Hogarth Press, 1953–74. Vol. 14, pp. 243–58.

—— (1927) *The Future of an Illusion*. Standard edition 24 vols. London: Hogarth Press, 1953–74. Vol. 21, pp. 57–147.

Girard, R. (1977) *Violence and the Sacred*. Baltimore: Johns Hopkins University Press.

Goff, S. (2004) *Full Spectrum Disorder*. New York: Soft Skull Press.

Grand, S. (2000) *The Reproduction of Evil*. Hillsdale, NJ: Analytic Press.

Greenblatt, S. (2001) *Hamlet in Purgatory*. Princeton: Princeton University Press.

Greven, P. (1992) *Spare the Child*. New York: Random House.

Hardt, M. and Negri, A. (2000) *Empire*. Cambridge, MA: Harvard University Press.

Hegel, G. (1910) *The Phenomenology of Mind*. Trans. J.B. Baillie. London: George Allen and Unwin.

Heidegger, M. (1962) *Being and Time*. New York: Harper and Row.

—— (1977) *The Question Concerning Technology, and Other Essays*. New York: Garland.

Hersh, S. (2004) "The Gray Zone." *New Yorker*, May 24.

Hiro, D. (2002) *War Without End*. London: Routledge.

Hobsbawm, E. (1999) *On the Edge of the New Century*. New York: The New Press.

Hoge, J. and Rose G. (eds) (2001) *How Did this Happen? Terrorism and the New War*. New York: Public Affairs.

Huntington, S. (1996) *The Clash of Civilizations and the Remaking of World Order*. New York: Simon and Schuster.

Jacoby, R. (1975) *Social Amnesia*. Boston: Beacon Press.

Jensen-Stevenson, M. (1990) *Kiss the Boys Goodbye*. New York: Dutton.

Johnson, C. (2000) *Blowback*. New York: Henry Holt.

Jones, J.W. (2002) *Terror and Transformation: The Ambiguity of Religion in Psychoanalytic Perspective*. New York: Taylor and Francis.

Juergensmeyer, M. (2000) *Terror in the Mind of God*. Berkeley: University of California Press.

Kant, I. (1960) *Religion Within the Limits of Reason Alone*. New York: Harper and Row.

—— (1964) *Groundwork of the Metaphysic of Morals*. New York: Harper and Row.

Kaplan, E. (2004) *With God on Their Side*. New York: The New Press.

Keats, J. (1966) *The Selected Poetry of Keats*. New York: NAL.

Kennedy, R. Jr. (2004) *Crimes Against Nature*. New York: HarperCollins.

Khalidi, R. (2004) *Resurrecting Empire*. Boston: Beacon Press.

Klein, M. (1967) *Envy and Gratitude*. New York: Delta.

—— (1975) *Love, Guilt and Reparation*. New York: Delta.

—— *The Psychoanalysis of Children*. New York: Dell.

Koenigsberg, R. (1977) *The Psychoanalysis of Racism, Revolution and Nationalism*. New York: The Library of Social Science.

Kohut, H. (1971) *The Analysis of the Self*. New York: International Universities Press.

Lacan, J. (1966) "Kant avec Sade." In *Ecrits*. Paris: Editions de Seuil.

—— (1972) "Of Structure as an Inmixing of Otherness Prerequisite to Any Subject Whatever." In K. Macksey and E. Donato (eds) *The Structuralist Controversy*. Baltimore: Johns Hopkins University Press.

—— (1977) *Ecrits: A Selection*. New York: Norton.

—— (1992) *The Seminar of Jacques Lacan, Book VII, The Ethics of Psychoanalysis*. New York: Norton.

—— (1994) *Le Seminaire. Livre X. L'Angoisse, 1962–63*. Paris: Editions du Seuil.

—— (1998) *Encore. The Seminar of Jacques Lacan, Book XX*. New York: W.W. Norton.

Lakoff, G. (2002) *Moral Politics: How Liberals and Conservatives Think*. Chicago: University of Chicago Press.

Leone, R. and Aurig, G. (2003) *The War on Our Freedoms*. New York: Public Affairs.

Lessing, D. (1962) *The Golden Notebook*. New York: Simon and Schuster.

Levi, P. (1961) *Survival in Auschwitz*. New York: Collier.

Lichtman, R. (2005) "The Consolations of George Lakoff." *Counterpunch*, May 28/30.

Lifton, R.J. (1976) *The Life of the Self*. New York: Simon and Schuster.

—— (1979) *The Broken Connection*. New York: Simon and Schuster.

—— (1993) *The Protean Self*. New York: Basic Books.

—— (2003) *Superpower Syndrome: America's Apocalyptic Confrontation with the World*. New York: Thunder's Mouth Press.

—— (2004) "Conditions of Atrocity." *Nation*, May 31.

Lifton, R.J. and Mitchell, G. (1995). *Hiroshima in America: A Half Century of Denial*. New York: Putnam.

Lowell, R. (1967) *Near the Ocean*. London: Faber.

Mamdani, M. (2004) *Good Muslim, Bad Muslim*. New York: Pantheon.

Mansfield, S. (2003) *The Faith of George W. Bush*. London: Penguin.

Marcuse, H. (1962) *Eros and Civilization*. New York: Vintage.

—— (1966) *One-Dimensional Man*. Boston: Beacon Press.

Marty, M.E. and Appleby, R.S. (eds) (1993–95) *The Fundamentalism Project*. 5 vols. Chicago: University of Chicago Press.

Marx, K. (1956) *Early Writings*. Trans. Ian Bottomore. Cambridge: Cambridge University Press.

McGowan, T. (2004) *The End of Dissatisfaction*. New York: SUNY Press.

McKeon, R. (1954) *Thought, Action and Passion*. Chicago: University of Chicago Press.

Merleau-Ponty, M. (1969) *Humanism and Terror*. Boston: Beacon Press.

Miller, M.C. (2004) *Cruel and Unusual: Bush/Cheney's New World Order*. New York: Norton.

Mitchell, S. (1993) *Hope and Dread in Psychoanalysis*. New York: Basic Books.

Mulvey, L. (1989) *Visual and Other Pleasures*. London: Macmillan.

Nabokov, V. (1997) *Lolita*. New York: Vintage Books.

*New York Times*, August 3, 2003, "Week in Review."

Nieman, S. (2002) *Evil in Modern Thought*. Princeton: Princeton University Press.

Nietzsche, F. (1966) *Thus Spake Zarathustra*. New York: Viking.

Nussbaum, M. (2001) *Upheavals of Thought*. Cambridge: Cambridge University Press.

Oppenheimer, P. (1996) *Evil and the Demonic*. New York: New York University Press.

Orwell, G. (1949) *1984*. New York: Signet.

Patai, R. (1973) *The Arab Mind*. London: Macmillan.

Rhodes, R. (1986) *The Making of the Atomic Bomb*. New York: Simon and Schuster.

Rilke, R.M. (1984) *Letters to a Young Poet*. Boston: Shambhala.

Ruppert, M.C. (2004) *Crossing the Rubicon*. Canada: New Society Publishers.

Said, E. (2000) *Orientalism*. New York: Vintage.

Sartre, J.-P. (1956) *Being and Nothingness*. New York: Philosophical Library.

—— (1981–93) *The Family Idiot*. 5 vols. Chicago: University of Chicago Press.

Schafer, R. (1976) *A New Language for Psychoanalysis*. New Haven: Yale University Press.

—— (1992) *Retelling a Life*. New York: Basic Books.

—— (2003) *Bad Feelings*. New York: Other Press.

Stein, R. (2002) "Evil as Love and as Liberation: The Religious Terrorist's Mind." *Psychoanalytic Dialogues*, 12, pp. 393–420.

—— (2003) "Vertical Mystical Homoeros: An Altered Form of Desire in Fundamentalism." *Studies in Gender and Sexuality*, 4(1), pp. 38–58.

Stern, D. (1977) *The First Relationship*. Cambridge: Harvard University Press.

Stimson, H. (1947) "The Decision to Use the Atomic Bomb." *Harper's*, February.

Stolorow, R. and Atwood, G. (1992) *Contexts of Being*. Hillsdale, NJ: Analytic Press.

Strozier, C.B. (1994) *Apocalypse: On the Psychology of Fundamentalism in America*. Boston: Beacon Press.

Strozier, C.B. and Flynn, M. (eds) (1996) *Trauma and Self*. Maryland: Rowman and Littlefield.

Taylor, C. (1975) *Hegel*. Cambridge: Cambridge University Press.

Terkel, S. (2002) *Guardian*, August 5.

Tibbets, P.W., Stebbens, C., and Franken, H. (1978) *The Tibbets Story*. New York: Stern and Day.

Vendantam, S. (2004) "The Psychology of Torture." *Washington Post*, May 20.

Wasserman, H. (1982) *Killing Our Own: The Disaster of America's Experience with Atomic Radiation*. Ohio: Delacorte.

Weinstein, M. (2004) "Abu Ghraib Means Impunity." PINR, May 24.

Weiss, P. (1972) *The Persecution and Assassination of Jean-Paul Marat as Performed by the Inmates of the Asylum of Charenton under the Direction of the Marquis de Sade*. New York: Atheneum.

Williams, R. (2000) *Marxism and Literature*. Oxford: Oxford University Press.

Williams, R. (2000) *Marxism and Literature*. Oxford: Oxford University Press.

Wills, G. (2004) "God in the Hands of Angry Sinners." *New York Review of Books*, 51(6), April 8, pp. 68–74.

Winnicott, D.W. (1958) *Collected Papers: Through Paedatrics to Psycho-Analysis*. New York: Basic Books.

—— (1980) *Playing and Reality*. London: Penguin.

—— (1974) "Fear of Breakdown." *International Review of Psycho-Analysis*, 1, pp. 103–07.

—— (1987) *Holding and Interpretation*. New York: Grove Press.

—— (1988) *Human Nature*. New York: Schocken Books.

*Wired News*, July, 30, 2003, Business section.

Wittgenstein, L. (1958) *Philosophical Investigations*. London: Macmillan.

Woolf, R.P., Moore, B., and Marcuse, H. (1969) *Critique of Pure Tolerance*. Boston: Beacon Press.

Wordsworth, W. (1979) *The Prelude*. New York: Norton.

Zirin, D. (2005) "Pat Tillman, Our Hero." *Nation*, October 24.

Žižek, S. (1989) *The Sublime Object of Ideology*. London: Verso.

—— (1991) *For They Know Not What They Do*. New York: Verso.

—— (1996) "Fantasy as a Political Category: A Lacanian Approach." *Journal for the Psychoanalysis of Culture and Society*. 1(2), Fall, pp. 77–85.

—— (1997) *The Plague of Fantasies*. London: Verso.

—— (1999) *The Žižek Reader*. Oxford: Blackwell.

—— (2002) *Welcome to the Desert of the Real*. London: Verso.

Zupančič, A. (2000) *Ethics of the Real*. London: Verso.

# Index